SPIRITUALITY IN COLLEGE STUDENTS' LIVES

Spirituality in College Students' Lives draws on data from a large-scale national survey examining the spiritual development of undergraduates and how colleges and universities can be more effective in facilitating students' spiritual growth. In this book, contributors from the fields of education, psychology, sociology, social work, and religion present research-based studies that explore the importance of students' spirituality and the impact of the college experience on their spiritual development. Offering a wide range of theoretical perspectives and worldviews, this volume also includes reflections from distinguished researchers and practitioners which highlight implications for practice. This original edited collection explores:

- emerging theoretical frames and analytical approaches;
- differences in spiritual expressions and experiences among sub-populations;
- the impact of campus contexts;
- how college experiences shape spiritual outcomes.

Spirituality in College Students' Lives is an important resource for higher education and student affairs faculty, administrators, and practitioners interested in nurturing the inner lives of college students.

Alyssa Bryant Rockenbach is Associate Professor in the Department of Leadership, Policy, and Adult and Higher Education at North Carolina State University, USA.

Matthew J. Mayhew is Associate Professor of Higher Education at New York University, USA.

SPIRITUALITY IN COLLEGE STUDENTS' LIVES

Translating Research into Practice

Edited by Alyssa Bryant Rockenbach and Matthew J. Mayhew

Routledge
Taylor & Francis Group

NEW YORK AND LONDON

First published 2013
by Routledge
711 Third Avenue, New York, NY 10017

Simultaneously published in the UK
by Routledge
2 Park Square, Milton Park, Abingdon, Oxon OX14 4RN

Routledge is an imprint of the Taylor & Francis Group, an informa business

Library of Congress Cataloging in Publication Data
Spirituality in college students' lives : translating research into
practice / edited by Alyssa Bryant Rockenbach, Matthew J.
Mayhew.
       p. cm.
   Includes bibliographical references and index.
   1. College students – Religious life. 2. Spiritual formation.
   I. Rockenbach, Alyssa Bryant. II. Mayhew, Matthew J.
   LB3609.S67 2012
   378.1´98-dc23   2012002382

ISBN: 978-0-415-89505-7 (hbk)
ISBN: 978-0-415-89506-4 (pbk)
ISBN: 978-0-203-11897-9 (ebk)

Typeset in Bembo
by HWA Text and Data Management, London

SUSTAINABLE
FORESTRY
INITIATIVE

Certified Sourcing
www.sfiprogram.org
SFI-01234

Printed and Bound in the United States
of America on sustainably sourced paper
by IBT Global

To Miranda, Sarah, Eli, and Sawyer

CONTENTS

FOREWORD

The Spirituality in Higher Education project was initiated in 2002 with a generous grant from the John Templeton Foundation to UCLA's Higher Education Research Institute. The major goal of this project was to examine the spiritual growth of college undergraduates and to assess the role that the college experience plays in facilitating students' spiritual development.

To pursue this project our research team assembled a large and complex database that included extensive longitudinal data on the spiritual and religious life of some 14,527 college students who were attending 136 diverse colleges and universities. Students were initially assessed when they entered college as new freshmen in the fall of 2004, and again as they were completing their third undergraduate year. In addition to extensive data on their spiritual and religious lives, we also assembled detailed data on the students' colleges and college experiences. (Further details regarding the database are discussed by our colleague Jennifer Lindholm in Chapter 2.) Major findings from this study were subsequently reported in the book, *Cultivating the Spirit: How College Can Enhance Students' Inner Lives* (Jossey-Bass/Wiley, 2011), which was coauthored jointly by the two of us and Jennifer Lindholm.

As we began writing up our findings, it became clear to us that there was no way that the three of us could do justice to the full research potential of this remarkable database in a single book. Accordingly, with support from the John Templeton Foundation, in the fall of 2008 we initiated a national competition to award small grants to selected investigators across the country who were interested in conducting original studies using this database. The basic goal of this competition was to expand the impact of our Templeton project by encouraging other researchers from across the country to devote their talents to the study of students' spiritual and religious development by means of original studies that utilized our unique database.

We announced the competition in November 2008 with an advertisement in the *Chronicle of Higher Education* and by emailing the membership lists of national scholarly organizations such as the Association for the Study of Higher Education. All applications had to be received by February 2009. We eventually received 68 complete proposals and were able to fund 12 of them with grants in the amount of $10,000 each.

We employed an elaborate review procedure to ensure not only that the most promising proposals would be funded but also that the process would be as fair and as free from bias as possible. Each proposal was first examined by a UCLA research analyst who stripped away all information that might identify the researcher who submitted it. The proposals were then read by members of our research team to ensure that they fell within our guidelines—that is, that they focused on issues of religiousness and/or spirituality in higher education and that the study design was adequate to answer the questions being posed—and in order to eliminate any that were logistically unfeasible (e.g., available data were not well matched to the proposed project, the proposal required the collection of additional data, or the study could not realistically be completed within our specified time frame of eight months). We were also looking to eliminate proposals that duplicated studies currently underway by members of our research team, but no proposals were eliminated for this reason.

Following this initial screening, a total of 45 proposals remained for more intensive review. For this purpose we recruited five members of our Technical Advisory Panel[1] to serve as reviewers. Copies of the proposals, stripped of identifying information, were sent to each reviewer with a request to rate each proposal according to the following criteria:

- Purpose, rationale, theoretical framework;
- Research questions, hypotheses, proposed methodology;
- Dissemination plan;
- Quality of presentation and writing.

Reviewers assigned numerical ratings to each proposal. The project staff prepared summaries of these ratings and forwarded them to the reviewers, who were then brought to the UCLA campus for a day-long meeting in April 2009 where they worked to adjudicate any differences in the ratings. The project staff joined the reviewers for this final session, although the proposals remained anonymous until the final selections were made. The twelve winners were notified shortly thereafter.

Authors of the twelve winning proposals were invited to an initial May meeting at UCLA where they were encouraged to exchange information about their projects with each other and to raise any questions with the UCLA project staff that they might have had concerning the database, our expectations, or other aspects of the award program.

In December 2009 we hosted a symposium at UCLA where all twelve awardees presented the findings from their studies. There were three panels consisting of four papers each, and three of the original reviewers (Hill, McLennan, and Pargament) served as discussants for the panel presentations. This edited volume reports findings from nine of the original twelve presentations at the symposium.

We are especially pleased that two of the original awardees, Alyssa Bryant Rockenbach and Matthew Mayhew, agreed to serve as editors of this unique volume. They have worked closely with the original investigators to produce a volume that is beautifully edited and creatively organized into three sections that nicely reflect the major content emphases of the studies: *Student Characteristics and Group Differences, College Contexts,* and *Outcomes.* These sections are further enriched by the insightful commentary and reflections of researchers and practitioners.

We particularly encourage readers to begin by reading the opening chapter by Mayhew and Bryant Rockenbach, where they provide an excellent account of the essence of the book, stressing the importance of studying students' spirituality and assessing the impact of the college experience on students' spiritual and religious development. The chapter also includes an insightful discussion of the theoretical underpinnings of the constructs of spirituality and religiousness, of the dilemmas of measuring how these aspects of the student's life unfold, and of some of the implications for institutional practice.

We expect that this volume will generate a good deal of discussion with the higher education community about the importance of understanding student development from a holistic perspective and of how we can become more responsive to students' search for purpose and meaning in their lives. We also hope that other investigators will become inspired to pursue further this important area of inquiry so that we can enlarge our understanding of student growth and development and thereby serve them better.

This book extends our own work and knowledge in this growing field of research, and we would like to take this opportunity to extend our personal congratulations and thanks to the investigators for carrying out such thoughtful and original research. We hope that other researchers and practitioners will be as challenged and enlightened as we were by their scholarship.

Helen S. Astin
Alexander W. Astin

Note

1 Scotty McLennan (Stanford), Arthur Chickering (Goddard), Peter Hill (Biola), Ellen Idler (Emory), and Kenneth Pargament (Bowling Green).

ACKNOWLEDGMENTS

As editors of this volume, we are grateful to the UCLA Spirituality in Higher Education project team for the generous research awards and access to the data that made these studies possible. The Spirituality in Higher Education project was funded by the John Templeton Foundation and led by Alexander W. Astin, Helen S. Astin, and Jennifer A. Lindholm. The opinions expressed in this volume are those of the authors and do not necessarily reflect the views of the John Templeton Foundation.

PART I

Introduction and Methodological Overview

1

INTRODUCTION

Matthew J. Mayhew and Alyssa Bryant Rockenbach

On April 25, 2011, Christiane Amanpour asked Eboo Patel, "What do you think are the key, pressing spiritual issues of our time?" His answer was quick and clear. He said, "The role religion is going to play in the 21st century is going to be one of the key issues. Faith can either be a barrier of division, a bomb of destruction, or a bridge of cooperation. Our job is to make it a bridge of cooperation."

This brief exchange exemplifies the spirit in which this book is offered, as a cooperation among contributors, unified in a quest to understand college student spiritual development, and representing many faith and non-faith-based traditions. In the spirit of building a bridge of cooperation, the purpose of this chapter is to provide an overview of some of the ways, both ideologically and methodologically, in which volume contributors came together to make meaning of college student spirituality and the collegiate conditions, educational practices, and student experiences that influence its development.

To achieve this purpose, we, as co-editors of this volume, approach this chapter with three interwoven goals. First, we introduce readers to the commonalities volume contributors experienced, either implicitly or through our explicit directive, as a means for providing some interpretive context for each chapter. Second, to improve volume parsimony, we discuss common chapter elements, such as arguments related to the importance of studying student spirituality and to the use of post-positive research paradigms for examining the influence of college on student spirituality. Finally, for the sake of transparency, we share our perspectives as co-editors; indeed some of the choices, such as integration of the authors' voices into the chapter narrative, were based in our ontological and epistemological approaches to the study of spirituality and may not reflect the normative scholarly practices of the many authors contributing to this volume. With these goals as our guide, we turn to a discussion of some of the common elements embedded in chapters of this volume.

Framing the importance of the study of spirituality was a key consideration of volume contributors. The authors of each chapter offered a distinctive approach to the study of student spirituality and its importance, ranging from, but not limited to, responding to President Obama's charge for college campuses to serve as the breeding ground for interfaith dialogue (see Bryant Rockenbach & Mayhew, Chapter 6), to adapting empirical studies to include examination of the inner-self (see Faigin, Chapter 10), to considering social justice advocates' concerns with re-framing certain cultural norms that sustain faith-based privilege by silencing the voices of other faith and non-faith-based worldviews (see Bowman & Small, Chapter 3), to disrupting monolithic spiritual development models that fail to account for students' rich racial and cultural diversity (see Gehrke, Chapter 4), to recognizing implicit values of care and compassion within diverse faith traditions (see Brandenberger & Bowman, Chapter 7; Chenot & Kim, Chapter 8). Our intent is not to argue that one of these approaches is more appropriate than another; instead, we describe them here to highlight that the authors, with a distinctive set of experiences on which to draw, considered the empirical study of student spirituality a worthwhile endeavor.

Another solidarity shared among contributors was the epistemic and ontological frames used to approach the spirituality studies contained in this volume. Is spirituality a reality that can be accessed? Can it be measured? Although potential responses to these questions were, are, and continue to be fodder for scholarly debate and are much too broad to address within the confines of this introductory chapter, the contributors of this volume concede, at least implicitly through their participation in the research effort, that spirituality is real, existent, and to some degree measurable. Voices not represented in this volume may not share this assumption, as there are many who question that any dimension of spirituality, however defined, is not something that can be empirically examined, citing that spirituality is too subjective to be of value in the objective world. Rather than ask volume contributors to respectively take up this argument, we assert on their behalf that spirituality, at least in part, has definable characteristics that can be articulated, accessed, measured, and analyzed through quantitative means.

Spanning many academic disciplines, the volume contributors shared pragmatic paradigmatic approaches to the study of spirituality, with each author locating part of the research effort in improving spiritual practices on college campuses. From this solidarity emerged the title of the volume, *Spirituality in College Students' Lives: Translating Research into Practice*, and our decision to ask a series of researchers and practitioners to respond to each of the book's sections. Indeed, it is a shared assumption among volume contributors that the utility of the research ultimately lies in how it informs practice.

Although the use of research paradigms and the relative weight each contributor gave to their influence varied, nuanced by each researcher's experience, we asked contributors to include their "voice" as part of the chapters. Consistent with many post-positive paradigmatic approaches to empirical explorations of this kind and with recently emerging insights into the role author position plays in framing quantitative research lines (see Stage, 2007), the voice contributors offered was intended to contextualize their research endeavors with the texture needed for readers to understand why the research questions were asked; how the authors approached the data in an effort to answer these questions; and what the authors learned as a result of their respective inquiries. Again, authors interpreted this voice element differently, with some using it to frame the entire study and reflect on its conclusions and others inserting it into the methods section. How the authors integrated their respective voices into each chapter provides yet another layer of meaning through which readers can interpret findings.

Readers may also glean additional insight into the authors' findings by closely examining the different theoretical orientations volume contributors used to explain the relationship between college-going and spirituality. For example, authors focusing on race and religious minorities and their relationship to spirituality adopted, either explicitly or implicitly, a critical theoretical frame for understanding how spiritual experiences and outcomes are often subjected to cultural systems that privilege some at the expense of oppressing others. Authors highlighting environments were more likely to turn to philosophical and sociological reasons for explaining the occurrence of particular phenomenon within a specific social context, like evangelical institutions (see Rine, Chapter 5) or institutions with peer environments oriented toward particular spiritual traits (see Bryant Rockenbach & Mayhew, Chapter 6). Authors motivated by interests in spiritual outcomes grounded explorations in psychosocial theories of human development, ranging from Fowler's and Park's model for faith development, to prosocial development (see Brandenberger and Bowman, Chapter 7), to the intersections of moral, prosocial, and spiritual development (see Chenot and Kim, Chapter 8), to Gilligan's work on the ethic of care (see Fleming, Purnell, & Wang, Chapter 9), to the developmental implications of spiritual struggles and substance use (see Faigin, Chapter 10). Distinctive and innovative, the authors' choices of theoretical orientations as frames for examining student spirituality clearly reflects the interdisciplinarity represented in this volume and showcase the informed creativity that can emerge from a variety of perspectives linked by common interest, which, in our case, involved college and its influence on student spirituality.

Although authors varied in their theoretical approaches to the study of spirituality, a common theme emerging from contributors was the need to draw on the literature as a means for defining spirituality as something related to but distinct from religiosity. Such a need mirrors empirical data suggesting that students often make nuanced distinctions between religion and spirituality, as student patterns of self-identification with religion decrease during college while self-identification with spirituality increases (see Astin, Astin, & Lindholm, 2011). Perhaps, the reasons for needing to define spirituality as separate from religion reflect these empirical findings; alternatively, the authors may share a desire to make their studies more inclusive, accessible to an audience wider than that espousing a particular faith tradition.

Including as many voices as possible to develop working understandings of spirituality was a hallmark of the UCLA researchers responsible for creating and administering the College Students' Beliefs and Values survey to the students participating in the study. Although united, at least implicitly, in the notion that spirituality or at least its constituent dimensions can be articulated and subsequently measured, Alexander Astin, Helen Astin, and Jennifer Lindholm allowed response patterns to naturally occur, thus empowering students to give meaning to the spiritual dimensions that became the outcomes of interest to volume contributors. These twelve dimensions, including, for example, Ecumenical Worldview, Ethic of Care, Religious Commitment, Spiritual Identification, and Spiritual Struggle, are described in full in Chapter 2. (The methods used to construct and validate these dimensions are also discussed in detail in Chapter 2.) We contend that empirical explorations of these constructs represent one way that spirituality can be examined. Surely, other ways, unfettered by the limitations inherent with central tendency theory, are equally valid, but are not reflected in this volume.

The most obvious point of connection among contributing authors was in the use of an existing dataset for asking and answering research questions related to college student spirituality. Although the dataset will be described in much more detail in the next chapter, volume contributors shared a common experience related to accessing the existing dataset and using it as a vehicle for pursuing their respective lines of inquiry. As part of the award process (described in the Foreword), contributing authors were invited to participate in a training workshop that provided detailed instruction on how to work with the data, including the variables (e.g., institutional religious type) that could not be altered or changed for reasons of maintaining confidentiality among participants and participating institutions. Clearly, this experience accentuated pre-existing dispositions concerning the use of these data; researchers self-selected into a competition that examined spirituality as a set of related constructs measured by existing variables and then were given some guidelines regarding how to use these variables in strategic ways to answer research questions.

In tandem with the common experience of performing secondary data analysis on a pre-existing dataset come a series of limitations each volume contributor likely experienced as a result of participating in this competition. First, authors were not able to ask participants questions perhaps better suited for each particular line of inquiry. Often, this limitation may have made authors feel as though they were fitting a square peg into a round hole as existing variables may not have captured elements of theorized constructs needed to substantiate claims. Second, data were collected at only two time points, once when respondents were in their first year of college and subsequently when they were third-year students. This limitation clearly affects data interpretations, as seniors may have reported differently than juniors and only a modicum of information can be gleaned concerning the stability of change scores over time. Third, the survey used to measure collegiate experiences related to religion and spirituality was based on general collegiate environments known to exert influence on student outcomes. Environmental measures that explicitly reflect myriad campus climate properties and programmatic interventions involving spirituality and religion were not, for the most part, included on the survey. Despite these limitations and the many others left unsaid, the studies contained in this volume are certain to illumine the relationship between college and student spirituality. We turn now to a discussion of the organizational strategy adopted for this volume.

Organization of the Volume

At the heart of each study, although not always explicit, was a common practice among contributors of deconstructing the college experience for its influence on spiritual outcomes. Each author interrogated a series of inputs, environments, and outcomes in hopes of understanding the relationship between college-going and student spirituality.

For this reason, we organized the volume into sections loosely aligned with Astin's Input-Environment-Outcome (IEO) model for understanding college and its influence on students. Loose alignment leaves room for variability among studies with regard to the amount of emphasis each author placed on a particular dimension of the Astin model. Although contributors of each study investigated all three dimensions, certain authors (see Bowman & Small, Chapter 3; Gehrke, Chapter 4) focused more on inputs than either environments or outcomes; while other authors (see Rine, Chapter 5; Bryant Rockenbach & Mayhew, Chapter 6) emphasized environments more than inputs or outcomes; and the remaining authors (see Brandenberger & Bowman, Chapter 7; Chenot & Kim, Chapter 8; Fleming, Purnell, & Wang, Chapter 9; and Faigin, Chapter 10) highlighted outcomes to a greater degree than inputs or environments.

The organization of the volume consists of four parts. The first part, comprised of this chapter and an overview of the methodology, outlines how volume contributors were selected; some of the common approaches contributors shared in developing their research lines; and a description of the dataset that each author used to answer the proposed research questions. The second part of the volume, *Student Characteristics and Group Differences*, focuses on inputs, the characteristics students bring with them to college, and how these characteristics inform conversations about spirituality. The third part, *College Contexts*, emphasizes distinctive college environments and experiences as they relate to spiritual dimensions. The fourth part, *Outcomes*, highlights outcomes related to spiritual development. Following each input, environment, and outcome part, scholars and practitioners share their reflections on the empirical, theoretical, and practical implications of the work presented. Kathy Goodman provides the practitioner reflection for the part on inputs, while Peter Magolda provides the part's researcher reflection. Contributing the practitioner reflection for the environments section is Scotty McLennan; and Peter Hill, Keith Edwards, and Jonathan Hill offer the researcher reflection. Finally, Donna Talbot and Diane Anderson provide the practitioner reflection for the outcomes section, and Mike Waggoner provides the researcher reflection. Carney Strange closes with an epilogue at the end of the volume to offer concluding reflections and overarching implications for this emerging line of research.

References

Astin, A. W., Astin, H. S., & Lindholm, J. A. (2011). *Cultivating the spirit: How college can enhance students' inner lives.* San Francisco, CA: Jossey-Bass.

Stage, F. K. (2007). Answering critical questions using quantitative data. In F. Stage (Ed.), *Using quantitative data to answer critical questions* (pp. 5–23). San Francisco, CA: Jossey-Bass.

2

METHODOLOGICAL OVERVIEW OF THE UCLA SPIRITUALITY IN HIGHER EDUCATION PROJECT

Jennifer A. Lindholm

In 2003, Alexander Astin, Helen Astin, and I launched a multi-year research program to examine the spiritual development of undergraduate students during the college years. Funded by the John Templeton Foundation, the project was designed to enhance understanding of how college students conceive of spirituality, the role it plays in their lives, and how colleges and universities can be more effective in facilitating students' spiritual development. The primary reason for undertaking the study was our shared belief that spirituality is fundamental to students' lives and yet, despite the extraordinary amount of research that has been done on college students, very little systematic study has focused on their spiritual development, particularly at the national level. We were also compelled by a shared sense that the relative amount of attention that colleges and universities devote to the "inner" and "outer" aspects of students' lives is largely out of balance. This chapter offers a brief methodological summary of the research.[1]

From the project's outset, we have conceptualized spirituality as pointing to people's inner, subjective lives, as contrasted to the objective domain of observable behavior and material objects that we can readily point to and measure. We believe that spirituality involves our affective experiences at least as much as it does our reasoning and logic. It is reflected in the values and ideals we hold most dear, our sense of who we are and where we come from, our beliefs about why we are here— the meaning and purpose we see in our lives—and our connectedness to each other and the world around us. Spirituality also captures those aspects of our experience that are not easy to define or talk about, such as intuition, the mysterious, and the mystical.

In undertaking this work, our expectation was that individuals will view their spirituality in somewhat unique ways. For some, traditional religious beliefs will comprise the core of their spirituality; for others, such beliefs or traditions may play little or no part. For us, how students define their spirituality or what particular meaning they make of their lives was not at issue. Rather, we were interested to understand the nature and degree of students' spiritual inclinations, learn how students change spiritually during the college years, and identify ways in which college does, and could, contribute to this developmental process. Our quantitative work encompassed three national surveys of college students (2003, 2004, and 2007) and a national survey of college faculty (2004–05). We also conducted focus group discussions with students along with individual interviews with students and faculty.

Assessing Spirituality and Religiousness

As we developed items that addressed students' spiritual qualities, we were guided by two basic principles: (1) spirituality is a multidimensional construct and no single measure can adequately capture all that we mean when we use the term; and (2) while many students no doubt express their spirituality in terms of some form of organized religion, the fact that others do not requires that we view religiousness and spirituality as separate qualities, and that we attempt to develop separate measures of each. In short, the fundamental task we set for ourselves was to design a survey questionnaire that could provide us with a comprehensive look at each student's spiritual and religious qualities. Toward that end, we worked closely with members of the project's Technical Advisory Panel and reviewed previous studies and instruments. Although our evaluation of these instruments indicated that they contained a number of interesting and potentially useful items, no single instrument appeared to be well suited to the purposes of this project.

We began our survey development process by exploring various definitions of "spirituality" as proposed by scholars in business, education, health, psychology, sociology, and related fields. Because a number of psychologists and measurement specialists have also attempted to develop measures of "spirituality" and "religiousness" we reviewed that critical body of work as well. The limitations inherent in many of these instruments were expressed in different ways. For example, "spirituality" is often equated with traditional religious practices and beliefs, and questions tend to assume a monotheistic, Judeo-Christian belief system. Additionally, no distinction is typically made between "inner" and "outer" manifestations of spirituality (i.e., between spiritual attitudes, beliefs, or perspectives, and spiritual action or behavior).

In developing the new survey instrument, our research team sought to design a set of questions that would meet the following requirements: (1) all students— regardless of their theological/ metaphysical perspective or belief system—should be able to respond to items in a meaningful way; (2) references to "God," a "supreme being," or similar entity would be held to a minimum; rather, students would be given an opportunity to specify what such a concept means to them, including the option to reject the concept; (3) both religious beliefs/perspectives and religious practices/behaviors would be covered, although the use of specific denominational or sectarian terminology would be avoided (e.g., we used "sacred texts" instead of "Bible" or "Koran"); and (4) the items would accommodate those who define their spirituality primarily in terms of conventional religious beliefs and practices, as well as those who define their spirituality in other ways.

Through our preliminary work, we identified twelve content areas or "domains" to be considered in designing items and scales to measure spirituality and religiousness. These included: spiritual or religious orientation/worldview, wellbeing, behavior, quest, experience, emotions, attitudes, and self-assessments. The domains also encompassed theological/metaphysical beliefs, attitudes toward religion and spirituality, and religious affiliation/identity along with perceived facilitators/inhibitors of spiritual development.

Using these domains as a framework, we developed a large number of potential survey items. In addition to modifying many of the items developed by earlier investigators, we also created a number of new items. Throughout this process, the project's Technical Advisory Panel members helped serve as judges in finalizing the relevant domains and selecting the most appropriate items for each domain. This preliminary work led to the development of the College Students' Beliefs and Values (CSBV) Pilot Survey, which included approximately 175 items having to do with spirituality and religion and 50–60 other items covering students' activities and achievements since entering college. The survey also post-tested selected items from the Cooperative Institutional Research Program (CIRP) Freshman Survey questionnaire that these students had completed three years earlier (Fall 2000) when they entered college. In Spring 2003, 3,680 students who were completing their junior year at 46 colleges and universities across the country participated in the CSBV Pilot Survey. To help further contextualize our pilot survey findings, we also conducted focus group interviews with 90 students at 6 campuses across the country.

Longitudinal (2004–07) Survey Procedures

In Fall 2004, we undertook a much larger scale survey involving entering freshmen. That survey was comprised of the traditional four-page CIRP Freshman Survey, which queries students' backgrounds, high school experiences, expectations about college (including majors and careers), and attitudes about social issues, plus a two-page addendum. This addendum, the CSBV Survey, contained 160 specially-designed questions that pertained directly to students' perspectives and practices with respect to spirituality and religion. Most addendum questions were taken from the 2003 CSBV Pilot survey. The Fall 2004 survey was completed by 112,232 first-year students at 236 baccalaureate-granting institutions nationally. Data from the resulting normative sample were subsequently weighted to approximate the responses we would have expected had all first-time, full-time students attending baccalaureate colleges and universities across the country participated in the survey.

In Spring 2007, 14,527 students who were completing their junior year at 136 of these institutions participated in a follow-up survey that repeated most of the 160 questions contained in the CSBV Survey addendum to the 2004 CIRP Survey. This approach enabled us to measure change in students' spiritual and religious qualities during college. Respondents included sizable numbers of students from most religious denominations and racial/ethnic groups, and their colleges represent all types of public, private nonsectarian, and private religiously affiliated institutions (mostly Roman Catholic, mainline Protestant, and Evangelical). A complex weighting scheme allowed us to estimate how the entire population of juniors attending baccalaureate institutions would have responded to the survey.

Because the 2007 CSBV Survey was created as a follow-up to the 2004 CIRP/ CSBV Survey, it was particularly important to post-test key items from the 2004 survey, including those that were used to construct the ten factor scales measuring different aspects of spirituality and religiousness (discussed below). To understand how students' undergraduate experiences may impact their spiritual development, questions concerning college activities, classroom teaching methods, interactions with faculty, discussions on religion and spirituality, and other academic and nonacademic experiences, as well as satisfaction with college, were added to the follow-up survey. As they did during earlier data collection efforts in association with this research, members of the project's Technical Advisory Panel provided valuable feedback during the survey design process. The Spring 2007 follow-up questionnaire was four pages in length, including 150 items having to do with spirituality and/or religion, 59 items covering students' activities and achievements since entering college, and post-tests of selected items from the 2004 CIRP Freshman Survey, such as students' degree aspirations and political orientation.

Developing Measures of Spirituality and Religiousness

One of our goals in conducting the Spirituality in Higher Education study was to develop measures, or "scales," that address various dimensions of spirituality and religiousness by searching for clusters of survey items that form coherent patterns of student responses. All scales were developed using factor analysis and item analysis. Possible scales (i.e., groups of similar items) were identified using principal components analysis with Varimax rotation. Subsequently, each potential scale was subjected to an item analysis (Cronbach Alpha) to eliminate items that were not contributing to scale reliability. Considerations of item content appropriateness were also applied in each stage of scale development. Ultimately, we identified five spiritual measures:

- *Spiritual Quest* is a nine-item measure that assesses an individual's interest in searching for meaning and purpose in life, finding answers to the mysteries of life, attaining inner harmony, and developing a meaningful philosophy of life. Each of the individual items that comprise this heavily process-oriented measure includes words such as "finding," "attaining," "seeking," "developing," "searching," or "becoming."

- *Equanimity* includes five items reflecting the extent to which an individual is able to find meaning in times of hardship, feels at peace or centered, sees each day as a gift, and feels good about the direction of his or her life. Equanimity plays an important role in the quality of people's lives because it helps shape how they respond to their experiences, particularly those that are potentially stressful.

- *Ethic of Caring* is an eight-item measure that assesses an individual's sense of caring and concern about the welfare of others and the world around us. These feelings are expressed in wanting to help those who are troubled and to alleviate suffering, and include a concern about social justice issues and an interest in the welfare of one's community and the environment, as well as a commitment to political activism.

- *Charitable Involvement* is a seven-item behavioral measure that includes activities such as participating in community service, donating money to charity, and helping friends with personal problems.

- *Ecumenical Worldview* is a twelve-item measure that indicates the extent to which the individual is interested in different religious traditions, seeks to understand other countries and cultures, feels a strong connection to all humanity, believes in the goodness of all people, accepts others as they are, and believes that all life is interconnected and that love is at the root of all the great religions.

Framed by these five measures, we developed the following definition:

> Spirituality is a multifaceted quality that involves an active quest for answers to life's "big questions" (Spiritual Quest), a global worldview that transcends ethnocentrism and egocentrism (Ecumenical Worldview), a sense of caring and compassion for others (Ethic of Caring) coupled with a lifestyle that includes service to others (Charitable Involvement), and a capacity to maintain one's sense of calm and centeredness, especially in times of stress (Equanimity).

We also developed five measures of religiousness:

- *Religious Commitment* is an internal measure comprising twelve items. It reflects an individual's self-rating on "religiousness" as well as the degree to which he or she seeks to follow religious teachings in everyday life, finds religion to be personally helpful, and gains personal strength by trusting in a higher power.

- *Religious Engagement* is an external measure that represents the behavioral counterpart to Religious Commitment, includes nine items reflecting behaviors such as attending religious services, praying, engaging in religious singing/chanting, and reading sacred texts.
- *Religious/Social Conservatism* is a seven-item measure reflecting the individual's degree of opposition to such things as casual sex and abortion, a belief that people who don't believe in God will be punished, and a propensity to use prayer as a means of seeking forgiveness. It also involves a commitment to proselytize and an inclination to see God as a father figure.
- *Religious Skepticism* includes nine items reflecting beliefs such as "the universe arose by chance" and "in the future science will be able to explain everything," and disbelief in the notion of life after death.
- *Religious Struggle* includes nine items that represent, for example, the extent to which an individual feels unsettled about religious matters, feels distant from God, or has questioned his or her religious beliefs.

To enhance the measures' applicability to a wide variety of potential religious and non-religious respondents, we avoided using terminology in the survey items that refers to particular faith traditions. Ultimately, we found that these ten measures constitute a reasonably comprehensive set for assessing the spiritual and religious qualities of college students. As detailed in *Cultivating the Spirit*, while substantial differences in survey design make it difficult to directly compare our ten core measures and most of the measures developed by earlier investigators, some scales do incorporate parallel dimensions of spirituality.

Our scales, which were initially developed through the 2003 pilot survey, were replicated in the 2004 freshman survey and in the 2007 longitudinal follow-up. We considered that a pilot scale had been "replicated" if, in an independent sample, it yielded an alpha coefficient and corrected item-scale correlations that were comparable with those obtained in the original pilot sample. The scales' concurrent validity is evidenced through cross-sectional analyses which show that the scales differentiate in meaningful ways among students with different religious affiliations. Evidence of predictive validity is provided by longitudinal analyses showing that scale scores obtained when students first entered college as freshmen correlate significantly with selected college outcomes as assessed at the end of the junior year.

Given that raw scores on the ten factor scales have no absolute meaning, it is useful for research and policy purposes to be able to classify students according to their scores. Since any student's score on one of our measures of spirituality or religiousness reflects the degree to which the student possesses the quality being measured, defining high or low scores is to a certain extent an arbitrary decision. Nevertheless, we made an effort to introduce a certain amount of rationality into such definitions by posing the question: "In order to defend the proposition that someone possesses a 'high' (or 'low') degree of the particular trait in question, what *pattern* of responses to the entire set of questions would that person have to show?" This approach enabled us to identify the percentages of "high" and "low" scores on each measure and to analyze corresponding changes over the course of students' undergraduate careers.[2]

The 2004–05 HERI Faculty Survey

In an effort to understand the role that college faculty play in affecting students' spiritual development, we also collected extensive survey data (via the 2004–05 Higher Education Research Institute's triennial national faculty survey) from individual faculty members, including those at the same institutions where we collected longitudinal student data. In addition to demographic information, the questionnaire focused heavily on topics such as how faculty spend their time, how they interact with their students, how they view their institutions, their preferred methods of teaching, and their primary sources of stress and satisfaction. Spirituality items highlighted faculty perceptions of the intersections between spirituality and higher education and the extent to which faculty personally prioritize addressing spiritually-oriented aspects of student learning and development. The extent to which faculty themselves self-identify as spiritual and religious, and their perspectives on whether the spiritual dimension of their lives has appropriate place within the academy were also addressed.

That survey administration, the largest to date in HERI Faculty Survey history, enabled us to collect information from roughly 61,000 faculty at more than 500 institutions nationwide. Normative data from a subsample of respondents enabled us to approximate as closely as possible the results that would have been obtained if all teaching faculty in all two- and four-year colleges and universities in the United States had responded. Survey content provided considerable information that enabled us to analyze relationships between faculty members' personal inclinations and professional practices. We included some of those findings, particularly as they relate to students' spiritual growth and development, in *Cultivating the Spirit*. Perspectives from individual interviews with faculty provided additional context. Future research to be conducted with respondents who gave their permission to be contacted again for research purposes will enable us to glean additional insight into faculty perspectives and practices. This work will also enable us to evaluate the extent to which our measures of spirituality and religiousness can be replicated with additional populations.

Conclusion

As noted at the outset of this chapter, one of our primary motivations for undertaking the Spirituality in Higher Education project was to learn about the spiritual lives and development of undergraduate students. As work in this realm continues, our hope is that other researchers—like those whose projects are featured in this volume—use the data we have collected to understand in greater depth the spiritual and religious lives of traditionally-aged college students who attend baccalaureate degree-granting institutions. We also encourage colleagues to broaden our existing efforts to include populations that were not the focus of our work, such as adult learners, graduate and professional school students, and two-year college attendees.

Notes

1 Readers who are interested in additional details are encouraged to consult the project website (www.spirituality.ucla.edu) and *Cultivating the Spirit*, a book based on project findings that the Astins and I co-authored in 2011 (Jossey-Bass).
2 For more detailed information on these and other scales we developed over the course of the project, see Astin, A. W., Astin, H. S., & Lindholm, J. A. (2011). Assessing students' spiritual and religious qualities. *Journal of College Student Development, 52*(1), 39–61.

PART II

Student Characteristics and Group Differences

3

THE EXPERIENCES AND SPIRITUAL GROWTH OF RELIGIOUSLY PRIVILEGED AND RELIGIOUSLY MARGINALIZED COLLEGE STUDENTS

Nicholas A. Bowman and Jenny L. Small

Recently, scholars and practitioners have called for colleges and universities to consider the religious and spiritual lives of college students (e.g., Chickering, Dalton, & Stamm, 2005). These attempts to promote spiritual development among all students are complicated by the presence of substantial religious diversity within and across higher education institutions. For instance, Catholic students attending a Catholic college may feel "at home" in practicing their religious beliefs, but they may perceive a lack of institutional support at a public university or a Baptist college. Non-Christian students (e.g., Muslims, Jews) are likely to face challenges at almost any institution, and these difficulties may be particularly pronounced at Christian schools. Thus, students who are religious minorities at their college or university may have reduced spiritual development and well-being when compared with religious majority students.

As researchers, we care deeply about students' spiritual lives and whether their college environments promote, or perhaps hinder, their spiritual growth. As we have explored these questions in our previous work, we have learned that, relative to students from majority religions, those from minority religions have decreased mental well-being and increased religious skepticism at all schools (Bowman & Small, in press; Small & Bowman, 2011), and they do not fare as well spiritually at religious institutions (Bowman & Small, 2010). However, these differences largely disappear when controlling for college religious experiences, an effect which implies that these experiences mediate the relationship between minority/majority status and college outcomes. In other words, we have been able to describe a cycle in which affiliation with a religious minority group is presumably associated with fewer religious experiences, which then leads to reduced well-being and spiritual growth. As a member of a religious minority group, Judaism (Jenny), and of no formal religious affiliation (Nick), we identify personally with these students and their complicated relationship to exploring their spiritual identities while in college.

Religious Majority and Minority Students

Until very recently, religious diversity on college campuses has received little empirical attention (Nash, 2007; Patel, 2007), and religious minority groups have generally been overlooked in research on religiosity, spirituality, and well-being (Raiya, Pargament, Mahoney, & Stein, 2008; Tarakeshwar, Pargament, & Mahoney, 2003). It is critical this situation be rectified, as students from marginalized religious affiliations have been on the negative, receiving end of Christian privilege. Christian privilege is comprised of "the conscious and subconscious advantages often afforded the Christian faith in America's colleges and universities" (Seifert, 2007, p. 11), and this issue remains problematic in higher education (Watt, Fairchild, & Goodman, 2009).

Although Christian students may be unaware of their privilege (Schlosser, 2003), Small (2011) demonstrates that religious minority students are acutely aware of their marginalization, and this consciousness distinguishes their ways of viewing the world from those of majority students. In Small's study, students from all faith backgrounds described a three-tier structure of religious privilege in society, with Christians at the top, atheists at the bottom, and other religions in the middle. This structure caused stress for Jewish and Muslim students, who struggled to reconcile their beliefs with those of the mainstream; for atheist students, who often took a defensive posture; and for Christian students, who tried to understand their own roles in perpetuating their privilege.

For the most part, there is agreement about which religious affiliations constitute majority and minority (or privileged and marginalized) groups in American society. The privileged majority is comprised solely of Christian denominations, which include the mainline Protestant faiths Presbyterian, Methodist, Lutheran, Episcopalian, and United Church of Christ/Congregational (Bonderud & Fleischer, 2005; Roof & McKinney, 1987). Other relatively privileged Christian groups include Roman Catholic, Baptist, Church of Christ, and "other Christians." This classification is consistent with Beaman's (2003) conception, in that "Protestantism, and to some extent Catholicism, are constructed as the normal against which the 'other' is established" (p. 313).

Evangelical Christians, an important, growing group in the United States (Boorstein, 2009), can alternatively be considered privileged (as adherents of the most prevalent religion in the country) or marginalized (as somewhat outside of the mainstream ideologically). These students may disavow their privileged status, perceiving themselves as an oppressed minority on secular college and university campuses (Moran, Lang, & Oliver, 2007), and evangelical student organizations often position themselves as outsiders to campus cultural norms (Magolda & Gross, 2009).

Religious affiliations that are considered to be minorities include all non-Christian religions, such as Buddhist, Hindu, Islamic, Quaker, and Jewish. We describe these students as *double religious minorities*, as they are minorities both on their campuses and in society at large. Double religious minority students often do not receive the support they need from practitioners on campus and through current research. For instance, Jewish students may be less involved in student religious groups on campus, leading to fewer experiences of community support for their beliefs (Sax, 2002). Muslim students may find themselves and their religion grossly misunderstood, even by faculty members (Speck, 1997). Certain groups of students have been studied so little that it is difficult to locate any research about them (for example, see Kurien, 2005, on the topic of Hindu college students).

Moreover, LDS (Mormon) and Unitarian/Universalist students are considered marginalized minorities due to their separation from traditional Christian religious roots (Swatos, 1998) and their unique pattern of beliefs (Higher Education Research Institute, 2005). Seventh Day Adventists and Mormons, while defined by their adherents to be Christian, do not enjoy overall acceptance within the larger Christian base; they have fewer members, their beliefs are often stereotyped, and these groups may be considered cults (Schlosser, 2003). Eastern Orthodox students are considered minorities due to their significant ideological differences from Roman Catholicism (Flanagan, 1998) and their extremely low numbers on college campuses. Finally, those students with no religious affiliation, in particular atheists, have often been near-invisible minorities both on campus and in research on college students (Nash, 2003).

Despite the prevalence and prominence of these power dynamics, few studies have examined how students' spiritual beliefs and identities vary across religious affiliations. The most widely recognized theories of faith development (Fowler, 1981; Parks, 2000) have not integrated the possible differential impact of religious marginalization. Some authors have offered in-depth descriptions of the beliefs of students from particular religious minority groups (Nash, 2003; Peek, 2005; Sax, 2002), and one examination of non-religious students and students from five minority religions found that each group has its "own unique perspectives, principles, and foundational ideologies and values" (Bryant, 2006, p. 21). However, beyond Bryant's study, the lack of comparative analysis based on religious minority/majority status leaves one to question the broad applicability of certain findings.

Recent evidence, some of which we have collected ourselves, suggests that affiliation with a religious minority group or no organized religious group is adversely related to college student outcomes. For instance, college students from several minority religious groups experience greater religious and spiritual struggle than majority students (Bryant & Astin, 2008; Small & Bowman, 2011), and spiritual struggle, in turn, is negatively associated with religious growth and well-being (Bryant & Astin, 2008). Students who do not identify with any organized religion are generally less satisfied with their college experience than are Protestant students (Bowman & Toms Smedley, 2011). The link between minority status and student outcomes can also vary by institutional type; for instance, at secular and Catholic schools, Catholic students experience greater increases in spiritual identification than their mainline Christian peers, but the opposite pattern occurs at non-Catholic religious schools (Bowman & Small, 2010; also see Hill, 2009).

Present Study

This study further explores the links between several types of religious minority/ majority status and students' experiences and spiritual growth. In our previous research (Bowman & Small, 2010, in press; Small & Bowman, 2011), many of the effects of religious affiliation at the individual and institutional levels disappeared when controlling for students' college experiences, which implies that these experiences mediate the relationship between religious affiliation and subsequent outcomes. Therefore, in this study, we employed a multi-level path analysis approach to examine (a) the associations between college students' religious affiliations and spiritual identification and quest and (b) the extent to which these associations were explained by students' religious/spiritual experiences during college. In doing so, we conducted an empirical examination of a conceptual framework that may account for the relationship between religious affiliation and student spiritual growth. This study also examined whether and how individual-level relationships differ across institutional contexts. Because some colleges and universities are affiliated with particular religious organizations and denominations, the relationships between religious minority status and college experiences are likely to be more pronounced at religiously affiliated schools.

Methods

Dependent Variables

The existing measures of *spiritual identification* and *spiritual quest* were used (see Chapter 2). Two college experiences were included as dependent variables in some analyses and predictors of spiritual growth in others. *Faculty support of spiritual/religious development* was assessed with a five-item index ($\alpha = .82$). These items gauged the extent to which faculty "encouraged exploration of questions of meaning and purpose," "encouraged discussion of religious/spiritual matters," and "acted as spiritual role models for you" (Bowman & Small, 2010, in press). The existing scale for *religious engagement* was also used (see Chapter 2).

Independent Variables

Double religious minorities were defined as those who are considered minorities in mainstream society and on their college campus; these include students who identify as Buddhist, Eastern Orthodox, Hindu, Islamic, Jewish, LDS (Mormon), Quaker, Seventh Day Adventist, Unitarian/Universalist, and "other religion." One institution contained a majority of students who identified as Mormon; therefore, the Mormon students on this campus were not considered double religious minorities. As with all variables pertaining to religious affiliation and institutional type, double religious minority status was represented with a dichotomous variable (1 = double minority, 0 = other). *Non-religiously affiliated students* were those who reported their current religious affiliation as "none." Another dummy-coded predictor variable indicated students who identified as Roman Catholic. Moreover, a separate item on the expanded CIRP survey asked students whether they consider themselves to be "born-again Christians." To maintain mutually exclusive groups for religious affiliation, a variable was created to denote students who identified as born-again Christians and were affiliated with a mainline Christian denomination (e.g., not double minorities, such as Seventh Day Adventists). Mainline Christians (e.g., Lutherans, Methodists, Presbyterians) who did not identify as born-again were the referent group. For brevity's sake, students in these latter two groups will be described as *born-again Christians* and *mainline Christians*, respectively. Institutional type was gauged with a dummy-coded variable representing Catholic schools and another representing other religious (i.e., non-Catholic) schools. Secular schools served as the institutional referent group.

We used both existing indices of initial *ecumenical worldview*: one that characterized each individual student's views and another that represented the average of all students who completed the initial questionnaire at her/his institution (see Chapter 2). By including both of these indices, the unique effects of individual and average institutional perceptions can be examined.

Other precollege variables included gender (0 = male, 1 = female), age (1 = 16 or younger, to 10 = 55 or older), and parental education (mean of mother's and father's education; 1 = grammar school or less, to 8 = graduate degree). Several dichotomous variables indicated race/ethnicity: African American/Black; American Indian/Alaska Native; Asian American/Asian and Native Hawaiian/ Pacific Islander (a combination of two categories from the CIRP survey); Mexican American/Chicano, Puerto Rican, and Other Latino (a combination of three CIRP categories); and Other. White/Caucasian served as the referent group. Pretest or initial values of spiritual identification and spiritual quest were also used. The dependent variables and continuous independent variables were then standardized with a mean of zero and a standard deviation of one for inclusion in the analyses. As a result, the unstandardized regression coefficients for continuous independent variables can be interpreted as standardized coefficients, and those for dichotomous independent variables can be interpreted in terms of adjusted effect sizes (Cohen, Cohen, West, & Aiken, 2003).

Analyses

Because the current sample contained students nested within institutions and because some of the primary research questions dealt with the relationship between institutional and individual characteristics, hierarchical linear modeling (HLM) analyses were used. Two HLM models were examined for each outcome variable. In all analyses, independent variables in Model 1 included gender, age, race/ethnicity, parental education, double religious minority, Catholic, born-again Christian, and non-religiously affiliated student at level 1; Catholic institution, other religious institution, and the institution's average ecumenical worldview were included at level 2. Because the relationships among religious affiliation, college experiences, and student outcomes are conceptualized in terms of a path model, some predictors differ across the HLM analyses. Specifically, faculty support for spiritual/religious affiliation predicted religious engagement, and both faculty support and religious engagement were predictors of the spirituality variables. Moreover, the pretest for each spirituality variable was used as a predictor in the relevant analyses. A diagram that conveys these associations appears in Figure 3.1.

Two models predicting each student experience were examined. Model 1 held the level-1 slopes constant across institutions, whereas Model 2 contained the same variables and allowed the slopes to vary for student religious affiliations, student ecumenical worldviews, and faculty support for spiritual/religious development (when predicting religious engagement). The level-2 variables of Catholic school and other religious school were also added as predictors of the slopes of these level-1 variables. In other words, this slopes-as-outcomes model examines whether the effect of being a Catholic student, for example, depends upon the institution's religious affiliation. This model is conceptually similar to the moderated mediation approach described in Muller, Judd, and Yzerbyt (2005).

Moreover, for analyses predicting spiritual growth, the indirect effects of student and institutional religious affiliation (which were mediated through faculty support and religious engagement) were computed. These indirect effects from religious affiliation to spiritual growth occur through three separate paths (through religious engagement, through faculty support, and through both faculty support and religious engagement). Significance tests for indirect effects of path analyses are generally designed for only one mediating variable (e.g., MacKinnon, Lockwood, Hoffman, West, & Sheets, 2002) or for multiple mediators that do not directly affect one another (e.g., Preacher & Hayes, 2008). Therefore, the significance of the total indirect effect through all paths was calculated using the difference in HLM coefficients between the model that contained both mediators and the model that did not (Freedman & Schatzkin, 1992; MacKinnon et al., 2002). Because the

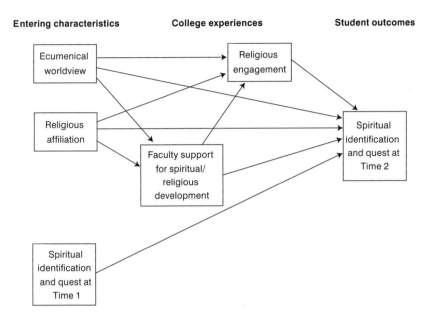

Entering characteristics   College experiences   Student outcomes

FIGURE 3.1 Diagram of predicted relationships between precollege characteristics, college experiences, and desired outcomes (e.g., spiritual identification and spiritual quest).

dependent variables were standardized while the dichotomous predictors were not, the HLM coefficients take the form of a partially standardized indirect effect (Preacher & Kelley, 2011). As a result, some of the coefficients for the indirect effects are small in magnitude—and in practical significance—but they are highly statistically significant within this large sample.

Intra-class correlations (ICCs) were computed for each HLM outcome. The proportion of variance that occurred at the institutional level was quite high for religious engagement (24 percent) and faculty support for spiritual/religious engagement (34 percent), and these were lower for spiritual identification (13 percent) and spiritual quest (5 percent).

Limitations

Some limitations should be noted. First, although the label of "born-again Christian" serves as a reasonable proxy for Christian fundamentalism, it does not perfectly capture the religious affiliation of students whose beliefs are more extreme than the majority of mainline Christians (and are thus more likely to view themselves as marginalized). Second, the proportion of variance that occurred between institutions was somewhat low for spiritual quest. HLM analyses are less likely to yield significant findings for level-2 predictors and for predictors of slopes when the proportion of between-group variance is low. However, as shown below, some institutional characteristics were still significant predictors.

Findings

Here, we discuss our examination of the relationship between religious minority/ majority status, college experiences, and spiritual development, focusing primarily on the key findings. The HLM analyses demonstrate that students' religious affiliations are strongly related to their religious engagement and to perceived faculty support for spiritual/religious development (see Table 3.1). Most notably, students attending religiously affiliated institutions report substantially higher levels of this form of faculty support (particularly at "other" religious institutions), and religious affiliation is strongly related to religious engagement during college. Although previous research had established this general pattern for religious engagement (Higher Education Research Institute, 2005), the current study demonstrated that these differences occur among students attending the same institution and across diverse institutional types. Moreover, religious engagement and faculty support for spiritual/religious development are both directly associated with gains on both spirituality outcomes (see Table 3.2). Thus, these experiences seem to play an important role in promoting spiritual growth. The following discussion explores these dynamics for several religious minority and majority groups.

Double religious minority students are less religiously engaged than mainline Christians, and religious engagement is positively associated with spirituality in the junior year; thus, an indirect, negative effect on spiritual identification exists for double religious minority status. However, this indirect effect is reasonably small, and no direct effect is observed for either of the spirituality outcomes. Therefore, these minority students—most of whom likely grew up as religious minorities before college—may have already adapted to their marginalized religious status. As a result, they may not be substantially affected by their minority status, particularly within secular colleges and universities. However, these students seem to suffer at Catholic schools, where the effect of double religious minority status is substantial and negative (Bowman & Small, 2010).

As expected, the experiences of Catholic students vary tremendously across institutional type, because these students constitute the privileged majority on Catholic campuses, but a potentially marginalized minority at other religious institutions. In the entire sample, Catholics perceive greater faculty support for their spiritual/religious development than do mainline Christians, but this pattern is essentially reversed at other religious schools. Furthermore, the effect of being Catholic on religious engagement is more positive at Catholic schools than at secular schools, but this effect is more negative at other religious schools than at secular schools.

TABLE 3.1 Unstandardized coefficients for hierarchical linear models predicting spiritual experiences

Independent variable	Faculty support for spiritual/religious development Model 1	Faculty support for spiritual/religious development Model 2	Religious engagement Model 1	Religious engagement Model 2
Catholic school	.608***	.622***	−.069	−.172
	(.072)	(.102)	(.071)	(.105)
Other religious school	1.068***	1.003***	.372***	.568***
	(.117)	(.137)	(.078)	(.136)
Average ecumenical worldview	.164***	.168***	.064+	.005
	(.038)	(.031)	(.034)	(.019)
Double religious Intercept	.088	.055	−.190*	−.136
minority	(.063)	(.071)	(.075)	(.100)
Catholic school		−.188		.079
		(.121)		(.163)
Other religious school		.054		−.138
		(.117)		(.140)
Catholic Intercept	.153*	.127	.041	.052+
	(.077)	(.098)	(.029)	(.028)
Catholic school		.000		.243***
		(.124)		(.055)
Other religious school		−.296+		−.152**
		(.152)		(.047)
Born-again Christian Intercept	.144**	.114	.628***	.746***
	(.043)	(.059)	(.071)	(.090)
Catholic school		.157		−.022
		(.110)		(.115)
Other religious school		.165+		−.363**
		(.091)		(.134)
No organized religion Intercept	.056+	.078*	−.824***	−.777***
	(.032)	(.035)	(.047)	(.073)
Catholic school		−.113		.190
		(.098)		(.125)
Other religious school		−.309**		−.273*
		(.090)		(.125)
Ecumenical worldview Intercept	.155***	.148***	.049**	.058*
	(.015)	(.016)	(.016)	(.022)
Catholic school		.048		.058+
		(.033)		(.032)
Other religious school		.009		−.063*
		(.040)		(.028)
Faculty support for Intercept			.193***	.184***
spiritual/religious development			(.016)	(.017)
Catholic school				.009
				(.030)
Other religious school				.056*
				(.026)

Note: Gender, race/ethnicity, age, and parental education were also included as level-1 predictors.
+ p < .10 , * p < .05, ** p < .01, *** p < .001

TABLE 3.2 Unstandardized coefficients for indirect and direct effects of religious affiliation and experiences on spiritual growth

	Dependent variable			
	Spiritual identification		Spiritual quest	
Independent variable	Indirect effect	Direct effect	Indirect effect	Direct effect
Catholic school	.089***	−.068*	.127***	−.061
Other religious school	.396***	−.167***	.291***	−.163**
Average ecumenical worldview	.064***	−.009	.046***	−.027
Double religious minority student	−.074***	.031	−.007***	.100
Catholic student	.051***	−.007	.040***	.104*
Born-again Christian student	.334***	.063	.120***	.008
Non-religiously affiliated student	−.389***	.025	−.103***	.090*
Ecumenical worldview	.055***	.072***	.042**	.051
Faculty support for spiritual/ religious development	.094***	.108***	.027**	.197***
Religious engagement	N/A	.485***	N/A	.140***

Note: With the exception of faculty support for spiritual/religious development, the coefficients for indirect effects are the sum of three distinct paths (through faculty support, through religious engagement, and through faculty support and religious engagement). The indirect path for faculty support for spiritual/religious development occurs only through religious engagement. Gender, race/ethnicity, age, parental education, and the pretest were also included as level-1 predictors in all models.
+ $p < .10$ * $p < .05$ ** $p < .01$ *** $p < .001$

Some of these findings are likely the product of self-selection (i.e., more religiously committed Catholics decide to attend Catholic schools), but the other patterns are more complex. On average, students from all religious backgrounds who attend other religious institutions are more religiously engaged than those at Catholic institutions. Although the difference in slopes seems to suggest that Catholics at other religious schools have relatively low levels of religious engagement, their engagement is actually much higher than Catholics who attend Catholic schools (see Figure 3.2). Moreover, Catholic students as a whole tend to experience greater gains in spiritual quest than do mainline Christians, and these patterns appear to be consistent across institutional types (see Bowman & Small, 2010). Therefore, in terms of the religious engagement and spiritual development measures used in this study, Catholic students do not receive greater benefits from attending Catholic colleges and universities than from attending other religious institutions. These findings echo those from a previous HERI-conducted

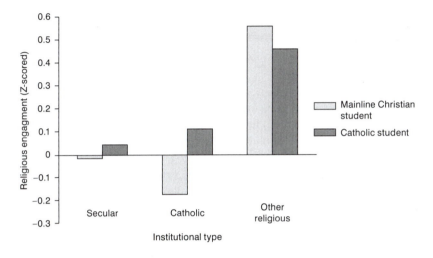

FIGURE 3.2 Hierarchical linear modeling results for student and institutional religious affiliation predicting religious engagement.

study, sponsored by the *Catholic World Report* and the Cardinal Newman Society; in response to those findings, a leader at a Catholic institution suggested that "administrators [at Catholic colleges] put their focus on comparisons with secular institutions, leaving little room for consideration of their Catholic identity" (Reilly, 2003, p. 45).

As noted earlier, many born-again and evangelical Christians often see themselves as being marginalized minorities (Moran *et al.*, 2007) or outside of the mainstream of secular campuses (Magolda & Gross, 2009). However, these students flourish religiously and spiritually on college campuses. Compared with mainline Christians, born-again Christians perceive greater faculty support for spiritual/religious development, and they report substantially greater religious engagement. Indeed, for both spiritual outcomes, the indirect, positive effects of identifying as a born-again Christian are notably larger than the direct effects.

In our earlier work (Bowman & Small, 2010), we found that non-religiously affiliated students had smaller gains in spiritual identification than mainline Christians. The current study finds massive differences in religious engagement between students who have no religious affiliation and mainline Christians, along with negative, indirect effects of non-affiliation on both spiritual outcomes, especially spiritual identification. Thus, religious engagement seems to largely account for the previously observed patterns (also note that faculty support appears to play some limited role in mediating the impact on spiritual identification). In the current analyses, not being affiliated with an organized religion has a direct, positive relationship with spiritual quest, but this is counteracted by a negative, indirect effect of approximately the same size. That is, there is no overall difference between non-religiously affiliated and mainline Christian students on changes in spiritual quest.

Reflections

The results of this study have important implications for college and university educators, many of which may be implemented in straightforward ways. We have demonstrated that through a combination of attending to the needs of specific types of students and emphasizing effective institutional characteristics, the development and maintenance of students' spiritual identities during their college years can be successfully supported. Given the positive relationships between spiritual activity and other desirable activities and outcomes (e.g., Kuh & Gonyea, 2005; Posner, Slater, & Boone, 2006), administrators working to improve students' spiritual development can help promote both spiritual involvement and the ensuing positive results. We do recognize, however, that this may be a foreign or novel goal for many educators, so we offer some introductory ways to begin this important work. Our focus is on the key factors of student religious engagement and faculty support.

Religious Engagement

At the fundamental level, educators need to understand that a student's level of religious engagement during college largely explains the relationship between his/her religious affiliation and spiritual identification. The findings suggest that all types of institutions can bolster their students' spiritual development by providing opportunities to become involved with relevant activities. For educators at religious institutions, it is clear that a continued emphasis should be placed on students' becoming involved in their religious communities or spending time in personal exploration and reflection upon their spiritual beliefs. At religiously affiliated schools in particular, educators must ensure that double religious minority and non-affiliated students have the chance to express and explore their spiritual and religious beliefs, as these minority viewpoints may often be overlooked. These students may even benefit from direct exploration of their differences from the environment around them, because "at least moderate levels of misfit may encourage creativity, independence, and a personal sense of control in life" (Pargament, 1986, p. 681).

We understand that for educators at public institutions, however, this type of promotion yields more perceived complications. As long as administrators do not favor either religious or non-religious organizations over one another, however, student groups that engage in religious or spiritual activities do have a legal right to utilize space and resources on public campuses (Lowery, 2004). Students may benefit from this important form of engagement due to this freedom for religious expression. Therefore, educators should not shy away from offering these opportunities.

Faculty Support

We identified another potential lever for fostering student spiritual development; students' perception of faculty support for their spiritual/religious development is also a key mediator of the link between religious affiliation and the outcomes of spiritual identification and quest. In other words, students who feel they have institutionalized approval for their religious beliefs (in this case, as represented by the faculty) will feel comfortable considering their spiritual identities and searching for meaning. Concerned faculty members can feel confident that they can make a direct difference in the quality of students' lives. They can actualize these concerns by engaging their students in conversations about religion and spirituality, and about personal purpose and meaning, either within or without the classroom setting, as appropriate and welcomed by students.

Directions for Practice and Future Research

This study provides a compelling picture of how educators and administrators can work to construct campus climates that foster student spiritual development, focusing on those key areas of student religious engagement and faculty support of students' questing behaviors. Ideally, allowing spiritual and religious student groups equal opportunities to use campus resources would give all students a chance to explore their spiritual selves. Educators at religiously affiliated schools, in particular, will have to establish an awareness of the needs of religious minority students that demonstrate lower levels of spiritual growth. Mentoring communities (Parks, 2000) and "safe spaces" (Magolda & Gross, 2009) are two avenues discussed in the literature that educators can help these students explore. Furthermore, working with faculty to ensure that they support the development of all students—even those whose religions differ from the institutional affiliation—will be a critical step for higher education administrators and practitioners.

As scholars who have helped develop this relatively new research area of college student spirituality, we know first-hand that fostering spiritual growth among college students from diverse religious backgrounds is not a simple task. Practitioners and administrators at public institutions may not feel comfortable being involved in spirituality or religiosity in any manner, and those at faith-based institutions may be inclined to focus on students with a particular religious affiliation or set of beliefs. Taken together, this leads to an overall blindness to the needs of double religious minority students during their college years, no matter the institutional type.

We recommend that future research on this topic delve more deeply into issues broached in this study, including the confluence and divergence between students' beliefs and the institutional mission and the potential relationship between faculty support and perceived institutional support for religious diversity. Some of these questions may be better answered by surveying faculty at a variety of institutions and/or through qualitative research. Knowing what we do now about the ways institutions can positively impact students' spiritual growth, researchers should continue to explore these types of questions, both to provide fundamental answers about religiously diverse college students and to provide additional insights and tools to campus practitioners.

References

Beaman, L. G. (2003). The myth of pluralism, diversity, and vigor: The constitutional privilege of Protestantism in the United States and Canada. *Journal for the Scientific Study of Religion, 43*(3), 311–325.

Bonderud, K., & Fleischer, M. (2005). *College students report high levels of spirituality and religiousness: Major study has implications for colleges, health, and politics*. Los Angeles: University of California, Higher Education Research Institute.

Boorstein, M. (2009). 15% of Americans have no religion. *The Washington Post,* March 9, p. A04.

Bowman, N. A., & Small, J. L. (2010). Do college students who identify with a privileged religion experience greater spiritual development? Exploring individual and institutional dynamics. *Research in Higher Education, 51*(7), 595–614.

Bowman, N. A., & Small, J. L. (in press). Exploring a hidden form of minority status: College students' religious affiliation and well-being. *Journal of College Student Development.*

Bowman, N. A., & Toms Smedley, C. (2012). *The forgotten minority: Examining religious affiliation and college satisfaction in the United States*. Manuscript submitted for publication.

Bryant, A. N. (2006). Exploring religious pluralism in higher education: Non-majority religious perspectives among entering first-year college students. *Religion & Education, 33*(1), 1–25.

Bryant, A. N., & Astin, H. S. (2008). The correlates of spiritual struggle during the college years. *Journal of Higher Education, 79*(1), 1–28.

Chickering, A. W., Dalton, J. C., & Stamm, L. (2005). *Encouraging authenticity & spirituality in higher education*. San Francisco: Jossey-Bass.

Cohen, J., Cohen, P., West, S. G., & Aiken, L. S. (2003). *Applied multiple regression/correlation analysis for the behavioral sciences* (3rd edn). Mahwah, NJ: Lawrence Erlbaum.

Flanagan, K. (1998). Eastern Orthodoxy [Electronic Version]. *Encyclopedia of Religion and Society*. Retrieved May 15, 2009 from http://hirr.hartsem.edu/ency/eastern.htm.

Fowler, J. W. (1981). *Stages of faith: The psychology of human development and the quest for meaning*. San Francisco: Harper Collins.

Freedman, L. S., & Schatzkin, A. (1992). Sample size for studying intermediate endpoints within intervention trials of observational studies. *American Journal of Epidemiology, 136*, 1148–1159.

Higher Education Research Institute. (2005). *The spiritual life of college students: A national study of college students' search for meaning and purpose*. Los Angeles: University of California, Higher Education Research Institute.

Hill, J. P. (2009). Higher education as moral community: Institutional influences on religious participation during college. *Journal for the Scientific Study of Religion, 48*(3), 515–534.

Kuh, G. D., & Gonyea, R. M. (2005). *Exploring the relationships between spirituality, liberal learning, and college student engagement*. Bloomington, IN: Indiana University. Retrieved September 11, 2006 from http://www.nsse.iub.edu/pdf/research_papers/teagle.pdf.

Kurien, P. A. (2005). Being young, brown, and Hindu: The identity struggles of second-generation Indian Americans. *Journal of Contemporary Ethnography, 34*(4), 434–469.

Lowery, J. W. (2004). Understanding the legal protections and limitations upon religion and spiritual expression on campus. *College Student Affairs Journal, 23*(2), 146–157.

MacKinnon, D. P., Lockwood, C. M., Hoffman, J. M., West, S. G., & Sheets, V. (2002). A comparison of methods to test ediation and other intervening variable effects. *Psychological Methods, 7*(1), 83–104.

Magolda, P., & Gross, K. E. (2009). *It's all about Jesus! Faith as an oppositional subculture.* Sterling, VA: Stylus.

Moran, C. D., Lang, D. J., & Oliver, J. (2007). Cultural incongruity and social status ambiguity: The experiences of evangelical Christian student leaders at two Midwestern public universities. *Journal of College Student Development, 48*(1), 23–38.

Muller, D., Judd, C. M., & Yzerbyt, V. Y. (2005). When moderation is mediated and mediation is moderated. *Journal of Personality and Social Psychology, 89*, 852–863.

Nash, R. J. (2003). Inviting atheists to the table: A modest proposal for higher education. *Religion and Education, 30*(1), 1–23.

Nash, R. J. (2007). Understanding and promoting religious pluralism on college campuses [Electronic Version]. *Spirituality and Higher Education Newsletter, 3*(4), 1–9.

Pargament, K. I. (1986). Refining fit: Conceptual and methodological challenges. *American Journal of Community Psychology, 14*(6), 677–684.

Parks, S. D. (2000). *Big questions, worthy dreams: Mentoring young adults in their search for meaning, purpose and faith.* San Francisco: Jossey-Bass.

Patel, E. (2007). Religious diversity and cooperation on campus. *Journal of College and Character, 9*(2), 1–8.

Peek, L. (2005). Becoming Muslim: The development of a religious identity. *Sociology of Religion, 66*(3), 215–242.

Posner, B., Slater, C., & Boone, M. (2006). Spirituality and leadership among college freshmen. *International Journal of Servant-Leadership, 2*(1), 165–180.

Preacher, K. J., & Hayes, A. F. (2008). Asymptotic and resampling strategies for assessing and comparing indirect effects in multiple mediator models. *Behavior Research Methods, 40*(3), 879–891.

Preacher, K. J., & Kelley, K. (2011). Effect size measures for mediation models: Quantitative strategies for communicating indirect effects. *Psychological Methods, 16*(2), 93–115.

Raiya, H. A., Pargament, K. I., Mahoney, A., & Stein, C. (2008). A psychological measure of Islamic religiousness: Development and evidence for reliability and validity. *International Journal for the Psychology of Religion, 18*, 291–315.

Reilly, P. J. (2003). Are Catholic colleges leading students astray? A nationwide survey raises concerns about the impact that American colleges have on the faith and morals of Catholic students. *The Catholic World Report*, March.

Roof, W. C., & McKinney, W. (1987). *American mainline religion: Its changing shape and future.* New Brunswick, NJ: Rutgers University Press.

Sax, L. (2002). *America's Jewish freshmen: Current characteristics and recent trends among students entering college.* Los Angeles: University of California, Higher Education Research Institution.

Schlosser, L. Z. (2003). Christian privilege: Breaking a sacred taboo. *Journal of Multicultural Counseling and Development, 31*(Jan.), 44–51.

Seifert, T. (2007). Understanding Christian privilege: Managing the tensions of spiritual plurality. *About Campus, 12*(2), 10–18.

Small, J. L. (2011). *Understanding college students' spiritual identities: Different faiths, varied worldviews.* Cresskill, NJ: Hampton Press.

Small, J. L., & Bowman, N. A. (2011). Religious commitment, skepticism, and struggle among college students: The impact of majority/minority religious affiliation and institutional type. *Journal for the Scientific Study of Religion, 50*(1), 154–174.

Speck, B. W. (1997). Respect for religious differences: The case of Muslim students. *New Directions for Teaching and Learning, 70*, 39–46.

Swatos, W. H. (1998). Unitarianism [Electronic Version]. *Encyclopedia of Religion and Society.* Retrieved May 15, 2009 from http://www.hartfordinstitute.org/ency/Unitarianism.htm.

Tarakeshwar, N., Pargament, K. I., & Mahoney, A. (2003). Initial development of a measure of religious coping among Hindus. *Journal of Community Psychology, 31*(6), 607–628.

Watt, S. K., Fairchild, E. E., & Goodman, K. M. (Eds.). (2009). *Intersections of religious privilege: Difficult dialogues and student affairs practice.* San Francisco: Wiley.

4

RACE AND PRO-SOCIAL INVOLVEMENT

Toward a More Complex Understanding of Spiritual Development in College

Sean J. Gehrke

"I am a spiritual person." These words can mean a wide variety of things. One can be a spiritual person through engaging in rituals prescribed by his religion. One might consider herself spiritual if she feels at peace when in nature. One could feel a longing or searching for what is transcendent but not have the words to describe it. However one describes what it means to be spiritual, I believe strongly that the act of defining spirituality is inherently a personal endeavor. I once found my spiritual fulfillment solely through the practices of Protestant Christianity, and I have since expanded my searching beyond the confines of organized religion and have looked for purpose and wholeness through a variety of life pursuits. I am a spiritual person, and while I often have difficulty putting into words how this spirituality plays out in my life, I know that I am searching for meaning in this world and find solace in pursuits that bring me into community with others and communion with the natural world that surrounds me. The period in my life where I experienced the most questioning and evaluation of my personal spirituality, which led me closest to my current understanding of it, was college. The impact that my college experience had on me and these inherent feelings is what draws me to the study of college student spirituality.

I first discovered the academic study of spirituality while researching developmental frameworks to apply to Christian college students as part of a first-year Master's course in higher education and student affairs. The works of Fowler (1981) and Parks (1980; 2000) immediately resonated with me as they gave me the language to describe my internal search for purpose and meaning. These scholars provided me with a framework through which to evaluate my own spiritual development. This discovery sparked an intense academic interest in exploring how college students develop spiritually and the relationships between college involvement experiences and spiritual development. Through this work, I have uncovered another facet of life experience that contributes to my spiritual fulfillment.

The fact that I have found inspiration and meaning in theories of spiritual development comes as little surprise because I resemble the participants that Fowler (1981) and Parks (1980; 2000) studied. I am White and was raised in the Christian faith tradition. While I choose to define my spirituality outside of a religious framework, I cannot deny the impact of my religious upbringing on my current beliefs. In early conversations as I began to study spirituality, both with people of color and those from underrepresented religious traditions, I was surprised to learn that they were drawn to the academic study of spirituality because *they did not resonate* with mainstream spiritual development theories. In fact, their experiences were not clearly represented in them. The lack of ethnic and religious diversity inherent in the studies that informed these theories (Mayhew, 2004) drew me to consider how individuals who come from different backgrounds may develop and be shaped by the collegiate experience in ways that are attuned to their backgrounds. While some work has been done to examine differences in spiritual development by race/ethnicity, there have been few or no opportunities to begin to answer these questions with a large, generalizable sample. The opportunity to use a large dataset to examine differences in spiritual development, specifically for students of different racial identities, is what led me to the work of the Higher Education Research Institute and was the impetus for this study.

Specifically, this study seeks to explore the dynamics of spiritual growth in college for students from different racial and ethnic backgrounds. In this study I examine differences in spirituality between African American/Black, Asian American/Pacific Islander, Latino/Hispanic, and White/Caucasian students both upon entrance to college and the completion of the junior year of college. I also examine the impact of pro-social college experiences on the spiritual growth of these students. This chapter will focus predominantly on the differences in spiritual growth between these groups of students while highlighting some of the key findings of the study examining pro-social involvement and its impact on spiritual development.

Spirituality in College

In order to accomplish the aforementioned purpose, I focused my literature review on two specific areas of empirical research on student spirituality: how researchers have explored spirituality with regard to race and ethnic identification and how scholars have examined the relationship between spirituality and pro-social involvement. In examining the literature, it quickly became apparent that race was not a specific component of many articles on spirituality, probably due to a lack of adequate ethnic diversity in their samples to make meaning of group differences. Those that do focus on race and ethnicity provide the groundwork upon which this study builds.

Spirituality and Race

Research has shown that college leads to changes in many facets of students' lives (Astin, 1993b), including spiritual and religious beliefs and values. Several scholars have examined changes in spirituality and religiosity (Bryant, 2007; Bryant, Choi, & Yasuno, 2003; Muller & Dennis, 2007; Zinnbauer & Pargament, 1998). However, their findings are limited by the lack of ethnic diversity in their samples. Others have shown that the spiritual experiences of college students do vary depending on other social identities and factors such as gender (Bryant, 2007), sexual orientation (Love, Bock, Jannarone, & Richardson, 2005), and worldview (Mayhew, 2004).

While race has not been the focus of many researchers of spirituality, several scholars have addressed it. Tisdell (2003) asserts that spirituality occurs in a cultural context. While research has shown how the interaction between multiple social identities informs the meaning one makes of the world (Jones & McEwen, 2000), Tisdell explores how spirituality mediates this meaning-making process. She describes a process by which people from ethnic minority backgrounds reclaim their oppressed identities as a means of spiritual fulfillment, whereas White individuals often strengthen their sense of spiritual wholeness through cross-cultural interactions. These findings suggest that individuals from different racial and ethnic backgrounds experience spirituality differently, although it is not possible to differentiate between experiences of various marginalized ethnic identities through Tisdell's study. While Tisdell's work provides insight into spirituality through an ethnic cultural lens, her participants consisted of 31 adult educators, not college students.

Two studies involving African American/Black participants support the relationship between ethnic identity and spirituality described by Tisdell. Watt (2003) interviewed 48 African American female college students and found that spirituality was used to help them cope with and psychologically resist oppression while shaping their identitiy. In a study involving five Black college students at a predominantly White institution, Stewart (2002) asserted that greater spiritual maturity was required for Black college students to integrate multiple facets of their identity. These studies provide insight into the spiritual lives of a specific population of college students, supporting work by Tisdell (2003), but do not provide comparisions of spirituality in the lives of students from different racial and ethnic backgrounds.

In a study comparing spiritual experiences of students from different ethnic backgrounds, Chae, Kelly, Brown, and Bolden (2004) found that ethnic group membership significantly affected "spirituality means" in a sample of 198 college students from four different ethnic groups. The spirituality means measure refers to "the internalized and fully lived experiential and transcendent components of spirituality that serve to guide an individual's life" (p. 17). Specifically, higher scores for spiritual means were found for African Americans ($p < .001$), Latino

Americans (p < .05), and Asian Americans (p < .05) compared with White American participants. These results suggest that spiritual experiences in college vary depending on ethnic group membership, but the findings are limited by the use of only one construct of spirituality. In addition, these findings do not explore the impact of college experiences on these group differences.

These studies begin to address an aspect of spirituality that remains relatively unstudied in the literature. They reveal differing roles of spirituality in the lives of students from different racial and ethnic backgrounds and point to differences in the spiritual experiences of these students. My study aims to reveal a deeper understanding of the differences in spiritual development in college for students from different backgrounds while also exploring the influences of some involvement experiences on this development.

Spirituality and Pro-Social Involvement

In recent years, scholars have drawn theoretical connections between service and spirituality (Koth, 2003; Sikula & Sikula, 2005). In addition, several studies have posited a connection between spirituality and service-oriented behavior (Bryant, *et al.*, 2003; Bryant, 2007; Kuh & Gonyea, 2006; Serow, 1990). Ciarrocchi, Piedmont, & Williams (2003) reported that spirituality correlated significantly with pro-social behavior, a construct including volunteerism, compassion, and fiscal responsibility. While they offer a cursory understanding of the effects of pro-social or community-oriented involvement on spirituality, these studies do so for predominantly White samples of college students and assume a narrow view of pro-social experiences in college. For the purpose of this study, I have defined pro-social involvement in college as involvement that contributes to building or serving one's community.

Taken together, this literature provides the foundation for this study, which seeks to examine the differences in spiritual development in college for students from different racial/ethnic backgrounds while exploring one set of experiences that may influence this development. In doing so, the study addresses some key limitations of prior research and paints a more complex picture of spiritual development within an ethnically diverse student body. The specific research question that guided this inquiry was: Do students from different racial/ethnic backgrounds exhibit different degrees of spiritual growth while in college? A second research question sought to further explore this complex area of study: Does pro-social involvement in college predict spiritual growth differently for students from different racial/ethnic backgrounds?

Methods

In order to answer the research questions posed, special consideration was given to coding participants' race/ethnicity and to which analyses were best suited to fully addressing the questions. Responses to demographic questions measuring respondents' ethnic background were re-coded utilizing a least prevalent single-race category classification scheme (see Soldner, Inkelas, & Szelenyi, 2009). White/Caucasian students accounted for over 75 percent of the sample while African American/Black, Asian American/Pacific Islander, and Latino/Hispanic students accounted for nearly 20 percent of the sample. American Indian/Alaska Native and students identifying as "other" ethnic backgrounds accounted for the remaining 5 percent. For the sake of data analysis, a smaller, random sample of 9 percent of the White/Caucasian students was selected using a random number generator in order to allow comparisons with the students from other ethnic backgrounds. Due to their small sample sizes, students who identified as Native American/Alaska Native or "other" ethnic background were not included in the data analysis for this study. The final sample utilized 3,698 college students attending 135 institutions. Of the participants, 19 percent identified as African American/Black; 31 percent were Asian American/Pacific Islander; 23 percent were Hispanic/Latino; and 28 percent were White/Caucasian. Over half (56 percent) of the sample was female, 80 percent identified with an organized religion, and 89 percent indicated average high school grades of B or better.

Three different methods of data analysis were used to address the research questions. First, ANOVA was used to assess ethnic/racial differences on three factor scales measured at the beginning of college and the end of the junior year—one factor pertaining to whether a student identifies as spiritual (spiritual identification) and two factors pertaining to spiritual processes or experience (spiritual quest and equanimity). The three factors, described in Chapter 2, were selected for this study based on findings from previous studies (Astin, 2004; Dalton, *et al.*, 2006; Fowler, 1981; Love, 2002; Mayhew, 2004; Parks, 2000; Tisdell, 2003), which suggest that spirituality is a universal human experience (i.e., all respondents have the capacity to identify with spiritually-related factors regardless of their religious background). In order to analyze spiritual growth in college, paired sample *t*-tests were used to determine growth from college entrance to end-of-junior-year on the three factors of spirituality.

The final set of analyses was a series of modified hierarchical regression analyses used to measure the effects of various types of pro-social college involvement, as well as other factors, on spiritual growth for students from different ethnic groups. The independent variables were entered in five blocks according to the I-E-O educational assessment framework (Astin, 1993a). The regressions were modified by entering the final block of variables (those pertaining to pro-social involvement) in a step-wise fashion, in which variables were entered one at a time and in an order in which the variable that contributed most to variance was entered first, followed by the one that contributed the second most and so on. Experiences that did not contribute to variance in the model were removed through the step-wise procedure. This allowed me to determine which pro-social variables statistically contributed to the regression model variance for the three spiritual factors. The method was chosen for its effectiveness in measuring significant contributions of college environment variables on other student outcomes (see Dugan, Garland, Jacoby, & Gasiorski, 2008, and Haber & Komives, 2009 for examples of modified hierarchical regression used to assess leadership outcomes).

The first four blocks entered into the regressions utilized data from the 2004 CSBV (pre-test of dependent variable, background and demographic characteristics, pro-social involvement prior to college, and characteristics of insitutional type and selectivity), while the fifth block utilized data from the 2007 follow-up survey. It consisted of six pro-social involvement experiences in college: participation in organized demonstrations, discussing politics, working on a political campaign, charitable involvement, participation in student government, and participation in leadership training. These variables were entered in a step-wise fashion in order to determine which pro-social experiences contributed the most to variance in factor scale scores.

Limitations

Two primary limitations are evident in this study. First, while it examines differences in spiritual development for students from different racial/ethnic groups, identifying race or ethnic background is a complex process for each individual. This study utilized a specific coding scheme for classifying students based on racial demographic responses. For the purpose of data analysis, some ethnic groups were collapsed into one group (for instance, Asian American students were grouped with Pacific Islander students). This coding scheme may produce biased results because it aggregates students from groups that may experience spirituality in unique ways. In addition, the sample for this study contained very few responses from ethnic groups other than the four studied, such as Alaska Natives or Native Americans, and failed to account for students who identify as more than one race. Second, this study examines a small number of college environment/experience variables in relation to spiritual development and was guided by a specific set of previous research studies. Other experiences in college may lead to greater spiritual development but were not the focus of this study.

Findings

Comparing Racial/Ethnic Groups' Levels of Spirituality

Students from different racial/ethnic backgrounds enter college with different predispositions toward spirituality, as well as significantly different levels of

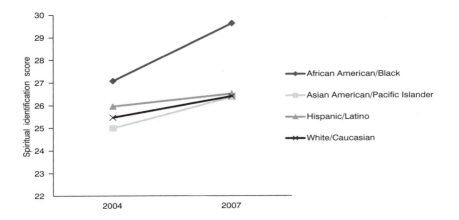

FIGURE 4.1 Spiritual identification scores at college entrance (2004) and junior-year completion (2007) by ethnic background.

spirituality upon the completion of their junior year. ANOVA results reveal significant between-group differences in spiritual identification upon entrance to college, F (3, 3395) = 16.37, p < .001, and at completion of the junior year, F (3, 3579) = 49.69, p < .001. Post-hoc comparisons reveal that Black students enter college with a higher spiritual identification than their Asian, Latino, and White counterparts; Latino students also exhibit higher scores than Asian students. Upon completion of the junior year, Black students continue to rate themselves more highly in spiritual identification than their peers while the remaining three groups exhibit no differences between them (see Figure 4.1).

The picture changes slightly when examining spiritual processes. Significant differences in spiritual quest were found both at the beginning of college, F (3, 3295) = 14.68, p < .001, and the end of the junior year, F (3, 3586) = 24.41, p < .001. At entrance to college, Black students score significantly higher than both Latino and White students in spiritual quest, while Asian students score higher than only White students. Latino students also exhibit higher scores than White students. No differences are found between Black and Asian students or Asian and Latino students. By the end of the junior year, Black students are still stronger in spiritual quest than Latino and White students and Asian students remain stronger than White students, but Latino students no longer exhibit differences from their White counterparts. As in the first year of college, no differences exist between Black and Asian students and Asian and Latino students at the end of the junior year (see Figure 4.2).

Similar to the other spiritual factors, group differences in equanimity were found both upon entry to college, F (3, 3240) = 34.84, p < .001, and at the conclusion of the junior year, F (3, 3545) = 19.13, p < .001. At the beginning of college, Black students exhibit higher levels than the other groups in equanimity. While

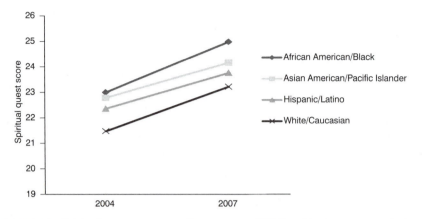

FIGURE 4.2 Spiritual quest scores at college entrance (2004) and junior-year completion (2007) by ethnic background

no differences are found between Latino and White students, Asian students score significantly lower on this scale than both of these groups. By the completion of the junior year, Black students score significantly higher than only Asian and White students. Latino students exhibit significantly higher scores than their White and Asian counterparts by their junior year. Whereas Asian students score lower than White students before college, they show no difference with White students at the completion of the junior year (see Figure 4.3).

Trends within these findings begin to paint a picture of differing spiritual experiences for students from different backgrounds. In general, Black students are significantly more spiritually-identified and exhibit spiritual quest and equanimity at higher levels than other students. These findings are consistent with previous research that has shown the integral role that spirituality plays in identity development for Black students (Stewart, 2002; Watt, 2003). Latino students reported higher scores than their White and Asian counterparts on several factors at both time points, while Asian students reported higher levels than only White students on some factors. On the other hand, White students exhibited levels either at or below all other students at both times for most factors. Prior research has shown that individuals of ethnic minority backgrounds reclaim their oppressed identities through spiritual fulfillment, whereas increased cross-cultural interaction strengthens spiritual wholeness for White individuals (Tisdell, 2003). These results may point to fewer cross-cultural experiences for White students in relation to their peers who may utilize spirituality to make meaning of their experiences with oppression.

These results clearly indicate that students from different racial/ethnic backgrounds exhibit differing levels of spirituality both prior to entering college and three years later. The following sections will further examine spiritual growth in college and experiences that contribute to this growth for each racial group.

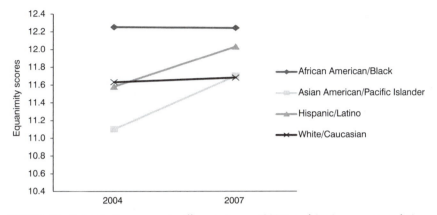

FIGURE 4.3 Equanimity scores at college entrance (2004) and junior-year completion (2007) by ethnic background

Spiritual Growth in College for Black Students

Black students grow significantly in their spiritual identification and spiritual quest in college but do not exhibit significant changes in equanimity during college. These results suggest that experiences in college contribute to strengthening Black students' spiritual identity and spiritual searching for meaning but do little to influence their ability to connect to others and find meaning in hardships. Interestingly, the scores on equanimity upon entrance to college for Black students were higher than the junior levels of equanimity exhibited by the other three groups of students. It may be that college does not impact growth in equanimity for Black students because life experiences prior to college have more impact on their development in this spiritual process.

What contributes to Black students' spiritual development through college? Not surprisingly, Black students' levels of spiritual identification and equanimity at college entry are the strongest predictors of how they score at the end of their junior year. In other words, students who enter college with higher scores on these factors will have higher scores in their junior year than those with lower scores. However, the block that accounted for the most variance in the spiritual quest factor was not the score at entrance to college but background characteristics. Unpacking this block for all three factors reveals that being a male was a significant positive predictor of spiritual identification and spiritual quest. Identifying with an organized religion had a positive influence on spiritual identification and equanimity and a negative influence on spiritual quest. This suggests that identifying with a religion does not strengthen all aspects of spiritual searching for Black students. As for pro-social involvement in college, participating in organized demonstrations and charitable involvement are positive predictors for all spiritual factors while working on a political campaign is a positive predictor for all factors but equanimity.

Spiritual Growth in College for Asian Students

Asian students experience significant growth in college on all three spiritual factors and exhibit the greatest relative growth in equanimity of all racial groups. Their levels of spiritual identification and spiritual quest at the outset of college are the strongest predictors of scores in their junior years but pro-social experiences in college are the strongest block for predicting equanimity. This suggests a considerable impact of pro-social involvement on equanimity for Asian students and is the only instance in this study where pro-social involvement experiences in college accounted for the most variance in any factor for any group.

In evaluating trends in regression models, the input and environment blocks provide little that is noteworthy in understanding spiritual development in Asian students. Charitable involvement in college is a significant positive predictor of all three spiritual factors, while student activism through organized demonstrations is a significant positive predictor for spiritual identification and equanimity. Leadership training contributes positively to all three spiritual factors for Asian students, while student government participation is a negative predictor of spiritual identification and equanimity.

Spiritual Growth in College for Latino Students

Similar to their Asian peers, Latino students experience significant growth in all three spiritual factors while in college. Spiritual identification and spiritual quest levels upon entrance to college account for the most variance in junior-year levels. However, not only did pre-college pro-social involvement account for the most variance in equanimity scores for Latino students, but Latino students were the only students for whom initial equanimity scores do not predict junior-year equanimity scores. The fact that the regression model for Latino students' equanimity experience had the smallest percentage of variance indicates a much more complicated picture of Latino equanimity than the factors included in this study can explain. Once in college, leadership training and organized demonstrations are the strongest positive predictors of all three spiritual factors for Latino students.

Spiritual Growth in College for White Students

White students experience significant growth through college in spiritual identification and spiritual quest but show no significant growth in equanimity. The greatest growth in spiritual quest in this study is evident in White students. Students' scores upon entrance to college are the greatest predictor of junior-year scores for all factors for White students. While several pro-social experiences in college contribute positively to some spiritual factors, no single experience contributes significantly to all three factors for White students.

Reflections

The first and arguably most notable finding of this study is that spiritual growth in college varies significantly for students from different racial and ethnic backgrounds. This has far-reaching implications for both higher education scholars and practitioners. First, it is worth noting that none of these groups experience decline through college in the spiritual factors measured. In fact, throughout college, most students exhibit growth in spiritual values but often do so differently than their peers from other racial/ethnic groups. This finding points to the transformative nature of the college experience described by previous research (Astin, Astin, & Lindholm, 2011) but calls for further exploration of the complexities of this development for diverse students.

The regression models in this study explained a considerable amount of variance in most cases. Only three models accounted for less than 50 percent of variance in factor scores: spiritual quest for Asian students and equanimity for Asian students and Latino students. For these models, students' pre-college scores for these factors accounted for little to no variance in their junior-level scores. These results reveal that the complex picture of spiritual development for these students is largely still not understood. Further examination of both pre-college measures and college experiences and environments are necessary for us to better understand what life experiences impact spiritual development for these students.

Certain pro-social involvement experiences in college tend to impact spiritual development across groups. Charitable involvement activities and participation in organized demonstrations were positive predictors of spiritual development for most groups and most factors of spirituality. Leadership training was a positive predictor of spiritual development for all groups but Black students. These findings contribute to an understanding of the types of involvement activities that can contribute to the spiritual fulfillment of college students. Engaging students in service, activism, and leadership development activities impact this development, allowing most students to better fulfill their spiritual needs. While some experiences were positive, participation in student government was a negative predictor of spirituality for most groups in this study. These findings reveal that not all community-engaging activities contribute to spiritual development and suggest that further qualitative inquiry into the specific processes inherent in these experiences will further reveal the reasons for their influence on spiritual development.

When taken as a whole, what do these findings offer us as we seek to uncover a clearer picture of spiritual development for college students from different racial/ethnic backgrounds? In examining the two factors that deal with spiritual processes (spiritual quest and equanimity), it is worth noting that White students scored the lowest in spiritual quest at both time points and exhibited no growth through college in equanimity. Students of color, on the other hand, entered college with higher levels on spiritual quest than White students and either entered significantly higher in equanimity but didn't grow (as with Black students) or exhibited significant growth through college (as with Latino and Asian students). These findings serve to reinforce the differing role that spirituality plays in the lives of White students versus students of color (Chae *et al.*, 2004; Tisdell, 2003). The role of spirituality in the lives of students of color combined with the transformative experience of college seems to be a powerful influence on spiritual development of students of color. However, this phenomenon may not reflect the experiences of White students.

This study also contributes to a better understanding of different groups of students of color. By comparing differing experience of specific racial/ethnic groups, this study can carry the conversation on spirituality beyond the binary of White students and students of color. For example, while Black students enter college with significantly higher levels of equanimity than Latino students, they are not impacted by the aspects of the college experience assessed in this study. On the other hand, Latino students exhibit tremendous growth in equanimity in college, leading them to exhibit no differences from their Black peers by the time they complete their junior year. While college has a large impact on Black students, it clearly does not contribute to a deepening sense of equanimity as it does for Latino students. Findings such as these further the understanding of the impact of college on spiritual development and point to the need for more research.

The theories of faith and spiritual development offered by Fowler (1981) and Parks (2000) have been integral in my and others' approaches to the study of the spiritual experiences of college students. The results of this study, which utilized a far more diverse sample than the studies informing these theories, essentially bring into question the generalizability of existing theories to an ethnically and racially diverse student body. The theories may provide frameworks for practitioners in their work with college students, but this study suggests that not only do students come to college with differing degrees of spiritual searching and feelings of centeredness or peace, they also develop in differing ways, depending on their race or ethnicity. Acknowledging that students will be informed by cultural experiences that affect the ways in which they engage their inner lives is a first step in providing guidance to students from all backgrounds. It is the obligation of practitioners to frame conversations on spirituality with an understanding of the multicultural experiences of both students of color and White students, recognizing how students may utilize spirituality in differing ways and how the college experience may impact these students differently.

The natural next steps beyond this study involve continuing to examine the different ways that students from different racial/ethnic backgrounds engage spirituality in order to develop more accurate theories of spiritual development to guide practitioners and scholars alike. Utilizing a critical lens that acknowledges the differing spiritual experiences of students from different backgrounds will contribute to a body of literature designed to inform decisions and practice. In addition, this critical lens should be used to better understand not only the experiences of students of color but also the experience of White students. While studies informing current theories of spiritual development utilized predominantly White samples and generalized the findings to all students, studying White students as their own population while not generalizing their results to the entire population of students places them as a group among a multicultural student population, not *the entire* group. It is crucial to use a cultural lens that acknowledges the intersectionality of social identities (Jones & McEwen, 2000) to explore how students of color and White students develop spiritually. In doing so, scholars and researchers can further evaluate the importance of culture and experience for students from both dominant and oppressed social groups.

This study is significant because it provokes more questions than provides answers. While some generalizations can be drawn around specific experiences in college and their impact on spiritual development, the bottom line is that there is little consistency in the predictive nature of these experiences across racial groups. The varying impact of pro-social involvement on spirituality points to the most important finding of this study, which is that students from different racial and ethnic backgrounds engage their spiritual lives differently. How do they do so? What other aspects of the college environment impact students differently? Spiritual development is a complex process, and this study narrowly contributes to understanding this complexity.

Perhaps the most intriguing aspect of this study is that it leads me to further question my spiritual life. How have I developed spiritually? How is my understanding of spirituality evolving? How do I find common spiritual understanding with those who are different from me? How can I learn from them? As I mentioned earlier, the study of spirituality is not only interesting from an academic perspective but contributes to my spiritual fulfillment and encourages my continued spiritual search.

References

Astin, A. W. (1993a). *Assessment for excellence: The philosophy and practice of assessment and evaluation in higher education.* Westport, CT: Oryx Press.

Astin, A. W. (1993b). *What matters in college? Four critical years revisited.* San Francisco: Jossey-Bass.

Astin, A. W. (2004). Why spirituality deserves a central place in liberal education. *Liberal Education, 90* (2), 34–41.

Astin, A. W., Astin, H. S., & Lindholm, J. A. (2011). *Cultivating the spirit: How college can enhance students' inner lives.* San Francisco: Jossey-Bass.

Bryant, A. N. (2007). Gender differences in spiritual development during the college years. *Sex Roles, 56,* 835–846.

Bryant, A. N., Choi, J. Y., & Yasuno, M. (2003). Understanding the religious and spiritual dimensions of students' lives in the first year of college. *Journal of College Student Development, 44,* 723–745.

Chae, M. H., Kelly, D. B., Brown, C. F., & Bolden, M. A. (2004). Relationship of ethnic identity and spiritual development: An exploratory study. *Counseling and Values, 49,* 15–26.

Ciarrocchi, J. W., Piedmont, R. L., & Williams, J. E. (2003). Love thy neighbor: Spirituality and personality as predictors of prosocial behavior in men and women. *Research in the Social Scientific Study of Religion, 14*, 61–75.

Dalton, J. C., Eberhardt, D., Bracken, J., & Echols, K. (2006). Inward journeys: Forms and patterns of college student spirituality. *Journal of College & Character, 7* (8), 1–22.

Dugan, J. P., Garland, J. L., Jacoby, B., & Gasiorski, A. (2008). Understanding commuter student self-efficacy for leadership: A within-group analysis. *NASPA Journal, 45*, 282–310.

Fowler, J. W. (1981). *Stages of faith: The psychology of human development and the quest for meaning.* San Francisco: Harper & Row.

Haber, P., & Komives, S. R. (2009). Predicting the individual values of the social change model of leadership development: The role of college students' leadership and involvement experiences. *Journal of Leadership Education, 7* (3), 133–166.

Jones, S. R., & McEwen, M. K. (2000). A conceptual model of multiple dimensions of identity. *Journal of College Student Development, 40*, 405–414.

Koth, K. (2003). Deeping the commitment to serve: Spiritual reflection in service-learning. *About Campus, 7* (6), 2–7.

Kuh, G. D., & Gonyea, R. M. (2006). Spirituality, liberal learning, and college student engagement. *Liberal Education, 92* (1), 40–47.

Love, P. G. (2002). Comparing spiritual development and cognitive development. *Journal of College Student Development, 43*, 357–373.

Love, P. G., Bock, M., Jannarone, A., & Richardson, P. (2005). Identity interaction: Exploring the spiritual experiences of lesbian and gay college students. *Journal of College Student Development, 46*, 193–209.

Mayhew, M. J. (2004). Exploring the essence of spirituality: A phenomenological study of eight students with eight different worldviews. *NASPA Journal, 41*, 647–674.

Muller, S. M., & Dennis, D. L. (2007). Life change and spirituality among a college student cohort. *Journal of American College Health, 56*, 55–59.

Parks, S. D. (2000). *Big questions, worthy dreams: Mentoring young adults in their search for meaning, purpose, and faith.* San Francisco: Jossey-Bass.

Parks, S. L. (1980). *Faith development and imagination in the context of higher education.* Unpublished doctoral dissertation, Harvard Divinity School.

Serow, R. C. (1990). Volunteering and values: An analysis of students' participation in community service. *Journal of Research and Development in Education, 23* (4), 198–203.

Sikula, J., & Sikula, A. (2005). Spirituality and service learning. *New Directions for Teaching and Learning, 104*, 75–81.

Soldner, M., Inkelas, K. K., & Szelenyi, K. (2009). Select all that apply? The pitfalls of various racial classification schemes in higher education research. *Paper presented at the Annual Meeting of the American Educational Research Association*, April. San Diego, CA.

Stewart, D. L. (2002). The role of faith in the development of an integrated identity: A qualitative study of Black students at a White college. *Journal of College Student Development, 43*, 579–596.

Tisdell, E. J. (2003). *Exploring spirituality and culture in adult and higher education.* San Francisco: Jossey-Bass.

Watt, S. K. (2003). Come to the river: Using spirituality to cope, resist, and develop identity. *New Directions for Student Services, 104*, 29–40.

Zinnbauer, B. J., & Pargament, K. I. (1998). Spiritual conversion: A study of religious change among college students. *Journal for the Scientific Study of Religion, 37* (1), 161–180.

Researcher Reflection on Part II
RISKY BUSINESS
Studying and Supporting Collegians' Spiritual Development

Peter M. Magolda

> There has been a lot of ugly talk in the campaign lately about the faith that you and Mitt Romney share—Mormonism. What do you make of people calling Mormonism a cult? And by the way, I am a Catholic and you are a Mormon. Let's not argue over who is right and who is not a Catholic. Let Jesus decide—the last judgment. Why do you feel like it is okay for people to attack Mormons?

On October 24, 2011 during the *Colbert Report*, a television comedy show that lampoons politics, Stephen Colbert (performing as a faux right-wing pundit) made this comment during his interview with Jon Huntsman—the former Governor of Utah and Ambassador to China—an aspiring Republican party nominee for the President of the United States. Huntsman replied:

> First of all, you get in a whole lot of trouble talking about religion. So you should never go there, particularly when you are seeking votes and running for a public office. When John F. Kennedy ran in 1960, what were people calling Catholicism? A cult. As they become more mainstream people learn about them. John F. Kennedy wins and his religion goes mainstream. It will probably be the same thing with Mormonism. It will become more mainstream over time as people kind of look at it and understand it a bit better.

This Colbert–Huntsman comedic exchange reminds television viewers that intermixing religion and national politics—despite the prospect of a humor goldmine—is fraught with prejudicial landmines. Religious diversity in America produces many serious challenges. Huntsman's *solution* is for politicians—especially those who aspire to win elections—to avoid talking about religion, because these conversations are simply too risky.

Avoiding conversations about faith and spirituality are not unique to America's presidential campaigns. Risk management, as it relates to faith and spirituality, is alive and well in American higher education. When conversations do occur, divisive campus rhetoric (e.g., Mormonism is a cult) and polarizing talking points (e.g., Catholicism is better than Mormonism) masquerade as intellectual discourse. Such efforts yield futile and contentious debates about whose religion or conceptualization of spirituality should reign, which represent squandered learning opportunities for all.

Educational researchers, too, avoid the topic of faith. Religion is a contentious topic, spirituality is indefinable and hard to pin down, and the elusive and personal nature of one's faith and spirituality are some contributing factors that make it difficult to design high-quality empirical studies (both qualitative and quantitative). Lee (2002) concluded: "For the most part, religion has been neglected in higher education research, even though most would agree that religion is a powerful force for many in shaping individual values, providing an overall sense of purpose, forming connections with others, and building a sense of community" (p. 369). Jon Huntsman's assertion—"You get in a whole lot of trouble talking about religion"—partially explains this scholarly void. Still, collegians consistently yearn to search for meaning and enhance their inner lives (e.g., values, spirituality, and self-understanding) (Astin, Astin, & Lindholm, 2011).

To address these challenges and voids, Nicholas Bowman and Jennifer Small, in their chapter entitled *The Experiences and Spiritual Growth of Religiously Privileged and Religiously Marginalized College Students,* as well as Sean Gehrke, in his chapter entitled *Race and Pro-Social Involvement: Toward a More Complex Understanding of Spiritual Development in College,* sought to identify aspects of both pre-college and college environments that strongly predict spiritual growth. They refute Huntsman's claim and concur with Lee's declaration. Unlike Huntsman, these scholars recognize the importance of college students' faith and spiritual development and talk about it (using their research findings as a foundation for these conversations). Unlike Huntsman, they argue universities "get in a whole lot of trouble" if their faculty and staff ignore empirical research studies centering faith and spirituality, fail to recognize the unique experiences and needs of faith/spirituality-oriented students, and repress collegians' expressions of their faith/spirituality.

In the remainder of this essay I discuss the three theoretical contributions that transcend these two research studies. Specifically I examine how their research foci, findings, and reflections: 1) influence current thinking about these topics, 2) augment existing knowledge about faith and spirituality in the academy, and 3) may influence future research endeavors. I refrain from commenting on the research design, sampling, and data collection and analysis procedures, due to the narrow scope of this essay. Instead I answer the question, "How can these newfound insights benefit the higher education community—most importantly collegians?"

Majority Minority Rules

The most surprising, refreshing, and potent aspect of these two studies is the researchers' emphasis on marginalized collegiate subcultures. Both studies examine the roles that student characteristics (e.g., religious affiliation, ethnicity) play in expressions of religious and spiritual dimensions during college. Bowman and Small—whose sample includes infrequently studied and less powerful student enclaves—explore how spiritual beliefs and identities vary across religious affiliations. Gehrke explores the dynamics of spiritual growth in college for students from different racial and ethnic backgrounds. He recognizes that race was seldom a specific component of many quantitative faith/spirituality research studies, because of a lack of adequate ethnic diversity in research samples to make meaning of group differences. His dataset was sufficiently robust to examine any subculture, yet he narrowed his sample to examine the spiritual development of collegians from diverse racial and ethic backgrounds.

Researching *the margins* is risky business in these uncertain economic times. With dwindling financial support for research, accrediting agency assessment frenzy, and governing boards' accountability preoccupations, conventional wisdom suggests that researchers (especially those with access to a national dataset with a highly generalizable sample) would get the "best bang for their bucks" by concentrating on the majority—subscribing to a variation of utilitarianism, which aspires to provide the greatest good for the greatest number of people.

Instead, these researchers take the proverbial road less taken—focusing on historically understudied groups. These two studies clarify subculture differences and identify campus environments that impede and enhance students' spiritual development during college. For example, Gehrke's findings refute some mainstream spiritual and faith development theories. He questions the appropriateness of generalizing mainstream spiritual and faith development theories to particular ethic minorities—because the students who participated in these studies did not include a sufficient number of non-white students to make ethnic generalizability claims. This finding has theoretical and practical implications—cavalierly generalizing these theories can de-legitimatize the veracity of the theories and harm the very students they intend to support. Gehrke's broad conclusion that students from different racial/ethnic backgrounds exhibit different degrees of spiritual growth while in college makes clear that a *one size fits all* approach to supporting students' faith/spiritual growth is as flawed as simply ignoring these subculture differences.

Bowman and Small introduce the concept of the double religious minority (i.e., minorities both on their campuses and in society at large) and a schema organizing religious minority status: being in the minority on a majority campus (e.g., Muslims at Vanderbilt University), the minority on a minority campus (e.g., Quakers at Liberty University), and the majority on a minority campus (e.g., Mormons at Brigham Young University). This framework reveals religious diversity hierarchies, illuminates the importance of understanding context, and warns against treating minorities as a uniform group.

Bowman, Small, and Gehrke recognize the urgency to understand the unique religious and spiritual experiences and needs of the privileged *and* the marginalized. They resist simplistic categories (e.g., majority/minority) that treat members of that group as a monolithic entity with essentialized characteristics (e.g., students of color) and instead favor the nuanced examination of less powerful subcultures. These studies provide glimpses into the (hidden) political nature of research that coexists with seemingly rigorous research techniques. This is an invaluable revelation for researchers, especially those who work with large datasets, value objectivity, and seek explanations.

One way that researchers can reveal the hidden political nature of their work more is to continually ask the question, "Whose interests are being served as a result of this research?" Posing this question reminds all researchers that their rigorous and ethical methodological undertakings are also political acts that privilege some and not others. I do not intend for this assertion to cast aspersions on the quality of educational research, or alarm or paralyze inquirers—for no single study can be all-inclusive and attend to everyone's interests. Instead, the two studies remind researchers that research should be more purposeful and inclusive and that educational research is both a methodological and moral undertaking—making it risky business.

Should a *majority rules* ideology prevail when studying students' inner lives? Bowman, Small, and Gehrke would probably respond, "No," because these scholars recognize the substantial religious and spiritual diversity within and across higher education institutions as well as understand the debilitating impact of universities ignoring faith/spirituality matters (especially for those on the margins). Yet they make clear that when minorities rule, it is not at the expense of the majority. Many of their findings about the marginalized students they studied benefit all students as well as faculty and staff.

Ruling Classes

A second theme that transcends these two essays is the authors' emphasis on the ruling class and its influences on minority students' spiritual quests. For example, Bowman and Small highlight the influence of faculty on students' faith and spiritual development as well as the power they possess to determine what is and is not discussed in the classroom. Faculty members rule classes and determine whether students can openly engage with religious or spiritual matters, what engagement is permissible, and what engagement will look like. On a more macro level, presidents and board of trustees of both faith-based and public colleges determine the degree to which faculty and staff infuse faith and spirituality doctrines in the curriculum and co-curriculum that conflict with institutional missions.

Gehrke, too, makes clear the influence of the ruling class on pro-social involvement experiences (i.e., involvement in college that contributes to serving one's community such as civic engagement or charitable involvement) aimed at enhancing students' spiritual development. University staff members define, sponsor, facilitate, and evaluate these activities such as leadership retreats and community service projects. Studying members of the campus community (such as faculty and senior university administrators), whose influences shape not only policy, but also the cultural ethos of campuses, dovetails nicely with these two studies that focus exclusively on students.

Bowman, Small and Gehrke infer that students who believe they have institutionalized approval for their faith and spiritual exploration will be comfortable considering their spiritual identities and searching for meaning. Studying individuals who give approval and determine students' comfort levels would further reveal the interplay of faculty/staff, institutional, and student values, and various stakeholders' levels of power and risk taking.

These authors' recognition of and attentiveness to ruling classes reveal numerous hierarchical relationships. The title of Bowman and Small's chapter—*The Experiences and Spiritual Growth of Religiously Privileged and Religiously Marginalized College Students*—exemplifies this student hierarchy theme present in both studies.

Research citations included in these two chapters are replete with binaries (e.g., majority vs. minority, sacred vs. secular institutions, religious vs. non-religious students, white students vs. students of color). Dichotomies in research and applied contexts are beneficial because they provide broad understanding of phenomena, simplify the complex matrix of interrelationships, and highlight stark differences. And these binaries are dangerous because the reinforced one-dimensional stereotypes create the illusion of equality and lead to simplistic and superficial analysis of "the other" (Weingarten, 2005). Most alarmingly, they mask hierarchical relationships as Aichele (1995) noted:

> Western thought has always based itself on binary oppositions ... Such oppositions are founded on repression, the relation between the two terms being one of hierarchical violence rather than equal partnership. The first term in each pair has been forcibly elevated over the second. (p. 122)

At the outset of this essay, Colbert positions mainstream religion against Mormonism. This distinction highlights stark differences between these two religions; he also intends this innocuous binary to privilege mainstream religion— making it the ruling class in this context. Colbert's glib comment represents an *individual's* construction of a faith hierarchy based on status. Likewise, when

Bowman and Small mention the challenges that public universities face when trying to respond to the faith and spiritual demands of students, secularism trumps the sacred in this particular juxtaposition; this example represents a collective construction of a faith-hierarchy on status. The power of these *accessible* and simplistic categories often goes unnoticed.

While both studies include binaries to educate readers (e.g., Bowman and Small's focus on privileged vs. religiously marginalized students and majority vs. minority status), they work to modestly rupture these discrete categories, revealing differences—especially power differences. For example, Gehrke avoids the White student–student of color binary and instead assesses how students' different racial/ethnic backgrounds (e.g., Black, White, Latino, and Asian) and spiritual levels upon entering college differ upon the completion of their junior year—revealing differing spiritual experiences for students from different backgrounds. Bowman and Small's double minority discussion accomplishes a similar aim. These frameworks modestly challenge binaries and focus attention on power, which has implications for scholars and practitioners (pardon the binary).

Ruling classes and hierarchies inevitably exist in higher education settings as university presidents, faculty, and students jockey for power and influence. These ruling classes and hierarchies also exist within student-only subcultures as marginalized and privileged students continually negotiate what is *normal*. Huntsman's comments remind researchers that these power-determined hierarchies are fluid when he argued that Catholics were on the margins in the 1960s, but are now considered a mainstream religion, and Mormons will soon achieve mainstream religious status. The need to conduct on-going education research, especially critical studies as Gehrke advocates, paying particular attention to religious and faith ruling classes and faith and spiritual hierarchies, would augment these two studies.

Rules of Engagement

These two research summaries include everyday recommendations for practitioners (e.g., faculty, student affairs educators) interested in supporting students' faith quests during college. In Gehrke's study, no ethnic groups experienced decline through college in the spiritual factors measured; most reported an increase in spiritual values but this increase looked different for the various racial/ethnic groups. Gehrke posits that this finding points to the transformative nature of the college experience and the importance of *engagement*. Student engagement, inside and outside the classroom optimizes collegians' faith/spiritual development. It is difficult to counter this argument; intuitively it sounds *right* and these days student engagement is en vogue—a popular buzzword in the academy. Importantly, the authors reveal the complications and tensions associated with supporting students' faith/spirituality engagement both inside and outside of the classroom.

Public colleges and universities—often under the guise of the separation of church and state—mandate rules of engagement that restrict or control faith/spirituality dialogues by relegating these conversations to, for example, comparative religious studies seminars or campus lectures/speeches about the topic of faith. Another popular avoidance "solution" is for universities to outsource responsibilities for faith- and spirituality-based initiatives to non-university religious institutions, such as Newman Centers, Hillel Centers, or evangelical parachurches (Magolda, 2010; Miller & Ryan, 2001).

Managing risk associated with faith/spirituality-related discourses on religiously affiliated colleges is markedly different than their public counterparts, resulting in distinct rules of engagement, some of which pose threats to some students' development. Typically, religiously affiliated colleges encourage substantive and frequent, although focused, dialogues about religion and spirituality. Predictably, dialogues in these contexts privilege the religious denomination to which the university aligns itself, more so than other religious sects. For example, Catholic universities favor conversations about Catholic doctrine while evangelical colleges encourage conversations about evangelical perspectives. The benefits are obvious to collegians whose faith leaning aligns with their college's mission, as are the liabilities for those whose faith leanings are out of bounds.

While these engagement containment strategies lessen risks for the universities, they increase risks for students, especially students on the margins. Bowman, Small, and Gehrke describe these rules of engagement and document their influences on students' faith and spiritual development, but the scope of their research prohibited a more careful and thorough examination of the origins and rationales for these engagement practices. Understanding the gap between what institutions espouse versus what they enact as it relates to engagement rules involving faith and spirituality represents a future research topic and a good rule of thumb.

The Golden Rule

The Golden Rule—*treat others as one would like others to treat oneself*—is a guide that can aid different subcultures to resolve conflicts. In the faith and spirituality arena, subcultures exist and have unique creeds that clash with the unique creeds of other faith and spirituality subcultures. The illumination of unique faith and spirituality needs of marginalized collegiate subcultures is a unique contribution of the Bowman and Small as well as the Gehrke studies. These insights can help resolve conflicts—minimizing what Colbert calls "ugly talk."

Bowman, Small, and Gehrke persuasively argue that: students yearn to search for meaning and enhance their inner lives ... studying and supporting collegians' spiritual development by understanding their unique experiences and needs is essential ... aspects of both pre-college and college environment strongly predict spiritual growth ... when the *minority rules*, it is not at the expense of the majority ...

the political nature of research coexists with rigorous research techniques ... faculty and administrators determine the degree to which students can openly engage with religious or spiritual matters ... a need exists to conduct additional research about *the ruling classes* and their *rules of engagement* ... conducting research about faith and spirituality as well as mediating faith and spirituality interaction is risky business—a risk worth taking.

"College is a critical time when students search for meaning in life and examine their spiritual/religious beliefs and values" (Bryant, Choi, & Yasuno, 2003, p. 726). If colleges and universities aspire to support students' development (e.g., spiritual, intellectual, identity) and promote student success, they must take risks. Simply stated, faculty and administrators cannot: relegate conversation about faith or spirituality to niches in the curriculum and co-curriculum; sit on the proverbial sidelines acting as neutral observers of polarizing campus-wide debates; outsource their faith and spiritual development responsibilities; or ignore the religious or spiritual needs of the minority. All students who attend secular or faith-based universities deserve better.

References

Aichele, G. (1995). *The postmodern Bible*. New Haven: Yale University Press.

Astin, A. W., Astin, H. S., & Lindholm, J. A. (2011). *Cultivating the spirit: How college can enhance students' inner lives*. San Francisco: Jossey-Bass.

Bryant, A. N., Choi, J. Y., & Yasuno, M. (2003). Understanding the religious and spiritual dimensions of students' lives in the first year of college. *Journal of College Student Development, 44*(6), 723–745.

Lee, J. J. (2002). Religion and college attendance: Change among students. *Review of Higher Education, 25*(5), 369–384.

Magolda, P. M. (2010). An unholy alliance: Rethinking collaboration involving student affairs and faith-based student organizations. *Journal of College & Character, 11*(4), 1–5.

Miller, V. W., & Ryan, M. M. (2001). *Transforming campus life: Reflections on spirituality and religious pluralism*. New York: Peter Lang.

Weingarten, T. (2005). Campus Christians: Not always at ease. *Christian Science Monitor, 97*(42), 12.

DELIBERATE CAMPUS PRACTICES TO FOSTER SPIRITUALITY, PURPOSE, AND MEANING

Recognizing Student Characteristics and Group Differences

Kathleen M. Goodman

In 1936, psychologist Kurt Lewin presented his groundbreaking equation, $B = f(P, E)$, stating that behavior is a function of the person and her or his environment (Lewin, Heider, & Heider, 1936). This was a paradigm shift in that it suggested one must consider an individual's momentary situation (the environment), rather than relying entirely on the person's past, in order to understand a person's behavior. Due to Lewin's influence, the study of higher education has focused on creating campus environments to successfully engage college students, and the results of that research have proven useful to educators and student affairs practitioners interested in shaping learning environments. However, the focus on campus environments cannot come at the expense of understanding individual differences as they pertain to the college experience. How the environment affects non-majority populations is of great importance in this era of mass higher education. By focusing on the effects of student characteristics and group differences on spirituality, Bowman, Small, and Gehrke have moved the research in a direction that will serve practitioners well.

The authors of the chapters in this part provide compelling evidence that college experiences influence spiritual development. Within these authors' studies, involvement in charitable activities, participation in organized demonstrations, leadership training, religious engagement, and faculty support for spiritual and religious development all have positive effects on spiritual identification or personal quests for spirituality. However, these authors also demonstrate that personal characteristics such as race and religion influence the effects of campus practices on spiritual development. For example, Gehrke found that leadership training had a positive effect on spirituality for Asian, Latino, and White students, but had a negative effect on spirituality for Black students. Bowman and Small found that students who were Catholic or who had no religion made greater gains in their personal quest for spirituality, compared with mainline Protestant students. Furthermore, Bowman and Small also found that the effects of college experiences and personal characteristics such as religion on spirituality differ depending on whether the college/university attended is Catholic, affiliated with religions other than Catholicism, or secular.

While some college experiences may positively influence spirituality for many students, these findings provide strong evidence that personal and institutional characteristics substantially influence the spiritual development of students in differing ways. Understanding those differing effects is vital to practitioners concerned with meeting the spiritual needs of *all* students. Building on the recommendations provided by Bowman, Small, and Gehrke, I offer the following suggestions for deliberate campus practices to foster spirituality, while recognizing that the influences of race, religion, and institutional context moderate the effects of campus practices on spiritual development.

Deliberate Campus Practices

Pro-social Involvement

Gehrke found that "pro-social involvement" such as involvement in charitable activities, participation in organized demonstrations, and leadership training can have a positive influence on spirituality. Student affairs practitioners are often the guiding force behind community service, campus activities, and leadership training and can purposefully include aspects of spirituality within each of these activities. By providing opportunities for students to reflect on the purpose and meaning in life and connecting it to pro-social activities, practitioners can help students begin to articulate and make explicit the values that guide their behaviors. Because the link between pro-social involvement and spirituality already exists, practitioners need only be more deliberate about consistently incorporating opportunities for reflecting on spirituality, life purpose, and meaning, as well as normalizing the idea that it is natural for students to be searching for meaning and connections through involvement in pro-social activities. Student affairs practitioners working with students in pro-social contexts must be prepared to help students as their ideas and perceptions related to meaning and purpose change over time (Fairchild, 2009). It can be disconcerting to students if they find their spiritual beliefs changing, and student affairs practitioners must be ready to support students as they face that challenge. Seifert, Goodman, and Harmon (2009) suggest that, when it comes to spirituality, the individual conversations that arise between student affairs practitioners and students require the courage to meet students where they are and operate outside of the confines of structured programs in order to have meaningful, unstructured, and highly personal conversations.

Religious Engagement

Bowman and Small's research demonstrated that religious engagement, which includes behaviors such as attending religious services, praying, religious singing/chanting, and reading sacred texts, has a positive impact on student spirituality. However, religious engagement is not a concern of student affairs practitioners on many campuses and the responsibility of religious engagement is often left to nearby religious organizations, or to students themselves. Two factors may drive this phenomenon. First, of the approximately 20.4 million students enrolled in institutions of higher education in the U.S. in 2009, only 9 percent attended institutions with a religious affiliation, and the remainder attended private, non-religious institutions (18 percent), or public institutions (73 percent) (U.S. Department of Education, National Center for Education Statistics, 2010). Public institutions have a long history of separation from religion for legal and other reasons (see Glanzer, 2011 for an account of that separation). Additionally, we live in an era of contention concerning whether the U.S. is a "Christian nation" (Fairchild, 2009). Perhaps educators and administrators are less likely to partake in the engagement of religion with students in an effort to be secular *and* to avoid the religious contentions that exist in the broader society.

These factors leave educators in a quandary: should institutions provide more opportunity for religious engagement, at the risk of appearing non-secular, or should they allow the status quo to exist, leaving students to find their own way in religious matters, with or without guidance from nearby religious organizations? I agree with Magolda (2010) who summed up the situation as follows:

> "College is a critical time when students search for meaning in life and examine their spiritual/religious beliefs and values" (Bryant, Choi, & Yasuno, 2003, p. 726), and *higher education and parachurch staff can best support students in their quest for meaning by forging alliances* [emphasis added]. These partnerships can cultivate a spirit of critique, understanding, and respect for human dignity, whereby participants learn from each other, and reflect on and re-evaluate their own beliefs and practices. This is a much holier alliance than the status quo, and will model for students a way to engage with others in our diverse world. (p. 5)

While it may be simpler for educators and administrators to avoid the topic of religion in any form or manner, there is much to be gained by engaging students in religious conversations, especially across difference. Students who are exposed to other perspectives and provided the opportunity to reflect on their own beliefs are likely to develop spiritually and gain clarity about their beliefs, whether their beliefs are reinforced by encounters with religious difference or changed because of them. Furthermore, with appropriate guidance, students can learn to respect difference and gain greater skills to live in our diverse world when provided the opportunity to engage with religious difference. Creating partnerships between student affairs practitioners and off-campus religious organizations that serve students is one way to increase religious engagement on campus (Chickering, Dalton, & Stamm, 2006; Magolda, 2010). However, finding ways to enact those partnerships in a way that does not favor religion over non-religion (or one particular religion over others), and focusing on learning and development is vital to maintain religious neutrality, a concern to public institutions (Magolda, 2010).

Providing equal space, support, resources, and publicity for all students groups with religious and spiritual foci is another way that campuses can legally provide opportunities for students' religious engagement (Chickering, Dalton, & Stamm, 2006). Furthermore, developing an academic calendar that acknowledges multiple religious traditions and accommodating the needs of students from non-dominant religious groups can provide a welcoming environment that allows students to develop their spiritual and religious engagement (Fairchild, 2009; Seifert, 2007). For example, making sure that campus food services provide adequate late-night options during Ramadan is one way to accommodate a non-dominant religion and indicate campus commitment to religious engagement (Seifert, 2007).

Faculty Support for Spiritual and Religious Development

Bowman and Small's research demonstrated the importance of faculty support for religious and spiritual development. Students who felt that faculty encouraged exploration of questions of meaning and purpose and discussion of religious and spiritual matters made gains in their spiritual identification and quest, perhaps because they interpret faculty support as institutional approval of their religious beliefs. Student affairs practitioners can develop collaborations with faculty who are most likely to have an interest in discussing spirituality and religion with students, such as those in the field of anthropology, sociology, and history (Stewart & Lozano, 2009). Faculty in religious studies (McCarty, 2009) and philosophy are also likely collaborators. By engaging faculty from these departments to participate in structured conversations about religion and spirituality, student affairs practitioners simultaneously signal to faculty that these are legitimate topics of discussion and signal to students that the institution supports their personal quests for spiritual development.

The book *Why Read?* by Mark Edmundson (2004) could also be used to encourage faculty to discuss religious and spiritual matters with students. This brief book makes a compelling case for faculty in the humanities to address "big questions" of purpose and meaning by encouraging students to see themselves through characters in books. Edmundson (2004) believes that "the purpose of a liberal arts education is to give people an enhanced opportunity to decide how they should live their lives" (p. 5). He suggests that educators should provide opportunity for students' self-discovery, by asking questions such as "How do you picture your life ten years from now?"; "How do you imagine God?"; "What do you value?"; and "What gives meaning to life?". This book could be used in a reading group sponsored by the faculty development center on campus, or in a collaborative group of student affairs practitioners and faculty.

Individualized Approaches for Differing Groups

Gehrke's research suggests that there is a need for individualized approaches for groups based on race, whereas Bowman and Small suggest the need for individualized approaches based on religion. Both of these research projects demonstrate that individual differences exist and must be understood if campuses are to attend to the needs of all students rather than focusing solely on those students that are in majority populations (e.g., White, Christian). Student affairs practitioners must begin by developing self-awareness concerning their own spiritual development and beliefs in order to provide guidance to diverse populations regarding their spiritual development (Seifert & Holman-Harmon, 2009). Furthermore, it is necessary for student affairs practitioners to have considerable knowledge about many faith traditions, spiritual pathways, and atheism in order to create environments, programs, and relationships that help students develop spiritually (Watt, Fairchild, & Goodman, 2009). Through these efforts of self-knowledge and ecumenical understanding, student affairs practitioners increase the likelihood that they can help students feel validated and safe in their spiritual pursuits.

Stewart and Lozano (2009) explain that for people of color, faith and race/ethnicity are intertwined. This becomes especially important when it comes to the idea of Christian privilege, because people of color may not see their alignment with Christianity as part of a system of privilege, but rather they may view it as part of the struggle against racial oppression. Stewart and Lozano (2009) suggest that student affairs practitioners incorporate multicultural awareness, knowledge, and skills with their understanding of spirituality and faith. Incorporating spirituality and religious diversity into multicultural and diversity events (which often focus solely on race/ethnicity) on campus is one way to help highlight the complex relationships between race and spiritual development for some groups. Providing opportunities for discussing the importance for imperialized groups to retain their spiritual and cultural traditions is another means for highlighting the complex relationship between race and spiritualty (Stewart & Lozano, 2009). Purposefully incorporating discussions of spirituality and religion into programming designed specifically for students of color (e.g., Black student organizations, Latino/a cultural centers) can provide those groups a chance to explore the relationship between their culture and faith traditions in a safe space and deepen their spiritual engagement.

Providing opportunities for non-dominant religious groups to explore their spirituality and faith is of great importance, because, as Bowman and Small explain, students in non-mainline Protestant and non-Christian groups are often marginalized in both society-at-large and on campuses. In addition to learning about non-dominant religious traditions, student affairs practitioners can play an active role in creating opportunities for students of all backgrounds to feel safe and deepen their spiritual commitments. Blumenfeld and Klein (2009) provide specific suggestions for working with Jewish students, including providing opportunities to observe Jewish holidays, collaborating with Hillel to provide opportunities for Jewish students to explore their religious identities, and developing and maintaining a library of materials about Judaism, as well as other world religions. Ali and Bagheri (2009) provide suggestions for working with Muslim students, such as including Islamic religious holidays on the academic calendar, providing safe spaces for prayer, and assessing whether the religious dietary needs of Muslim students are being met.

Attending to the individualized approaches necessary for differing groups to make the most of their spiritual development may seem overwhelming to student affairs practitioners. Indeed, simply learning about the many religious traditions and secular avenues related to spiritual development can be a daunting task. One way to make this a little easier for new student affairs professionals is to incorporate more about spiritual development, including how it differs for non-dominant groups, into student affairs preparation programs. For those already working in the student affairs profession, it is important to remember that the effort to understand religious and worldview diversity is a work in progress. Much of the necessary learning can take place by asking questions and listening to students' responses. By acknowledging short-comings in knowledge while demonstrating a willingness to learn and engage in conversations about difference, student affairs practitioners add to their own knowledge, help students learn, and provide a good model for students who may be nervous about broaching the topic of spirituality and religion.

Institutional Context

Of all the findings from the studies described in this section of the book, perhaps the most difficult to address is the influence of institutional context on spiritual development. What is one to make of Bowman and Small's findings that that effect of being Catholic on religious engagement is more positive at Catholic schools than at secular schools, whereas religious minority students fair worse in their spiritual development at Catholic institutions? On one hand, the news is positive, showing that Catholic institutions are meeting their mission of serving Catholic students. On the other hand, just as secular institutions must do a better job of attending to the spiritual and religious needs of their students, so too must religiously-affiliated institutions consider the spiritual and religious needs of all students. All institutions can benefit from a formal assessment to see how students of different faith traditions, and non-theistic students as well, are faring at the institution. Likewise, all institutions must be willing to scrutinize their climate to see whether religious privilege (privileging of a particular religion over others, or privileging religion over non-religion) or Christian privilege prevail. Each institution will have to determine what to do with the information they find and to what extent they can create a campus environment welcoming to students of all backgrounds within the context of their mission.

Resources

While the reference list contains many resources that will be helpful to campuses as they seek to help all students with their spiritual development, the following organizations may be useful as well:

- Campus Compact (www.compact.org): dedicated to promoting community service in higher education
- Diversity Web (http://www.diversityweb.org/DiversityDemocracy/vol14no3/patel.cfm): dedicated to exploring issues of diversity, including *The Civic Power of Interfaith Cooperation*
- Interfaith Youth Core (www.ifyc.org): dedicated to bringing together young people of different religious and moral traditions for cooperative service and dialogue around shared values
- *Journal of College and Character* (www.collegevalues.org): dedicated to publishing scholarly articles and applied research on issues related to ethics, values, and character development in higher education
- Leadershape (www.leadershape.org): dedicated to transforming the world by increasing the number of people who *lead with integrity*
- Secular Student Alliance (www.secularstudents.org): dedicated to helping non-theist students organize, unite, educate, and serve
- Society for Values in Higher Education (www.svhe.org): dedicated to providing fellowship for teachers and administrators who care deeply about ethical issues in higher education, such as integrity, diversity, social justice and civic responsibility.

Questioning the Inherent Privilege Within Spiritual Development

A reflection of this sort would be incomplete without considering what forms of privilege are inherent in the concept of spiritual development. The research findings of Bowman, Small, and Gehrke demonstrate the impact of race and religion on spiritual development. If taken to heart, those findings will influence how student affairs practitioners work to meet the spiritual development needs of all students, including those in non-dominant groups, thus addressing one privilege related to spiritual development. Bowman, Small, and Gehrke also noted the limitations of current spiritual and faith development theories used in higher education. These theories (see for example, Fowler, 1981 and Parks, 1980, 2000) were developed based on the experiences of White, Christian individuals and have not been expanded to reflect group differences. Questioning the appropriateness of the theories, and demonstrating the need to expand the theories, is another good step in challenging privilege within spiritual development. I believe that a third area of privilege must also be addressed: it is a mistake to think that spiritual development is an outcome of college.

To be clear, I whole-heartedly agree with the concept of holistic development, and I believe that colleges and universities must be attentive to students' inner lives. However, to suggest that values, meaning, and life purpose equate to spirituality for all students is a form of privilege that must be dismantled. Spirituality, religion, and secularity are three distinct pathways to values, meaning, and life purpose. Secular pathways can include science, reason, humanism, and other non-spiritual, non-religious ways that individuals use to make meaning. The pathways are not mutually exclusive—certainly many recognize the strong link between spirituality and religion. However, those students who identify with secular pathways to purpose—typically atheists, agnostics, and freethinkers—often do not relate to the spiritual and religious pathways. To try to force "spiritual development" on these students, and insist that spirituality is an inclusive term, further marginalizes a group that already exists on the periphery of society (Goodman & Mueller, 2009). Therefore, I believe that developing values, meaning, and life purpose are outcomes of college, and spirituality is one means for developing those outcomes. Once spiritualty is thought of as a means versus an end, truly inclusive environments can be created.

Concluding Thoughts

Bowman, Small, and Gehrke have provided research findings that acknowledge that spiritual development differs depending on student characteristics and group differences. Student affairs practitioners can use the knowledge and the ideas provided in this part of the book to address spiritual development in distinct ways with different populations. I have expanded on their findings by suggesting that they uncovered certain types of privilege associated with spiritual development. Educators and student affairs practitioners must continue to think critically about the term spiritual development and consider how to adapt their language and campus practices to be inclusive of many types of students, including those with secular worldviews. Though secular students may not relate to the concept of spiritualty, education must support their development of values, meaning, and life purpose. A willingness to ascertain how student characteristics and group differences influence spirituality and to consider ways that privilege may be related to the notion of spirituality within higher education is vital to creating truly inclusive environments in which educators and student affairs practitioners will be able to help all students develop values, meaning, and life purpose in tailored ways that address differences.

References

Ali, S. R., & Bagheri, E. (2009). Practical suggestions to accommodate the needs of Muslim students on campus. *New Directions for Student Services, 2009*(125), 47–54.

Blumenfeld, W. J., & Klein, J. R. (2009). Working with Jewish undergraduates. *New Directions for Student Services, 2009*(125), 33–38.

Bryant, A. N., Choi, J. Y., & Yasuno, M. (2003). Understanding the religious and spiritual dimensions of students' lives in the first year of college. *Journal of College Student Development, 44*, 723–745.

Chickering, A. W., Dalton, J. C., & Stamm, L. (Eds.). (2006). *Encouraging authenticity and spirituality in higher education.* San Francisco, CA: Jossey-Bass.

Edmundson, M. (2004). *Why read?* New York: Bloomsbury Publishing.

Fairchild, E. E. (2009). Christian privilege, history, and trends in U.S. religion. *New Directions for Student Services, 2009*(125), 5–11.

Fowler, J. W. (1981). *Stages of faith: The psychology of human development and the quest for meaning.* San Francisco: Harper & Row.

Glanzer, P. L. (2011). Peter Magolda's proposal for an unholy alliance: Cautions and considerations regarding collaboration between student affairs and faith-based student organizations. *Journal of College & Character, 12*(3), 1–8. doi: 10.2202/1940-1639.1779.

Goodman, K. M., & Mueller, J. A. (2009). Invisible, marginalized, and stigmatized: Understanding and addressing the needs of atheist students. *New Directions for Student Services, 2009*(125), 55–63.

Lewin, K., Heider, F., & Heider, G. M. (1936). *Principles of topological psychology.* New York: McGraw-Hill.

Magolda, P. (2010). An unholy alliance: Rethinking collaboration involving student affairs and faith-based student organizations. *Journal of College and Character, 11*(4), 1–5. doi:10.2202/1940-1639.1734.

McCarty, R. W. (2009). Facilitating dialogue on religion and sexuality using a descriptive approach. *New Directions for Student Services, 2009*(125), 39–46.

Parks, S. D. (2000). *Big questions, worthy dreams: Mentoring young adults in their search for meaning, purpose, and faith.* San Francisco: Jossey-Bass.

Parks, S. L. (1980). *Faith development and imagination in the context of higher education.* Unpublished doctoral dissertation, Harvard Divinity School.

Seifert, T., Goodman, K., & Harmon, N. (2009). Methods for assessing inner development: Spirituality and beyond. *Journal of College and Character, 10*(7), 1–5.

Seifert, T. A. (2007). Understanding Christian privilege: Managing the tensions of spiritual plurality. *About Campus, 12*(2), 10–17.

Seifert, T. A., & Holman-Harmon, N. (2009). Practical implications for student affairs professionals' work in facilitating students' inner development. *New Directions for Student Services, 2009*(125), 13–21.

Stewart, D. L., & Lozano, A. (2009). Difficult dialogues at the intersections of race, culture, and religion. *New Directions for Student Services, 2009*(125), 23–31.

U.S. Department of Education, National Center for Education Statistics. (2010). Table 205. Fall enrollment and number of degree-granting institutions, by control and affiliation of institution: Selected years, 1980 through 2009. In U.S. Department of Education, National Center for Education Statistics (Ed.), *Digest of Education Statistics* (2010 edn). Retrieved from http://nces.ed.gov/pubs2011/2011015.pdf.

Watt, S., Fairchild, E., & Goodman, K. (Eds.). (2009). Religious privilege and student affairs practice: Intersections of difficult dialogues. *New Directions for Student Services, 2009*(125).

PART III

College Contexts

5

CHRISTIAN COLLEGE PERSISTENCE IN THE POSTMODERN TURN

P. Jesse Rine

For over a century, modernist epistemology provided a common framework for the pursuit of knowledge within the American academy. Modernist epistemology asserted "that there are universals that can be discovered through reason, that science and the scientific method are superior means for arriving at truth and reality, and that language describes and can be used as a credible and reliable means of access to that reality" (Bloland, 1995, p. 523). Moreover, modernists held that universals operated outside of any local frameworks, so that learning itself is a generically human process best practiced by checking one's own national, cultural, racial, gender, class, and religious particulars at the entryway of the academy (Wolterstorff, 2004a).

Recent decades, however, have witnessed the rise of a diffuse yet robust challenge to prevailing modernist assumptions regarding the nature and scope of human knowledge. Generally speaking, postmodern theorists have rejected the Enlightenment notion of an objective, over-arching, unified understanding of reality in favor of a more contextualized approach to knowledge. In particular, French Poststructuralist theorists such as Jacques Derrida and Michel Foucault have argued against the modernist notion that language serves as a constant and neutral medium of exchange for ideas about an objective reality, contending conversely that language is an indeterminate phenomenon in which word meanings are constantly negotiated in sociocultural contexts framed by power relations (Bloland, 1995). Moreover, postmodernists contend, these sociocultural contexts are not superficial lenses that can be removed at will; they fundamentally frame one's identity and consciousness, permeating one's personal experiences and interpretations of reality (Cahoy, 2002), so that "the place from which an observer observes determines what can be observed" (Lincoln, 1991, p. 17). From the postmodern perspective, knowledge can no longer be viewed as an external, pre-existing entity waiting to be discovered by an objective observer, but must be understood instead to be the subjective product of individuals who operate within social, cultural, historical, and ideological contexts (Tierney, 2001).

The emergent postmodern paradigm presents a challenge to the evangelical Christian college. Though the Christian college's theistic worldview never gained supremacy within the postsecondary sector as a whole, modernist epistemology did foster a common forum in which the Christian college could argue the merits of its particular truth claims. As American higher education has struggled in recent decades to address the implications of postmodern thought for postsecondary practice, the Christian college has continued to operate according to a sacred version of the widely challenged modernist approach (Beal, 2002).

In order to maintain its legitimacy within the wider sector of higher education, the Christian college must adjust its practices in light of postmodern cultural shifts. However, this adaptation must occur in a manner consistent with its fundamental faith commitments, lest the Christian college lose its institutional soul. Denton Lotz (2003) expresses well the essence of this dilemma: "Compromising the faith, by either wholesale adaptation or disengaged preservation, will doom Christian higher education to either extinction or irrelevancy. Christian education must always proceed in creative and self-critical engagement with the wider culture, but it must do so without yielding firm commitment to Jesus Christ as Lord" (p. 172).

As a Christian college alum (B.A., Grove City College), I care deeply about the future of Christian higher education and its unique contribution to the postsecondary sector. I have noted with concern the challenge the postmodern turn poses to these institutions, often wondering if an institutional type committed to exclusivist truth claims could long survive in the midst of a decidedly inclusive cultural context. In addition, I have observed a phenomenon among a number of recent Christian college graduates that suggests a similar struggle occurs among individuals who adhere to exclusivist truth claims. When first confronted with the heterogeneity, contingency, and ambiguity existing beyond the Christian college environment, many Christian college graduates respond in one of two ways: they either feel overwhelmed and withdraw from the wider culture, taking refuge within narrow enclaves of like-minded peers, or they feel misled and abandon their exclusivist beliefs, adopting a relativistic worldview in order to accommodate their present context. Though admittedly anecdotal in nature, this observation led me to ask whether Christian colleges adequately prepare their students to successfully navigate the challenges of postmodernity. Therefore, my research sought to develop an empirically-based institutional orientation that could position Christian colleges to achieve the delicate balance between adaptation to environmental demands and fidelity to core values, and in the process, teach their students how to lead lives of Christian commitment and cultural engagement in the postmodern turn.

Higher Education in the Postmodern Turn

To elucidate the challenge facing the Christian college, I will begin by providing a brief overview of how postmodern thought has shaped the contemporary academy. Postmodern perspectives on knowledge yield important implications for higher education. First of all, if one's knowledge of reality is fundamentally local and fluid, rather than universal and permanent, then no one particular approach, method, or story can legitimately account for the diversity of human experience. This element of the postmodern critique was most famously expressed by another French philosopher, Jean-François Lyotard (1984), who defined the postmodern condition as "incredulity toward metanarratives" (p. xxiv). In the postmodern university, the previously privileged modernist metanarrative of continual progress through reason and the scientific method has no more legitimacy than any other grand story purporting to encapsulate the totality of human experience (Bloland, 1995). Moreover, if there are as many ways to understand reality as there are human cultures, but no external criteria by which to objectively assess these understandings, then every worldview becomes as valid as the next (Ford, 2002).

Not only did Lyotard reject the possibility of an objective metanarrative, but he also held "an incurable suspicion that all grand, sweeping narratives perform their legitimation functions by masking the will-to-power and excluding the interests of others" (Peters & Lankshear, 1996, p. 3). In addition to failing in their attempts to accurately describe the whole of human experience, metanarratives create totalizing discourses that suppress "anomalies, differences, and the ordinary concrete particularity of the many that comprise the one" (Cahoy, 2002, p. 94). In order to redress this offense, postmodernism employs "difference" as its organizing concept and consequently seeks to orchestrate a multiplicity of diverse voices (Tierney, 1993). This highlights a second key implication of the postmodern critique for higher education. In the absence of a legitimate, organizing metanarrative, the university becomes an embattled terrain on which "a series of power positions and contested viewpoints [vie] for a place in academe with no real set of standards by which to judge their relative merits" (Bloland, 1995, pp. 535–536). The result has been what Wolterstorff (2004a) has called the pluralization of the academy, as critical theorists (Giroux, 1988) and multiculturalists (Banks, 1993) have sought to lower the drawbridge of the university to groups previously marginalized by the totalizing discourse of modernism.

In short, postmodernists have maintained that institutions of higher learning should embrace cultural diversity, giving equal voice to the entire spectrum of human perspectives rather than privileging a select few. This imperative has led to two consequential shifts in the postsecondary landscape. The first is an expansion of postsecondary curricula, beginning in the humanities with the creation of Black Studies in the 1960s (Gumport, 2002) and leading to the eventual establishment of additional academic disciplines such as Women's Studies, Postcolonial Studies, and Urban Studies. For example, a 1992 study of 196 colleges and universities stratified by Carnegie classification found that over a third of all institutions examined had a multicultural general education requirement and over half had added multiculturalism content to their departmental course offerings (Levine & Cureton, 1992). In 1996, a study conducted by the National Association of Scholars discovered that 32 of the top 50 institutions in the *U.S. News & World Report* annual rankings had instituted diversity distribution requirements as part of their general education programs (Balch & Zurcher, 1996). By 2000, a survey administered by the Association of American Colleges and Universities revealed that 54 percent of all colleges and universities had instituted diversity requirements, while an additional 8 percent of the institutions surveyed were in the process of developing such requirements (Humphreys, 2000).

A second shift in the postsecondary landscape involves the codification of diversity requirements by accreditation agencies. American accreditation agencies expect that institutions of higher education will foster a non-threatening environment for differing points of view, an expectation evidenced by the presence of provisions supporting intellectual freedom in the quality standards of every regional postsecondary accreditor (American Association of University Professors, 2009). Moreover, this expectation has been enlarged by some agencies to include explicit statements regarding institutional diversity. For example, one agency encourages its member organizations to "promote diversity in both concept and practice" and to "evaluate their respective missions, visions, values, and character to determine how well they address issues of diversity" (Higher Learning Commission, 2003, p. 3.4-1), while another expects member institutions to foster "a climate of respect for diversity of backgrounds, ideas, and perspectives" and to determine how "various forms of diversity [can] be understood, appreciated, and valued in the curriculum" (Western Association of Schools and Colleges, 2008, pp. 19–20). This expansion of accreditation standards, along with the transformation of the postsecondary curriculum, reflects an ethos of openness to diversity within the contemporary academy, so that "[p]luralism—the right of various subcultural groups to practice their distinctive patterns of feeling, thinking, and behavior ... is not merely tolerated in the university community; it is celebrated" (Claerbaut, 2004, p. 58).

The Christian College and the Postmodern Challenge

The postsecondary shifts outlined above present a significant challenge to the Christian college. Litfin (2004) defines the Christian college as an institution that "seek[s] to make Christian thinking systemic throughout the institution," and aims "to engage any and all ideas ... from a particular intellectual location, that of the sponsoring Christian tradition" (p. 18). While a Christian college's sponsoring tradition may be defined as broadly as widely accepted Christian creeds or as narrowly as an individual denomination's articles of faith (Litfin, 2004), it will necessarily affirm the existence of an ultimate reality that operates beyond particular cultural contexts. Not only is the Christian college founded on belief in an ultimate, transcendent reality, but it exists for the sole purpose of orienting students to that reality. This mission is achieved in part by hiring only professors who "live and work from [the sponsoring] tradition—indeed from those who embody it" (Litfin, 2004, p. 18). It is further advanced by employing a pedagogical paradigm known as the integration of faith and learning (Cooper, 1999; Hasker, 1992; Holmes, 1975, 1999, 2003; Litfin, 2004; Pressnell, 1996), a method in which the implications of the Incarnation of Christ are brought to bear on the academic disciplines, with the aim of cultivating a Christian worldview in students. This approach establishes the story of Christ as the Christian college's totalizing narrative, privileging cultural perspectives judged to be consistent with Christian doctrine, while jettisoning views understood to be beyond the realm of Christian orthodoxy.

Although the integration of faith and learning served to operationalize the mission of Christian colleges throughout the modern era, its approach to cultural diversity is clearly at odds with the now prominent postmodern perspective.[1] Continued adherence to the integration paradigm not only marginalizes Christian colleges within the broader sector of higher education, but it also compromises their effectiveness in preparing students for a life of Christian faith in a postmodern world. Thus, a new pedagogical paradigm is needed, one that is sensitive to the postmodern turn yet faithful to the Christian college's core principles. This reality led me to ask, is it possible for an institution to exhibit an open stance towards diversity while being committed to an exclusivist faith tradition?

Conceptual Framework

Commitment to Christian faith requires a metaphysics, or philosophy of being, that affirms exclusivist truth claims regarding the existence of an ultimate reality beyond our present world.[2] Thus, the fundamental question to be answered is whether there exists an epistemology, or philosophy of knowledge, that values pluralism while affirming the Christian understanding of ultimate reality. H. A. Alexander (1995) has identified three epistemological orientations that religious institutions can adopt in response to cultural diversity. The first option, "absolutism" (p. 378), redoubles institutional commitments to an unambiguous understanding of core doctrines regarding ultimate reality, while rejecting any perspective that fails to comply with institutional orthodoxy. In an absolutist Christian college, only those perspectives judged to be in accordance with and not contrary to the institution's statement of faith would be allowed on campus. In practice, this means that faculty would be expected to teach within the confines of the institution's statement of faith and to present differing perspectives from the vantage point of the institution's stated beliefs. Only individuals friendly to the values of the institution would be invited to visit as guest speakers at chapel or school assemblies, and they would be prohibited from challenging institutional orthodoxy while on campus. Students would also be expected to affirm the institution's statement of faith. While the absolutist orientation preserves institutional distinctiveness, it does so by adhering to an approach to difference that has largely been abandoned by the sector of higher education. Thus, absolutism essentially amounts to what Lotz (2003) terms "disengaged preservation" (p. 172).

In order to better align with the higher education sector at large, Christian colleges may instead welcome diverse perspectives unconditionally, an orientation Alexander (1995) calls "relativism" (p. 378). This approach allows all accounts of ultimate reality to be expressed according to the terms of their own conceptual frameworks, while refraining from making value judgments according to any outside criteria. A relativist Christian college would exhibit an open and nonjudgmental stance toward all perspectives, viewing diversity of thought not as a threat to institutional character, but rather as an enhancement of the campus environment. In practice, this means that though the institution may have a Christian founding, its heritage would not be understood as necessarily normative for all peoples and cultures. Consequently, members of the college community would not be required to conform to the institution's historic Christian tradition. Moreover, no institutional effort would be made to evaluate curricular content from a Christian viewpoint. The institution would maintain an open campus, so that individuals or groups of any persuasion would be welcome to interact with students. While the relativist orientation ushers Christian colleges into the epistemological mainstream of higher education, it does so by abandoning exclusivist truth claims, harkening back to what Lotz (2003) terms "wholesale adaptation" (p. 172). This capitulation to cultural norms strips the Christian college of its distinctiveness, thereby undermining its *raison d'être*.

A *via media* is needed, an orientation that would pair absolutism's commitment to core doctrines with relativism's openness to cultural diversity. Such an orientation would, as Lotz (2003) recommends, "proceed in creative and self-critical engagement with the wider culture" (p. 172). The third orientation Alexander (1995) describes, "fallibilism" (p. 379), does just that. On the one hand, like absolutism, the fallibilist orientation acknowledges that ultimate reality does exist and can be known, therefore allowing for a commitment to core beliefs. However, fallibilism asserts that our knowledge of that reality will always be incomplete, and often incorrect, thereby rejecting the wide-ranging certitude of absolutism. On the other hand, like relativism, the fallibilist orientation encourages the expression of differing perspectives. However, fallibilism embraces cultural diversity as a potential source of greater understanding of ultimate reality, thereby rejecting relativism's wholesale denial of an objective truth existing independent of cultural context. Thus, a fallibilist orientation brings two seemingly contradictory practices—affirmation of core faith commitments and openness to cultural diversity—into harmony. By adopting a fallibilist orientation, the Christian college can gain relevance within the sector of higher education while retaining its distinctive character.

Methods

From a philosophical perspective, the fallibilist stance appears to be an attractive option for Christian colleges seeking to balance commitment to core principles and adaptation to changing contexts. However, though philosophical soundness is a necessary precondition for Christian college policy, it is ultimately insufficient, for prudent institutional action is never grounded in theory alone. The theoretical is helpful in determining the bounds of acceptability (i.e., what is philosophically plausible), but it is less effective in ascertaining the limits of actuality (i.e., what is possible in the physical world). This reality highlights the need for empirical analysis, an area of exploration that tests the veracity of theoretical claims.

Analytical Strategy

Moving from philosophical analysis of institutions to empirical analysis of individuals, my analytical strategy included three general goals. I sought first to determine whether or not students could be simultaneously committed to evangelical Christian faith and open to pluralism. I hypothesized that a fallibilist epistemology grounded in provisionality of belief would enable students to exhibit an open stance toward difference within the context of their personal faith commitments. Assuming that my first hypothesis would be confirmed, I planned next to examine a number of institutional factors that I believed would foster elements of this fallibilist Christian spirituality among students attending evangelical Christian colleges. In particular, I explored the following hypotheses: 1) two personnel factors—having faculty who model their faith and having committed Christian friends—would predict for an increase in student commitment to Christian faith; 2) two curricular factors—experiencing dissonance between new information and currently held beliefs and participating in a cultural, rather than a performative or transmissive, pedagogy—would predict for an increase in student provisionality of belief; and 3) one cultural factor—a sense of campus community—would predict for an increase in student openness to pluralism. The hypothesis testing results for each of these predictors would reveal specific actions Christian colleges could take to foster a fallibilist Christian spirituality among their students. My final goal, then, was to fashion from these results an empirically-based theory of how Christian colleges could themselves embody a fallibilist orientation and thereby persist in the postmodern turn.

Analytical Procedures

I employed the following procedures in order to execute my analytical strategy. Selecting 27 items from the 2007 CSBV survey instrument (i.e., the junior survey), I began by creating a scale to measure the theoretical construct of fallibilist Christian

TABLE 5.1 Fallibilist Christian Spirituality Scale items

Commitment to Christian Faith	Provisionality of Belief	Openness to Pluralism
Internal	*Passive*	*Knowledge*
Integrating spirituality into my life	Self-reflection	Improve understanding of other cultures
Pray to be in communion with God	Question religious beliefs	Interest in different religious traditions
Pray to express gratitude	Beliefs formed through searching	Understanding of others
Pray for forgiveness	Humility	Empathy
Seeking to grow spiritually	*Active*	*Volition*
External	Develop philosophy of life	Socialize with other racial/ ethnic groups
Attend religious services	Find answers to mysteries of life	Get along with different races/cultures
Religious singing/chanting	Seeking	Acceptance of different religious beliefs
Reading sacred texts	Search for meaning in life	Accepting others as they are
Introduce people to my faith		Cooperativeness
Follow religious teachings		

spirituality, a personal orientation consisting of three independent yet correlated components: 1) Commitment to Christian Faith (10 items), evidenced by internal expressions such as a personal desire for spiritual growth, and external expressions such as attending religious services and reading sacred texts; 2) Provisionality of Belief (8 items), passively expressed by self-reflection and humility, and actively expressed by searching for meaning and purpose; and 3) Openness to Pluralism (9 items), characterized by a desire to gain knowledge about diverse cultures and religions, and a willingness to accept people with different backgrounds or beliefs (see Table 5.1). Because I wanted to know if fallibilist Christian spirituality was a personal orientation that occurred among the college student population at large, I utilized the full longitudinal sample of 14,527 students enrolled at 136 institutions in my analysis of the scale. Multiple imputation was used to address the issue of missing data and weighting was used to correct for response bias. To determine the scale's reliability, I tested its internal statistical consistency through the use of Cronbach's alpha, and to determine the scale's validity, I performed confirmatory factor analysis using three goodness-of-fit statistics: the root mean square error of approximation (RMSEA), the comparative fit index (CFI), and the Tucker–Lewis index (TLI).[3]

I continued my empirical analysis by examining how fallibilist Christian spirituality was produced among students who attended Christian colleges. Again, I used items from the 2007 CSBV survey instrument to create scales for the five institutional factors that I hypothesized would predict for elements of fallibilist Christian spirituality (see Table 5.2). I also selected a few items from the Higher Education Research Institute's Triennial National Faculty Survey that were related

TABLE 5.2 Construct items for institutional predictors

Personnel Predictors

Faculty Modeling

Faculty mean: Enhance spiritual development

Faculty mean: Facilitate search for meaning

Faculty mean: Consider yourself a religious person

Faculty mean: Consider yourself a spiritual person

Discussed religion/spirituality with professors

Professors acted as spiritual models

Committed Christian Friends

Discussed religion/spirituality with friends

Spent time with people who share your religious views

Friends share your religious/spiritual views

Friends are searching for meaning/purpose in life

Friends go to church/temple/other house of worship

Friends belong to a campus religious organization

Having discussions about the meaning of life with friends

Curricular Predictors

Dissonance

Feeling unsettled about spiritual/religious matters

Feeling disillusioned with religious upbringing

Felt distant from God

Struggled to understand evil, suffering, and death

Disagreed with family about religious matters

Felt angry with God

Experienced conflict between coursework and beliefs

Cultural Pedagogy

Co-construction

Cooperative learning

Class discussions

Group projects

Reflective writing/journaling

Student evaluations of each other's work

Student evaluation of own work

Student-selected topics for course content

Contemplation

Discussed religion/spirituality in class

Teaching method: Prayer

Teaching method: Contemplation/ meditation

Professors encouraged exploration of meaning/purpose

Professors encouraged discussion of religious matters

Professors encouraged personal expression of spirituality

Cultural Predictors

Campus Community

Sense of community on campus

Interaction with other students

Respect for diverse spiritual/religious beliefs

---

to spirituality and that had been included in the longitudinal dataset. Multiple imputation and weighting were again used to handle missing data and response bias. As with the fallibilism scale, I utilized the full sample to confirm the reliability and validity of the five hypothesized predictors through the use of Cronbach's alpha and standard goodness-of-fit indices, respectively.

The final step was to determine whether or not these five institutional factors actually predicted for an increase in fallibilist Christian spirituality among students.

To ensure that my results would generalize to the Christian college context, I narrowed this final analysis to a subset of 3,238 students attending 39 member institutions of the Council for Christian Colleges and Universities, an association of intentionally Christ-centered, evangelical colleges. As with the previous two analyses, I used multiple imputation to handle missing data and weighting to control for response bias. Because I ultimately wanted to formulate an initial theory of institutional fallibilism that could be applied across a broad array of Christian college contexts regardless of particular student body characteristics, I controlled for student demographic characteristics (race, class, gender, and religion), student baseline measures of fallibilist Christian spirituality (i.e., entering scores from the freshman survey), and institutional variation resulting from the nested data structure of students within institutions. Using multilevel structural equation modeling, which provided standardized coefficients and significance tests for the structural paths existing between each hypothesized predictor and its corresponding response construct, I tested whether students who were exposed to each of the five institutional factors were more likely to experience an increase in fallibilist Christian spirituality during their undergraduate years.[4]

Limitations

It is important to note a few study limitations. First, the CSBV included items that could be used to measure fallibilist Christian spirituality and many, but not all, of its theorized institutional predictors. Consequently, institutional predictors had to be examined individually rather than as part of a greater whole, making it impossible to examine possible interaction effects between predictors. For example, it is unknown how predictors of commitment to Christian faith, such as faculty modeling and having committed Christian friends, affect the predictive power of campus community with respect to openness to pluralism, and vice versa. Furthermore, this design limits comparisons of relative impact to only those institutional predictors that share the same outcome variable, such as faculty modeling and committed Christian friends (personnel factors) or dissonance and cultural pedagogy (curricular factors). Finally, baseline measures were not available for two of the 27 CSBV items used to construct the fallibilist Christian spirituality scale, and thus could not be included as covariates for the multilevel structural equation models, though any potential effect on the resulting regression weights is presumed to have been minimal.

Findings

Results of the above analytical procedures yielded a number of key findings regarding fallibilist Christian spirituality and its hypothesized institutional predictors. First, the scale I created to measure fallibilist Christian spirituality evidenced sufficient reliability and construct validity, as did the constructs I formed to measure its five hypothesized institutional predictors, thus indicating that these measures were acceptable for use in additional multivariate analyses and offering empirical evidence that each of these phenomena actually occurred in the physical world. Also of note were the magnitude and direction of the correlation coefficients existing between each of the scale's subcomponents. Somewhat surprisingly, a positive relationship was found to occur between all three subcomponents, suggesting that personal faith in Christ and a pluralistic disposition are mutually reinforcing, rather than antithetical, orientations. However, the relationship between provisionality of belief and these two orientations was found to be significantly stronger, confirming that students who are committed to Christian faith are more likely to be open to pluralism if they adopt a fallibilist epistemology that emphasizes provisionality of belief.[5]

Results from multilevel structural equation modeling confirmed that, at least within a Christian college context, all five institutional factors examined do predict for elements of fallibilist Christian spirituality among students. In particular, students who have committed Christian friends and, to a lesser extent, who experience faculty modeling of Christian faith, were found to be more likely to grow in their personal faith in Christ during the college years. In addition, dissonance and cultural pedagogy were both found to foster student increases in provisionality of belief, with dissonance measuring as the stronger predictor. Finally, students were found to be more likely to exhibit openness to pluralism when they participated in a welcoming campus community.[6]

Reflections

Having established that fallibilist Christian spirituality is an orientation that occurs within the college student population, and having explored a number of institutional factors that predict for increases in elements of this personal orientation, I will close by considering how these findings might inform institutional practice. In particular, I will propose an empirically-based theory of institutional fallibilism that can empower Christian colleges to adapt in the postmodern turn without veering toward the absolutist or relativist extremes, and in so doing, prepare their graduates for a life of Christian faith in a postmodern world. The findings presented in this chapter suggest that Christian colleges seeking to adopt a fallibilist institutional orientation should embody the characteristics of institutional partisanship, individual freedom, and inclusive community.

Institutional Partisanship

As noted earlier in this chapter, the postmodern perspective rejects the very possibility of objective thought, because the "guidance of others is inherent in every language and touches every language user, making all of our thinking, even our most basic thinking, perspectival" (Scriven, 1999, p. 44). Postmodern thought recognizes that all knowing is located in some context, so that "[w]hat we see is relative to where we stand" (Cahoy, 2002, p. 98). Given the absence of neutral cognition, the modern endeavor of constructing a universal, unified field of knowledge collapses, as does modernism's concept of the university as an objective producer of knowledge. Therefore, attention shifts from the modern question of how institutions of higher learning can remain nonpartisan, to the postmodern question of how these institutions will in fact express their inescapable partisanship (Scriven, 1999).

Cahoy (2002) provides a helpful illustration of the issue at hand. Drawing from the work of C. S. Lewis, Cahoy recounts that Lewis once noticed a beam of light after entering a dark toolshed. When Lewis moved into the beam of light, he realized that his perspective had changed, so that looking *with* the beam provided a completely different view on reality than looking *at* the beam. Lewis discovered that "you can step outside one experience only by stepping inside another" (Lewis, 2000, p. 215). Applying Lewis's metaphor to the Christian college, Cahoy (2002) reasons that "if our principle is that where I stand affects what I see and everybody stands someplace, the Christian place to stand is with Christ" (p. 105). Thus, the fallibilist Christian college will intentionally locate itself within the Christian tradition, using its full resources to "explore what it would be like to think rigorously from this place" (Cahoy, 2002, p. 105).

In contrast to relativist abandonment of explicitly Christian identity, the first characteristic of an institutional fallibilist orientation is an unambiguous institutional partisanship, which in the case of the Christian college means a commitment to the historic Christian understanding of ultimate reality. In particular, the fallibilist Christian college will be theologically anchored to the touchstone that grants access to this ultimate reality, the Incarnation of Christ. Historic Christianity presents the Incarnation as the moment in history when God became flesh and dwelt among humanity. Thus, the Incarnation serves as "the objective and empirical ground within which Christian faith is generated" (Martin, 2001, p. 253). It is therefore the *sine qua non* of the fallibilist Christian college.

Although fallibilist Christian colleges will share their absolutist peers' commitment to historic Christian orthodoxy, the nature of fallibilist partisanship differs in that it is responsible, a characteristic revealed in two ways. First, responsible partisanship extends beyond cultivation of mere mental assent to address the faculties of the whole person, equipping students with the "feelings, imagination, habits, and virtues necessary to the living-out of that assent" (Scriven, 1999, p. 51). In other words, the responsibly partisan Christian college will teach its members how to personally embody the faith tradition it seeks to defend. This objective is accomplished by situating students within a campus community of committed Christian friends and by providing faculty members who can serve as models of mature Christian faith. Second, responsible partisanship does not exclusively teach its own tradition, but instead "acknowledge[s], confront[s], and learn[s] from the clash of human perspectives" (Scriven, 1999, p. 53). The partisan institution adheres to a particular tradition, while the responsibly partisan institution recognizes rival perspectives, testing its account of reality against the strongest possible objections (Scriven, 1999).

Individual Freedom

While a fallibilist Christian college will be unabashedly committed to Christian faith, it will hold on to its particular beliefs less tightly. Whereas partisanship asserts a particular perspective, fallibilist partisanship recognizes the provisional nature of all particularities. Brelsford (1995) has shrewdly observed, "if the church is oriented toward a God who is really God, then it must consider all else, including itself, as contingent and provisional" (p. 187). The same provisional standard could be applied to institutions of Christian higher education. Given this contingency, fallibilist Christian colleges will embody an "appreciation and love for, as well as an understanding of, the provisionality of [its] particularities" (Brelsford, 1995, p. 187). This attitude toward an institution's particularities reflects the second characteristic of a fallibilist institutional orientation, individual freedom.

In addition to factors such as geographic location and cultural context, a Christian college's particularities often take the form of denominational creeds and customs, and fallibilist partisanship requires an acknowledgement of the limitations of such statements and practices. Such a move does not constitute an abandonment of denominational identity or convictions, but rather an admission that these phenomena have a contingent relationship to the primary object of institutional partisanship, the person and work of Christ. Every denominational statement of faith contains theological propositions representing a particular group's latest best understanding of Christ and his significance. As such, these treatises must be held provisionally, even as the historical fact of the Incarnation remains constant. As Benson (2000) cautions, boldness must always be coupled with circumspection, because "our claims to knowledge of God always run the risk of placing a conceptual schema on God that creates Him in our image" (p. 160). Cahoy (2002) calls the divine prohibition of conceptual idolatry "a profound call for humility that should open us up to new ideas from all sources" (p. 108). Thus, Christian colleges can avoid committing conceptual idolatry by first placing the person of Christ, rather than an expansive set of theological certitudes, at the heart of their institutional identity, and then remaining open to diverse perspectives.

By focusing on the Incarnation first and foremost, members of the Christian college are encouraged to develop what Wineland (2005) calls the "open, active, and dynamic construct" of faith instead of the "static, exclusive, and immovable" construct of belief (p. 9). He argues that the construct of belief is an insufficient framework for authentic Christian faith, because faith in Christ has always involved more than a mere assent to a set of theological propositions. In fact, Wineland notes, Scripture seems to suggest that authentic faith does not require propositional certainty, but rather a commitment to the "Jesus of skin and history and the cosmic Christ of faith" (p. 14). Furthermore, an emphasis on belief implies that individuals must meet an impossible standard of total theological certainty in order to exhibit authentic faith. Wineland rightly observes that "regardless of how much we apply ourselves to study and reflection … there are still going to be holes in our belief system … and in our worldview; there are going to be mysteries we simply cannot resolve" (p. 9).

Unlike an absolutist orientation that requires strict conformity to a set of theological propositions, a fallibilist orientation encourages intellectual freedom for all members of the Christian college community. As with fallibilist partisanship, fallibilist freedom is responsible. It avoids the absolutism of the dogmatist and the relativism of the skeptic, instead encouraging individuals to think for themselves in the search for truth (Holmes, 1975). Responsible freedom allows faculty to pursue truth from "within the framework of reference to which [they stand] committed, rather than acting like iconoclasts or teaching subversion" (Holmes, 1975, p. 85). In the fallibilist Christian college, faculty members employ a cultural pedagogy that positions them as fellow travelers on the journey of faith who help guide students in a contemplative co-construction of knowledge. In addition, responsible freedom extends to students as they struggle to understand the implications of the Incarnation of Christ. By having the option of propositional uncertainty, students are empowered to remain confident in their devotion to Christ as they progress through the developmental stages that Perry (1968), Parks (1986), and Fowler (1981) have described, widely-regarded developmental models that acknowledge questioning of accepted beliefs as a natural step toward moral, spiritual, and faith maturity (Mannoia, 2000). In order to teach students the provisional nature of propositional knowledge, the fallibilist Christian college will intentionally build into its curriculum opportunities for students to experience dissonance between classroom content and their currently-held beliefs.

Inclusive Community

By acknowledging the provisional nature of their denominational creeds and customs, fallibilist Christian colleges become communities of inclusion, the final characteristic of a fallibilist institutional orientation. While fallibilism's provisional view of particulars results from an appreciation of the limits of human knowledge, it does not impede the quest for further understanding. To the contrary, as institutions charged with the promulgation of the message of Christ, fallibilist Christian colleges will always seek new and better ways to refine and express their truth claims, and hence will remain receptive to cultural diversity as a resource for theological formulations. This openness to difference is a vital hallmark of the fallibilist orientation, because it serves as a counterbalance to the temptation toward absolutist parochialism that is inherent in the Christian college's affirmation of a particular tradition (Cahoy, 2002). Wolterstorff (2004b) has observed that institutions of Christian higher education will "be delivered from [their] parochialisms" only when they "interact with humanity beyond [their] own narrow horizons" (p. 133). Citing John Calvin's pronouncement that "[t]he Spirit of God broods over humanity's cultural endeavors," Wolterstorff argues that the Christian college should recognize all forms of cultural excellence by introducing its students not only to the particulars of the institution's geographical, cultural, and denominational context, but also "to the cultural inheritance of humanity" (pp. 132–133). Moreover, by exercising receptivity to the insights of other cultures, institutions of Christian higher education empower themselves and their members to "modify or abandon [their] own inadequate or incorrect ideas" (Siejk, 1999, p. 169).

Indeed, a Christian college's unyielding commitment to the Incarnation does not require institutional homogeneity. Sloan (1999) explains that the Christian notion of unity in Christ is "an eschatological oneness that allows us here and now to turn away from our tribal prejudices and not to fear the diversities we all embody" (p. 35). Thus, complete unity in Christ is an ideal that will not be realized in this life. In this context, the Christian college should facilitate genuine dialogue among differing perspectives. Because our own particular narrative identities may grant us unique access to certain aspects of reality, Wolterstorff (2004c) argues that "the ultimate point of such intraperspectival endeavors is that what is discerned and learned be shared with those of us whose narrative identity is different—so that all together we can arrive at a richer and more accurate understanding" (p. 238).

How then does the Christian college foster an inclusive community of cross-perspectival interaction? First of all, inclusive community results when the Christian college abandons Christian triumphalism and engages in the practice of hospitality. According to Newman (2002), "hospitality means we welcome the colleague or student who is different from us not because all 'values' are relative, but because welcoming the stranger, even the enemy, is one way to practice the conviction that all persons are children of God called to live in communion with each other" (p. 146). Moreover, genuine hospitality receives the other without precondition, "in all of his or her particularity," thereby creating a space for individuals to speak the truth as best they know it, wherein they appear before others as a person and not just a position (Newman, 2002, p. 146). Hospitality, then, affirms the value of perspectives outside of the institution's particular tradition, attempts to bring alternative voices into conversation, and seeks to learn from those with whom the institution disagrees (Phipps, 2004).

Inclusive community is fostered through structural, as well as attitudinal, elements of the institution. Lakeland (2002) notes that an institution's openness to difference should manifest itself in admissions practices. Building on the work of Strike (1993), Heie (1996) argues that an institution committed to cross-perspectival conversation will employ a democratic administrative and governance structure that "values the 'better argument' rather than power; equality and reciprocity rather than bureaucratic hierarchy; and autonomy and solidarity rather than domination and coercion" (p. 153). Furthermore, Heie (1996) argues that the Christian college curriculum should be redesigned to "maximize the educational benefits of disagreements" by adopting two strategies promoted by Gerald Graff (1992): teacher-swapping, or allowing faculty from differing disciplines to trade classes periodically or to combine their classes at scheduled points of time in the semester to discuss a common text; and thematic course clustering, or integrating the content of multiple courses around a common theme.

Conclusion

By adopting the fallibilist characteristics of institutional partisanship, individual freedom, and inclusive community, Christian colleges can achieve faithful persistence in the postmodern turn. Furthermore, I believe that the fallibilist orientation may actually position Christian colleges to exercise leadership among their institutional peers. A number of theorists have contemplated what form and function a truly postmodern university might take, and it appears that a fallibilist Christian college would exemplify many of the traits suggested by these scholars. For example, Tierney (2001) has proposed characteristics such as sector heterogeneity marked by localized interpretations, engagement of identities within and outside of the university, and an acknowledgement that truth claims are contingent in nature, while Bloland (2005) has argued that, in order to cope with the postmodern turn, colleges and universities must commit to institutional reflexivity and rededicate themselves to serving their clients and society.

In the postmodern turn, the Christian college "becomes not an anomaly or even the oxymoron some would claim but a variation on the structure common to all knowing and all colleges" (Cahoy, 2002, p. 101). Moreover, the fallibilist Christian college becomes a model of appropriate postmodern postsecondary practice. The fallibilist Christian college operates according to its own local needs and interests, seeking primarily to understand and promulgate the implications of the Incarnation of Christ. Furthermore, it attempts to serve the needs of its clients by preparing students for a life of faith in a postmodern world. Recognizing the provisional nature of belief, the fallibilist Christian college reflexively allows itself and its members the freedom to question current understandings. Finally, the fallibilist Christian college views diversity not as a threat to institutional orthodoxy but as a potential source of greater understanding, and therefore fosters a sense of campus community that welcomes differing perspectives and ways of knowing. In sum, a fallibilist institutional orientation not only empowers

Christian colleges to persist in the postmodern turn, but it also positions these distinctive institutions to serve as archetypes of postsecondary practice in the age of postmodernity.

Notes

1 For additional critique of the integration paradigm, see Downing (2004) and Glanzer (2008).
2 Examples include (but are not limited to) the doctrine of creation *ex nihilo,* the doctrine of the Trinity, and the doctrine of the Incarnation of Christ.
3 For complete details of procedures relating to scale construction, see Rine (in press).
4 For complete details regarding the development of latent constructs for each of the institutional factors, see Rine (under review).
5 For complete results related to scale validation, see Rine (in press).
6 For complete results of the multilevel structural equation model analysis, see Rine (under review).

References

Alexander, H. A. (1995). Religion and multiculturalism in education. *Religious Education,* 90 (3), 377–387.

American Association of University Professors (2009). Regional accreditation standards concerning academic freedom and the faculty role in governance: http://www.aaup.org/AAUP/comm/rep/acredacafree.htm. Last accessed September 25, 2009.

Balch, S. H., & Zurcher, R. C. (1996). *The dissolution of general education: 1914–1993.* Princeton: National Association of Scholars.

Banks, J. A. (1993). The canon debate, knowledge construction, and multicultural education. *Educational Researcher,* 22 (5), 4–14.

Beal, T. K. (2002). Teaching the conflicts, for the Bible tells me so. In S. R. Haynes (Ed.), *Professing in the postmodern academy: Faculty and the future of church-related colleges* (pp. 183–193). Waco: Baylor University Press.

Benson, B. E. (2000). The end of the fantastic dream: Testifying to the truth in the 'post' condition. *Christian Scholar's Review,* 30 (2), 145–161.

Bloland, H. G. (1995). Postmodernism and higher education. *Journal of Higher Education,* 66 (5), 521–559.

Bloland, H. G. (2005). Whatever happened to postmodernism in higher education?: No requiem in the new millennium. *Journal of Higher Education,* 76 (2), 121–150.

Brelsford, T. (1995). Christological tensions in a pluralistic environment: Managing the challenges of fostering and sustaining both identity and openness. *Religious Education,* 90, 174–189.

Cahoy, W. J. (2002). A sense of place and the place of sense. In S. R. Haynes (Ed.), *Professing in the postmodern academy: Faculty and the future of church-related colleges* (pp. 73–111). Waco: Baylor University Press.

Claerbaut, D. (2004). *Faith and learning on the edge: A bold new look at religion in higher education.* Grand Rapids: Zondervan.

Cooper, M. V. (1999). Faculty perspectives on the integration of faith and academic discipline in Southern Baptist higher education. *Religious Education,* 94 (4), 380–396.

Downing, C. L. (2004). Imbricating faith and learning: The architectonics of Christian scholarship. In D. Jacobsen & R. Jacobsen (Eds.), *Scholarship and Christian faith: Enlarging the conversation* (pp. 33–44). New York: Oxford University Press.

Ford, M. P. (2002). *Beyond the modern university: Toward a constructive postmodern university.* Westport: Praeger.

Fowler, J. W. (1981). *Stages of faith: The psychology of human development and the quest for meaning.* San Francisco: Harper & Row.

Giroux, H. A. (1988). Border pedagogy in the age of postmodernism. *Journal of Education,* 170 (3), 162–181.

Glanzer, P. L. (2008). Why we should discard the integration of faith and learning: Rearticulating the mission of the Christian scholar. *Journal of Education and Christian Belief,* 12 (1), 41–51.

Graff, G. (1992). *Beyond the culture wars: How teaching the conflicts can revitalize American education.* New York: W. W. Norton.

Gumport, P. J. (2002). *Academic pathfinders: Knowledge creation and feminist scholarship.* Westport: Greenwood Press.

Hasker, W. (1992). Faith-learning integration: An overview. *Christian Scholars Review,* 21 (3), 231–248.

Heie, H. (1996). The postmodern opportunity: Christians in the academy. *Christian Scholar's Review,* 26 (2), 138–157.

Higher Learning Commission (2003). *Handbook of accreditation* (3rd edn). Chicago: Higher Learning Commission.

Holmes, A. F. (1975). *The idea of a Christian college.* Grand Rapids: Eerdmans.

Holmes, A. F. (1999). Integrating faith and learning in a Christian liberal arts institution. In D. S. Dockery & D. P. Gushee (Eds.), *The future of Christian higher education* (pp. 155–177). Nashville: Broadman & Holman.

Holmes, A. F. (2003). The closing of the American mind and the opening of the Christian mind: Liberal learning, great texts, and the Christian college. In D. V. Henry & B. R. Agee (Eds.), *Faithful learning and the Christian scholarly vocation* (pp. 101–122). Grand Rapids: Eerdmans.

Humphreys, D. (2000). National survey finds diversity requirements common around the country. *AAC&U Diversity Digest,* fall.

Lakeland, P. (2002). The habit of empathy: Postmodernity and the future of the church-related college. In S. R. Haynes (Ed.), *Professing in the postmodern academy: Faculty and the future of church-related colleges* (pp. 33–48). Waco: Baylor University Press.

Levine, A., & Cureton, J. (1992). The quiet revolution. *Change,* 24 (1), 25–29.

Lewis, C. S. (2000). *God in the dock.* Grand Rapids: Eerdmans.

Lincoln, Y. S. (1991). Advancing a critical agenda. In W. G. Tierney (Ed.), *Culture and ideology in higher education: Advancing a critical agenda* (pp. 17–32). New York: Praeger.

Litfin, D. (2004). *Conceiving the Christian college.* Grand Rapids: Eerdmans.

Lotz, D. (2003). Christian higher education in the twenty-first century and the clash of civilizations. In D. V. Henry & B. R. Agee (Eds.), *Faithful learning and the Christian scholarly vocation* (pp. 158–175). Grand Rapids: Eerdmans.

Lyotard, J. F. (1984). *The postmodern condition: A report on knowledge.* Minneapolis: University of Minnesota.

Mannoia, V. J. (2000). *Christian liberal arts: An education that goes beyond.* Lanham: Rowman & Littlefield.

Martin, R. K. (2001). Having faith in our faith in God: Toward a critical realist epistemology for Christian education. *Religious Education*, 96 (2): 245–261.

Newman, E. (2002). Beyond the faith-knowledge dichotomy: Teaching as vocation. In S. R. Haynes (Ed.), *Professing in the postmodern academy: Faculty and the future of church-related colleges* (pp. 131–148). Waco: Baylor University Press.

Parks, S. (1986). *The critical years: The young adult search for a faith to live by.* San Francisco: Harper & Row.

Perry, W. G. (1968). *Forms of intellectual and ethical development in the college years: A scheme.* New York: Holt, Rinehart & Winston.

Peters, M., & Lankshear, C. (1996). Postmodern counternarratives. In H. Giroux, C. Lankshear, P. McLaren, *et al.* (Eds.), *Counternarratives: Cultural studies and critical pedagogies in postmodern spaces* (pp. 1–39). New York: Routledge.

Phipps, K. S. (2004). Epilogue: Campus climate and Christian scholarship. In D. Jacobsen & R. H. Jacobsen (Eds.), *Scholarship and Christian faith: Enlarging the conversation* (pp. 171–183). New York: Oxford University Press.

Pressnell, C. O. (1996). Assessing faith/learning integration among alumni at Taylor University. *Research on Christian Education*, 3, 1–32.

Rine, P. J. (in press). Committed to faith yet open to difference: validating a model for fallibilist Christian spirituality among college students. *Journal of College Student Development.*

Rine, P. J. (under review). Fostering commitment and openness: The institutional predictors of fallibilist Christian spirituality. Unpublished manuscript.

Scriven, C. (1999). Schooling for the tournament of narratives: Postmodernism and the idea of the Christian college. *Religious Education*, 94 (1): 40–57.

Siejk, C. (1999). Learning to love the questions: Religious education in an age of unbelief. *Religious Education*, 94 (2), 155–171.

Sloan, R. B. (1999). Preserving distinctively Christian higher education. In D. S. Dockery & D. P. Gushee (Eds.), *The future of Christian higher education* (pp. 25–36). Nashville: Broadman & Holman.

Strike, K. A. (1993). Professionalism, democracy, and discursive communities: Normative reflections on restructuring. *American Educational Research Journal*, 30 (2), 255–275.

Tierney, W. G. (1993). *Building communities of difference: Higher education in the twenty-first century.* Westport: Bergin & Garvey.

Tierney, W. G. (2001). The autonomy of knowledge and the decline of the subject: Postmodernism and the reformulation of the university. *Higher Education*, 41 (4), 353–372.

Western Association of Schools and Colleges (2008). *Handbook of accreditation.* Alameda: WASC.

Wineland, R. K. (2005). Incarnation, image, and story: Toward a postmodern orthodoxy for Christian educators. *Journal of Research on Christian Education*, 14 (1), 7–16.

Wolterstorff, N. (2004a). Can scholarship and Christian conviction mix? Another look at the integration of faith and learning. In C. W. Joldersma & G. G. Stronks (Eds.), *Educating for shalom: Essays on Christian higher education* (pp. 172–198). Grand Rapids: Eerdmans.

Wolterstorff, N. (2004b). The project of a Christian university in a postmodern culture. In C. W. Joldersma & G. G. Stronks (Eds.), *Educating for shalom: Essays on Christian higher education* (pp. 109–134). Grand Rapids: Eerdmans.

Wolterstorff, N. (2004c). Particularist perspectives: Bias or access?. In C. W. Joldersma & G. G. Stronks (Eds.), *Educating for shalom: Essays on Christian higher education* (pp. 226–240). Grand Rapids: Eerdmans.

6

HOW INSTITUTIONAL CONTEXTS AND COLLEGE EXPERIENCES SHAPE ECUMENICAL WORLDVIEW DEVELOPMENT

Alyssa Bryant Rockenbach and Matthew J. Mayhew

> For we know that our patchwork heritage is a strength, not a weakness. We are a nation of Christians and Muslims, Jews and Hindus—and non-believers. We are shaped by every language and culture, drawn from every end of this Earth; and because we have tasted the bitter swill of civil war and segregation, and emerged from that dark chapter stronger and more united, we cannot help but believe that the old hatreds shall someday pass; that the lines of tribe shall soon dissolve; that as the world grows smaller, our common humanity shall reveal itself; and that America must play its role in ushering in a new era of peace.
> —President Barack Obama in his Inauguration Address delivered on
> January 20, 2009

Exemplified by this excerpt from President Obama's inaugural address, there is an urgent need for interreligious understanding and cooperation. The recent controversy surrounding plans to establish an Islamic community center, Park51, within two blocks of the site of the September 11th attacks on the World Trade Center serves as one especially powerful illustration of the discord that religious and worldview differences can inspire. Deeply divided opinions about the Park51 project were expressed in protests, heated discourse, and acts of violence. The controversy has ignited questions about religious tolerance and free exercise of religion for believers of diverse faith traditions in conjunction with a desire to honor the memory of those who perished in the attacks. As these recent events attest, aggression motivated by religious and worldview difference is a long-standing problem in human history—and one that has not been readily solved even in the midst of democratic, technological, and humanitarian progress.

The college years represent a critical period of time in which people of different backgrounds and worldviews have an opportunity to engage one another in ways that may make lasting impressions on beliefs and values related to pluralism. Whether this engagement occurs in formal learning environments (e.g., religion classes) or through informal peer interactions (e.g., religious discussions with friends in the residence halls), the culmination of various forms of exposure to religious and worldview diversity may in fact engender compassion for and understanding of those outside one's particular religion or worldview. As college students are challenged by pluralism on campus, the possibility exists that they may be transformed in the process. With the expectation that students grow in promising ways as they encounter diverse people and ideas, we come to the study of ecumenical worldview development with the hope that the college experience can indeed create change in the world beyond the academy. If students learn to replace fear and mistrust with openness and good will in their relationships with diverse others, perhaps benevolent exchanges across difference will become the norm rather than the exception.

Our research examined the collegiate influences on students' ecumenical worldview development, which is an outcome that reflects having an interest in diverse worldviews, accepting others, and believing in human interconnectedness. Specifically, we addressed the following questions: How do institutional contexts, educational practices, and student experiences influence the development of an ecumenical worldview? Is ecumenical worldview development in college dependent on gender, race, or religion/worldview?

The Multiple Meanings of Pluralism

To bring the concept of ecumenical worldview into focus, consideration of the underlying meanings of pluralism is in order. Diana Eck (1993) articulated a thoughtful and multidimensional definition of pluralism that effectively entwined several critical elements. First, Eck noted that pluralism, importantly, is a *response* to diversity. Diversity can be understood as a reality of our multicultural society; human differences exist whether we choose to engage or ignore them. Pluralism is an approach to diversity that entails "active engagement with plurality" (p. 191). Second, pluralism extends beyond mere toleration of others representing different cultural backgrounds, beliefs, and values to encompass acceptance and good will. As pluralists we do not simply endure the presence of those who are different from us; we welcome them with expressions of generosity, kindness, hospitality, and respect. Two additional dimensions of Eck's (1993) understanding of pluralism underscore what pluralism is *not*. Importantly, pluralism does not demand that we deny the existence of truth or maintain a relativistic stance in which all truths are equally valid. Pluralism, instead, involves making commitments in the presence of diversity, all the while maintaining a disciplined openness to learning from others.

Lastly, pluralism does not necessitate "flattening" differences in search of a basic, underlying commonality that unites us all. Although we may (and probably will) discover common ground with others in our diverse society, pluralism allows authentic differences to exist—and, in fact, these differences contribute to the richness and vitality of the world in which we live.

Fostering the pluralistic orientations of students in college is a value embedded in numerous developmental frameworks. Although students' openness to religious and spiritual diversity is not uniformly the focus of such frameworks, they do emphasize compassionate citizenship within our multicultural society and receptivity to differences, thus connecting multiple conceptualizations of diversity. The theoretical illustrations that follow are not meant to be exhaustive, but make evident the point that notions of openness to diversity and pluralism have been both implicit and explicit elements in student development theory for some time.

For instance, Chickering and Reisser (1993) affirmed the importance of appreciating differences in one of seven developmental vectors: developing mature interpersonal relationships. In their view, relational maturity necessitates challenging one's (perhaps inaccurate) assumptions and learning to value cultural differences. Similarly, Braskamp (2008) stressed the significance of "global citizenship" as a critical developmental objective involving not only recognition of "differences across continents or countries, but rather integration of all racial, cultural, and religious backgrounds" (p. 4). In other words, global citizenship reflects the degree to which students are understanding of, open to, and appreciative of cultural differences, broadly defined. Parks's (2000) framework illuminating faith development more closely aligns with this chapter's discussion of ecumenical worldview in that she expressly denoted openness to others as a formative milestone in faith development. Specifically, Parks (2000) described "longing for communion with those who are profoundly other than self" (p. 102) as an important step toward a mature adult faith marked by interdependence and connectedness in the midst of plurality.

How Students Develop Pluralistic Perspectives

Given the multifaceted definition of pluralism and the ubiquity of this concept in student development theory, how is pluralism fostered among young adults in college? Our synthesis of previous research suggests that pluralism is a function of manifold aspects of the world undergraduates inhabit when they come to campus, including the institutional context, curricular experiences, peer and co-curricular engagement, and "crisis" experiences.

Institutional Contexts

Engberg (2007) examined how students' encounters with diversity in college work in concert to encourage the development of pluralistic orientation, a construct that reflects students' "ability to see multiple perspectives; ability to work cooperatively with diverse people; ability to discuss and negotiate controversial issues; openness to having one's views challenged; and tolerance of others with different beliefs" (p. 291). Although the outcome of interest did not explicitly incorporate religious or spiritual content, pluralistic orientation is arguably related to ecumenical worldview. The findings revealed that institutional characteristics are associated with students' development of pluralistic orientation. Specifically, structural diversity, which in Engberg's (2007) study was defined as the racial/ethnic composition of the student body, creates the opportunity for positive interactions across racial differences, which indirectly promotes intergroup learning and subsequently pluralistic orientation.

Reinforcing the importance of the collegiate context, a recent study of ecumenical orientation (e.g., believing world religions have more commonalities than differences, respecting people with different worldviews than one's own, believing religious tolerance and understanding will make the world a more peaceful place) in relation to campus climate underscored the significance of space for spiritual support and expression (Bryant Rockenbach & Mayhew, 2011). The presence of welcoming spaces that allow students to be themselves religiously and spiritually cultivates ecumenical perspectives. In short, institutional contexts set the stage for pluralistic development by generating opportunities for the type of engagements that further solidify openness to, interest in, and acceptance of religiously diverse others.

Curricular Diversity Exposure

Classroom and curricular experiences play a direct role in shaping students' attitudes toward diversity and pluralism. Pascarella and Terenzini (2005), in their thorough review of research on the impact of diversity-related coursework, illuminated overwhelmingly positive multicultural competence outcomes, "including awareness of other ethnicities and cultures, openness to diversity, and the importance attached to promoting racial understanding" (p. 312). Likewise, a plethora of individual research studies over the last decade confirm that diversity-infused curricular offerings are promising sources of students' cultural competency (Chang, 2002; Engberg, 2007; Gurin, Dey, Gurin, & Hurtado, 2004; Nelson Laird, Engberg, & Hurtado, 2005). Recent evidence further demonstrates that provocative encounters with worldview diversity (e.g., class discussions that challenge students to rethink their assumptions about another worldview, having discussions with someone of another worldview that result in a positive influence on one's perceptions of that worldview) and enrolling in a religion course designed to enhance one's knowledge of a different religious tradition are positively associated with ecumenical orientation (Bryant Rockenbach & Mayhew, 2011).

Peer and Co-Curricular Diversity Exposure

Experiences in college that foster pluralistic openness and understanding extend well beyond the academic sphere. Peer and co-curricular influences are known to have considerable impact on students' perceptions of diversity. For example, interracial interactions—ranging from casual contact to friendship—contribute to positive racial attitudes and values, including knowledge and acceptance of others and reduced prejudice (Antonio, 2001; Engberg, 2007; Pascarella & Terenzini, 2005). The *nature* of the interaction matters as well. When value-laden discussions of controversial issues occur among diverse peers, first-year students become increasingly open to diversity and challenge (Pascarella, Edison, Nora, Hagedorn, & Terenzini, 1996), and these effects are maintained over time (Whitt, Edison, Pascarella, Terenzini, & Nora, 2001).

The peer effect is not only evident in individual student-to-student interactions but also manifests in a broader fashion via the environment that is created by the student body at large. For example, according to Chang, Denson, Saenz, and Misa (2006), "the peer average [cross-race interaction] level has a significant positive effect on students' openness to diversity" (p. 449). Student engagement with peer diversity, in other words, opens the door to pluralistic appreciation on an individual level but also serves to create a campus environment in which pluralism is valued and perpetuated.

Co-curricular engagements that are known to influence students' pluralistic understanding include activities that remove students from their comfort zones and challenge the veracity of their assumptions about the world. Volunteer work and study abroad excursions are two pertinent examples that may encourage worldview dismantling and reconstruction. Research on the effects of volunteer work deems these encounters as effective catalysts in transforming students' awareness of and attitudes toward other groups (Pascarella & Terenzini, 2005). Similarly, studies addressing the impact of study abroad programs identify these challenging co-curricular experiences as provoking deeper awareness, tolerance, and cultural pluralism among college students (Pascarella & Terenzini, 2005). In the section that follows we turn our attention to the mechanism by which challenging diversity encounters in academic, peer, and co-curricular contexts influence students' pluralistic and/or ecumenical orientation.

Crisis

Encounters in college that provoke new and more reflective ways of understanding the world induce critical developmental moments that have been widely referenced in the developmental literature. The psychological "crisis" (Erikson, 1968; Marcia, 1966) that arises from engaging the unfamiliar has been variously characterized by theorists over the last six decades as cognitive disequilibrium (Rest, 1986), cognitive dissonance (Festinger, 1957; Perry, 1968), crossroads (Baxter Magolda, 2001), and shipwreck (Parks, 2000).

The psychological discomfort wrought by encountering religious, worldview, or other dimensions of human difference is an important catalyst for growth and development, so long as students find adequate support to negotiate the disquiet that may ensue in the midst of challenging experiences (Sanford, 1968). Bowman and Brandenberger (in press) explain that "experiencing the unexpected" in conjunction with diversity interactions is associated with subjective sense of belief challenge and subsequent attitude change. In the realm of religion and spirituality, crisis has been linked to faith development (Fowler, 1981; Parks, 2000). Moreover, experiences in college that challenge, disorient, and introduce students to new and unfamiliar worldviews predict religious and spiritual struggles, which in turn promote growth in "acceptance of people with different religious/spiritual views" (Bryant & Astin, 2008). Reiterating the need for support mechanisms during moments of religious and spiritual crisis, the negative effects of struggles—namely poor physical and psychological health—should not be overlooked or underestimated (Pargament, 2008).

Our research contributes more definitive answers regarding the mechanisms by which institutional context, curricular experiences, peer and co-curricular engagement, and, importantly, crisis influence ecumenical worldview development among college students. Past studies, for the most part, did not examine pluralism as defined by students' levels of openness to religious and spiritual diversity. Moreover, the studies of religious/spiritual struggles and ecumenical worldview that have been conducted were limited by their cross-sectional design, a problem that we have rectified in our research through the use of national, longitudinal data.

Theoretical Perspective

One of the important distinctions between previous studies of student outcomes related to diversity, pluralism, and general openness to others is the quantitative criticalist lens we adopted in designing and conducting our analyses (see Stage, 2007). Stage (2007) describes the quantitative criticalist approach as one that "question[s] the models, measures and analytical practices of quantitative research in order to offer competing models, measures and analytical practices that better describe the experiences of those who have not been adequately represented" (p. 10). In other words, critical quantitative researchers are mindful that scales and analyses may not equally represent the experiences of diverse groups; rather, researchers who assume the criticalist lens seek to illuminate the experiences of groups that do not enjoy the privileges of the statistical majority.

Higher education researchers are becoming ever more aware of the fallacies associated with theoretical models based uncritically on aggregated samples. Pascarella (2006) argued that one of the key directions for future scholarship involves careful consideration of conditional effects, particularly because "the same intervention or experience might not have the same impact for all students, but rather might differ in the magnitude or even the direction of its impact for students with different characteristics or traits" (p. 512). The reality that individual student characteristics, including gender, race/ethnicity, religion/worldview, political orientation, and career aspirations, significantly shape the ways in which students experience their spiritual and religious lives (Astin, Astin, Lindholm, Bryant, Szelényi, & Calderone, 2005; Bryant, 2007; Lindholm, Goldberg, & Calderone, 2006) compels us to attend to the differential effects of college on ecumenical worldview.

Given that the study of ecumenical worldview is itself value-laden and thereby potentially shaped by the interests, commitments, and worldviews of the researchers, our intent is to be transparent concerning our approach to the study's design and analysis. As part of this transparency process, we articulate some of our own biases and how they may have influenced our approach to the analyses.

Alyssa

My research perspective integrates several lenses that together influence the way in which I approach and analyze problems in higher education scholarship. As a mixed-methods researcher, I have discovered that both quantitative and qualitative methodologies are instrumental in exploring the many questions I have regarding religion and spirituality in higher education. The nature of the topics I study necessitates a balanced and pragmatic approach that recognizes the value of representative, "big picture" data as well as nuanced and particular data. I hold in tension the post-positivist assumptions implicit in quantitative methodologies and the social constructivist assumptions that underlie most qualitative research and acknowledge that my overarching assumptions lean toward the latter. I believe that subjective realities can still be explored quantitatively so long as ample attention is given to the unique ways that diverse groups experience various phenomena. In addition, I deem quantitative data as an imperfect representation of diverse lived experiences, but hold that it may begin to illuminate some important dimensions of those experiences.

My lens is further complicated by a complex blend of marginalized and privileged identities. As a White woman who is a member of a faith tradition that is privileged in the U.S. (Christianity), I recognize the advantages that stem from my racial and religious background and, likewise, disavow any presumptions that my experiences are similar to individuals of other races, ethnicities, religious traditions, or worldviews. Yet, as a woman and sexual minority, my experiences with sexism and heterosexism have inspired my criticalist lens—as I, too, have lived to some extent on the margins and can appreciate the differences in perception that derive from a minority status.

Matt

My own approach to inquiry has often been underscored by my affinity toward and use of post-positive paradigms, assuming that aspects of reality can be objectively accessed and measured, while acknowledging the important role contexts play in understanding that reality. Of course, this paradigm continues to be challenged, particularly by colleagues interested in diversity-climate research who often share a concern that post-positivism may misrepresent the voices and experiences of individuals whose worldviews fall outside of the statistical majority. Expressions of this paradigm, as well as my tendency to align with religious worldviews representing the "religious majority," are likely to have influenced my approach to this study: maintaining that ecumenical worldview is quantifiable and that there will be observed differences in these orientations based on self-identified religious worldview.

Methods

Our analytical procedures entailed constructing and testing a series of structural equations and hierarchical linear models in an effort to illuminate how college students develop an ecumenical worldview during the college years. The analyses involving structural equation modeling were based on the full longitudinal sample of 14,527 students enrolled at 136 institutions, while the hierarchical linear modeling analyses were based on a slightly smaller sample of 13,932 cases at 126 institutions to ensure an adequate number of cases per school. The procedures are detailed in full elsewhere (Bryant, 2011a, 2011b; Mayhew, 2012), but below we provide a summary of our analytical approaches.

Structural Equation Modeling

Structural equation modeling was used to evaluate a conceptual framework comprised of eight measures, including six latent constructs and two observed variables. The six latent constructs included religious/spiritual struggles at time 1 and time 2, religious reinforcers, salience of religion/spirituality in academics, and ecumenical worldview at time 1 and time 2. Religious/spiritual struggles and ecumenical worldview were described in Chapter 2, but religious reinforcers and the salience of religion/spirituality in academics were created for the express purpose of testing the effects of different aspects of the college experience on ecumenical worldview. The religious reinforcers factor ($\alpha = .79$), assessed as part of the 2007 CSBV follow-up survey, measures students' engagement with people and contexts expected to strengthen their religious worldviews. The construct includes attending religious services, participating in campus religious organizations, discussing religion/spirituality with family, going on a religious mission trip, spending time with people who share one's religious views, and having friends who share one's religious views. Salience of religion/spirituality in academics ($\alpha = .87$) is a latent construct that reflects the degree to which students encountered religion and spirituality in their classroom and faculty interactions. Specifically, the seven items include discussing religion and spirituality in class and with professors; having professors who encouraged discussion of religious/spiritual matters, personal expression of spirituality, exploration of questions of meaning and purpose, and discussion of ethical issues; and having professors who acted as spiritual role models.

The two observed variables in the model were challenging co-curricular experiences and perceptions of the campus spiritual climate. "Challenging co-curricular experiences," which are experiences that bring students into contact with new people and ideas and potentially promote struggle and pluralism (Antonio, 2001; Bryant & Astin, 2008; Engberg, 2007; Pascarella et al., 1996; Pascarella & Terenzini, 2005; Whitt et al., 2001), include studying abroad, performing volunteer work, socializing with someone of another racial/ethnic group, discussing religion/ spirituality with friends, and exploring religion online. "Perceptions of the campus spiritual climate" was measured by one item: "My campus allows for personal expressions of spirituality" (1 = "disagree strongly" to 4 = "agree strongly").

Five dichotomous variables, gender (female), race/ethnicity (minority), religious minority (versus religious majority), non-religious (versus religious majority), and institution type (religious), were included in the model to control for the effects of demographic and institutional characteristics on religious/spiritual struggles at time 1, ecumenical worldview at time 1, and college involvement.

The structural model (see details in Bryant, 2011a) was designed to test several conjectures. First, student demographic characteristics and tendencies toward spiritual struggles and ecumenical worldview were expected to be predictive of college involvement and time-2 struggles and ecumenism. Second, we anticipated that academic encounters with religion and spirituality, challenging co-curricular experiences, and "open" campus spiritual climates would expose students to people and experiences that would challenge their pre-existing worldviews, thereby amplifying religious/spiritual struggles. Third, we expected religious reinforcers to diminish the tendency to struggle because these experiences protect against crisis and disequilibrium by minimizing exposure to diverse worldviews. Fourth, we hypothesized religious/spiritual struggle at time 2 would mediate the relationships between campus context/college encounters and ecumenical worldview at time 2. In other words, religious/spiritual struggle was expected to serve an important developmental purpose in encouraging students to adopt inclusive and compassionate attitudes toward diverse others in a pluralistic society.

The fit of the model was evaluated using standard indices, including chi-square, the goodness-of-fit index (GFI), the comparative fit index (CFI), root mean residual

(RMR), and the root mean square error of approximation (RMSEA). Moreover, we tested for measurement invariance to determine whether model parameters differed significantly by gender, race, and worldview (religious majority, religious minority, and non-religious).

Hierarchical Linear Modeling

Hierarchical linear modeling (HLM) was used to examine the multi-level nature of students' ecumenical worldview development. Given that students are nested in particular peer and institutional contexts, the constructed models helped to unpack the unique influence of institution-level variables (e.g., institutional religious type, peer group religious struggle, peer group ecumenicism) and student-level variables (e.g., demographics, college experiences) (see Raudenbush & Bryk, 2002).

The variables used to construct the hierarchical linear models included structural demographic organizational characteristics (e.g., religious type, religious type by average amount of exposure to peers reporting religious struggles), peer group characteristics (i.e., the average amount of student exposure to peers reporting religious struggles at time 1, and the average amount of ecumenical worldview reported at time 1), student entry covariates (i.e., race, gender, reported disability, pre-college religious identification, pre-college spiritual identification, ecumenical worldview at time 1), student academic experience variables (i.e., college grade point average and participation in curricular experiences with religious or spiritual content), and social experience variables (i.e., participation in co-curricular experiences with religious or spiritual content and perceptions of religious struggle).

In order to accurately capture the amount of variance explained by institutional-level and student-level covariates, a series of models was built before constructing the final model. The fully unconditional model was used to compute the intraclass correlation coefficients to determine whether any proportion of the variance in ecumenical worldview significantly varied across institutions. Next, the random coefficient models were built progressively, beginning with analyses to establish whether any of the variance in ecumenical worldview could be explained by the relationships between student-level variables and institutional variability. These analyses revealed that gender differences in ecumenical worldview existed and could be explained by institution-level differences. Based upon the previous models, the intercept and slope-as-outcome model was constructed. For these models all institutional-level variables were included in an effort to explain the grand mean of ecumenical worldview at time 2. The final model constructed considered the complex relationships between student-level and institution-level variables in predicting ecumenical worldview at time 2 and were informed by previous models and variance component analyses. Further details regarding the HLM analysis can be found in Mayhew (2012).

Limitations

Our research on ecumenical worldview development has limitations that warrant attention in future investigations. First, the models we constructed provide an adequate reflection of how development unfolds among college students; however, there are likely other measures not available in the dataset that might help to further account for change over time. The study of ecumenical worldview development is emerging, and as a result, the theoretical and empirical bases of our research derived from studies that defined pluralism somewhat differently (often along the lines of appreciation of and openness to racial/ethnic diversity). Any imprecision in our measures (or absence of relevant measures altogether) will need to be addressed as the study of ecumenical development advances and gains momentum. Second, though our studies used longitudinal data, students were surveyed at only two points in time. More robust assessments of ecumenical development would ideally include three or more time points. Finally, despite the considerable size of the sample, we were still unable to examine ecumenical worldview development among specific racial/ethnic and religious sub-groups. Aggregating the smaller religion and race categories into "minority" groupings was necessary for statistical reasons, but likely obscured important nuances.

Findings

Institutional Contexts

The hierarchical linear models brought into focus the importance of institutional context in facilitating ecumenical worldview development from the first to third year of college. The religious affiliation of the college or university a student attends plays an instrumental role in fostering ecumenicism. According to the analysis, Catholic institutions and "other" religious colleges promote ecumenical worldview development to a greater extent than do evangelical Christian institutions. Perhaps the tendency within evangelical Christian colleges to instill in students particular religious truths counters aspects of pluralism that involve serious consideration of other truth claims. It may also be that modifications to the ecumenical worldview construct would better reflect the openness toward and appreciation of other faiths that is expressed in nuanced ways within exclusivist traditions (see Rine's notion of fallibilism in Chapter 5). For instance, the prevailing, unquestionable message within an evangelical Christian college might be that salvation is only possible through faith in Jesus Christ. However, a concurrent message might simultaneously encourage students to challenge their own conceptions of reality, learn about other faith traditions, and demonstrate compassion and good will toward people of diverse worldviews. Ecumenical worldview as defined in our research may not adequately capture this level of complexity.

The peer environment on campus is another influential dimension of institutional context. Specifically, the ecumenical worldview development of individual students is enhanced on campuses where the student body at large, upon entry to college, reports having religious/spiritual struggles and ecumenical perspectives. This finding illustrates the significance of peer socialization in the collegiate experience and demonstrates that a campus context characterized by spiritual challenge and openness to religious pluralism fosters ecumenicism within students to a greater extent than would be anticipated based on individual predispositions toward ecumenicism. Ecumenical worldview development is not a solitary journey for students; rather, the contours of the path are in part determined by the experiences and perspectives of others sharing the same space on campus. Students collectively create and in turn are influenced by religious and spiritual aspects of the peer context.

Importantly, institutional religious affiliation and peer contexts work in tandem to shape students' ecumenical worldview. The effects of the average peer religious/spiritual struggle on ecumenical worldview development are more pronounced for students attending evangelical Christian institutions when compared with those attending public or other religiously-affiliated institutions. In other words, although ecumenical worldview development is generally fostered on campuses in which religious struggle among students is the norm, ecumenicism is accentuated even further by peer religious struggles at evangelical institutions. In light of the definitive, universal truth claims that are prevalent in evangelical Christian colleges, it may be that any willingness on the part of students to question or wrestle with religious doctrine makes a distinct developmental impression on those around them—namely, students who, perhaps for the first time, are encountering peers with religious doubts and questions.

Educational Practices and Student Experiences

Turning to educational and experiential influences on ecumenical worldview development, the structural models revealed several significant relationships that may help inform college educators and administrators. Generally speaking, ecumenical worldview is enhanced by college experiences that connect students with religion, spirituality, and diversity in curricular and co-curricular contexts. Interestingly, simply providing space for spiritual dialogue in the academic sphere of campus life plays a role in ecumenicism; we learned that the salience of religion and spirituality in the classroom and in students' interactions with faculty (e.g., discussing religion and spirituality in class and with professors; having professors who encouraged discussion of religious/spiritual matters) fosters ecumenical development. Likewise, when students engage in challenging co-curricular activities, such as studying abroad, performing volunteer work, socializing with someone of another racial/ethnic group, discussing religion/spirituality with friends, or exploring religion online, they became more ecumenically-minded—even when these activities are not explicitly religious or spiritual. Apparently, it is the *challenge* embedded in an activity that promotes greater interest in and acceptance of religiously diverse others rather than the activity's religious or spiritual content. Students' perceptions of the campus spiritual climate also facilitate ecumenical worldview development; "warm" environments that encourage spiritual expression directly amplify students' capacity to understand and accept others of diverse perspectives. One construct, religious reinforcers (e.g., attending religious services, spending time with people who share one's religious views, having friends who share one's religious views) propels students away from ecumenicism, perhaps because such influences shield students from encountering challenges to closely held religious perspectives.

The mediating properties of religious/spiritual struggles became evident in our discovery that challenging co-curricular experiences and the degree to which religion and spirituality are salient in classroom and faculty encounters provoke struggles, which in turn enhance ecumenical worldview. What we can glean from this finding is that religious and spiritual struggles, while potentially challenging to navigate (Bryant & Astin, 2008; Pargament, 2008), are developmentally meaningful. When students face novel, unexpected, or challenging experiences during college, the religious/spiritual struggle that may ensue serves a distinctive purpose in deepening appreciation for, interest in, and openness to religious and worldview diversity.

Group Differences

Our study exposed differences in ecumenical worldview by gender, race/ethnicity, and worldview. Women, racial/ethnic minority students, and religious minority students exhibit higher levels of ecumenicism than do men, racial/ethnic majority students, religious majority students, and non-religious students. These differences resonate with the notion that being a member of a marginalized population creates a unique reality unlike that of privileged populations.

The hierarchical linear models and structural models enabled us to examine plausible explanations for the group differences we observed. The HLM analysis identified an important gender by peer socialization interaction effect. Although men generally have lower scores on ecumenical worldview than women, the average amount of religious/spiritual struggle reported by students on a given campus appears to reduce this gender gap. In other words, exposure to an environment in which peers are feeling challenged by religious/spiritual questions and conflicts is particularly influential in fostering men's ecumenical development—bringing them closer to women's ecumenical capacity than would otherwise be the case. The ecumenical worldview gender gap remains significant under such circumstances but is diminished.

The structural models revealed only very minor race and gender differences in the way college experiences shape ecumenical worldview. It may be that other life experiences not accounted for in the structural models might help explain the racial and gender discrepancies. As it stands, the constructs included in the model (e.g., salience of religion and spirituality in academics, challenging co-curricular experiences) generally have similar effects on ecumenical worldview regardless of race or gender.

We ascertained considerable differences in the relationship between college experiences and ecumenical worldview by students' religious identification. Indicative of a bias privileging Christian perspectives, the model most closely resembles the development of religious majority students. By contrast, the model was less applicable to religious minority and non-religious students. Some of the differences between groups are worth noting as areas for future exploration. First, challenging co-curricular experiences and religious reinforcers have similar but stronger effects on ecumenical worldview development among religious minority students compared with religious majority students. In other words, religious minority students are more sensitive to such experiences than are religious majority students, which may be related to their underrepresented status in American society. Religious majority students, even when faced with challenging co-curricular experiences, still have the advantage of holding to a normative perspective that is taken for granted in most U.S. institutions. Religious minority students, on the other hand, enter into these environments without a privileged status and likely notice and are affected by the sharp contrast between challenging co-curricular activities and the religious reinforcers in their life.

The most dramatic group differences in college impact were revealed by comparing religious (minority or majority) students and non-religious students. Through these comparisons we learned that college experiences influence the ecumenical worldview of these students in ways that defy theoretically-based expectations. In fact, challenging co-curricular experiences and the salience of religion/spirituality in academics actually appear to undermine religious/spiritual struggles among non-religious students, while religious reinforcers promote struggling. Moreover, none of the college experiences in the model—with the exception of religious reinforcers—significantly predict ecumenical worldview among non-religious students, and the constructs on the whole are less reliable and valid for non-religious students relative to religious students. As a result, we are left with very little insight into how non-religious students develop an ecumenical worldview or even how to appropriately measure ecumenical worldview among students with secular identities.

Reflections

On the whole, the meaning we make of our investigation of ecumenical worldview development during the college years can be expressed through multiple story lines. The majority narrative that emerges from this work provides a broad portrayal of the general effects of college environments and experiences on ecumenical worldview. It is a story that reinforces expectations that stem from theoretical conceptions regarding how pluralistic perspectives evolve (Braskamp, 2008; Chickering & Reisser, 1993; Parks, 2000), confirming that institutional contexts, including the religious affiliation of the institution and the orientation toward struggle and ecumenicism of the student body at large, impact ecumenical development. Moreover, the notion of novel experiences leading to crisis and subsequent transformation is apparent in our analyses. College experiences that expose students to worldviews and other forms of diversity stimulate acceptance of, interest in, and understanding of others. And, finally, religious/spiritual struggles, when appropriately supported, are developmentally beneficial for fostering students' pluralistic competence, despite the potential disruptions to students' lives that may accompany struggling. For the researcher, these findings extend our theoretical and empirical knowledge base to include religious and spiritual dimensions in the development of pluralistic openness and appreciation. For the practitioner, these findings confirm that our efforts to "challenge and support" (Sanford, 1968) in the realm of religious and spiritual experiences are as worthwhile as our intuition suggests.

But there are other stories not captured by the statistical majority's "grand narrative." The criticalist lens that informed our research provides a nuanced depiction of ecumenical worldview development, demonstrating to us that patterns of experience and change are not universal. Student identities shape college impact. Men and women respond to peer socialization in different ways; the degree of religious/spiritual struggle in the peer environment has greater bearing on men's ecumenical worldview development than women's. In addition, college experiences appear to impact the ecumenical worldview of religious minority and non-religious students in ways that vary substantially from religious majority students. Our structural model, in fact, had very limited meaning for non-religious students. Our hope is that the nuanced nature of these developmental story lines impresses upon researchers, educators, and practitioners the theoretical and practical value of identifying where our models fall short. When we question the validity of our tried-and-true theories, we open the door to understanding our students in a way that acknowledges the complexity of their backgrounds and identities. While our research raises new questions and provides imperfect answers, our intent has been to demonstrate that the "story" of ecumenical development in college is actually a collection of stories, each of which is distinct and worth exploring.

References

Antonio, A. (2001). The role of interracial interaction in the development of leadership skills and cultural knowledge and understanding. *Research in Higher Education, 42,* 593–617.

Astin, A. W., Astin, H. S., Lindholm, J. A., Bryant, A. N., Szelényi, K., & Calderone, S. (2005). *The spiritual life of college students: A national study of college students' search for meaning and purpose.* Los Angeles: Higher Education Research Institute, UCLA.

Baxter Magolda, M. B. (2001). *Making their own way: Narratives for transforming higher education to promote self-development.* Sterling, VA: Stylus Publishing.

Bowman, N. A., & Brandenberger, J. W. (in press). Experiencing the unexpected: Toward a model of college diversity experiences and attitude change. *Review of Higher Education.*

Braskamp, L. A. (2008). Developing global citizens. *Journal of College and Character, 10*(1), 1–5.

Bryant, A. N. (2007). Gender differences in spiritual development during the college years. *Sex Roles, 56,* 835–846.

Bryant, A. N. (2011a). The impact of campus context, college encounters, and religious/ spiritual struggle on ecumenical worldview development. *Research in Higher Education, 52,* 441–459.

Bryant, A. N. (2011b). Ecumenical worldview development by gender, race, and worldview: A multiple-group analysis of model invariance. *Research in Higher Education, 52,* 460–479.

Bryant, A. N., & Astin, H. S. (2008). The correlates of spiritual struggle during the college years. *Journal of Higher Education, 79,* 1–27.

Bryant Rockenbach, A. N., & Mayhew, M. J. (2011). How the collegiate religious and spiritual climate shapes students' ecumenical orientation. Unpublished manuscript.

Chang, M. J. (2002). The impact of an undergraduate diversity course requirement on students' racial views and attitudes. *Journal of General Education 51*(1): 21–42.

Chang, M. J., Denson, N., Saenz, V., & Misa, K. (2006). The educational benefits of sustaining cross-race interaction among undergraduates. *Journal of Higher Education, 77,* 430–455.

Chickering, A. W., & Reisser, L. (1993). *Education and identity* (2nd edn). San Francisco, CA: Jossey-Bass.

Eck, D. L. (1993). *Encountering God: A spiritual journey from Bozeman to Banaras.* Boston, MA: Beacon Press.

Engberg, M. E. (2007). Educating the workforce for the 21st century: A cross-disciplinary analysis of the impact of the undergraduate experience on students' development of a pluralistic orientation. *Research in Higher Education, 48,* 283–317.

Erikson, E. H. (1968). *Identity: Youth and crisis.* New York: W. W. Norton.

Festinger, L. (1957). *A theory of cognitive dissonance.* Stanford, CA: Stanford University Press.

Fowler, J. W. (1981). *Stages of faith: The psychology of human development and the quest for meaning.* San Francisco, CA: Harper & Row.

Gurin, P., Dey, E. L., Gurin, G., & Hurtado, S. (2004). The educational value of diversity. In P. Gurin, J. S. Lehman, & E. Lewis (eds), *Defending diversity: Affirmative action at the University of Michigan* (pp. 97–188). Ann Arbor, MI: University of Michigan Press.

Lindholm, J. A., Goldberg, R., & Calderone, S. (2006). The spiritual questing of professional career aspirants. *Seattle Journal for Social Justice, 4,* 509–560.

Marcia, J. E. (1966). Development and validation of ego identity status. *Journal of Personality and Social Psychology, 3,* 551–558.

Mayhew, M. J. (2012). A multi-level examination of college and its influence on ecumenical worldview development. *Research in Higher Education*, 53, 282–310.

Nelson Laird, T. F., Engberg, M. E., & Hurtado, S. (2005). Modeling accentuation effects: Enrolling in a diversity course and the importance of social action engagement. *Journal of Higher Education* 76(4): 448–476.

Pargament, K. I. (2008). Spiritual struggles as a fork in the road to growth or decline. *Plain Views, 4*(24). Retrieved February 4, 2008, from http://www.plainviews.org/v4n24/lv_p. html.

Parks, S. D. (2000). *Big questions, worthy dreams: Mentoring young adults in their search for meaning, purpose, and faith.* San Francisco, CA: Jossey-Bass.

Pascarella, E. T. (2006). How college affects students: Ten directions for future research. *Journal of College Student Development, 47,* 508–520.

Pascarella, E. T., & Terenzini, P. T. (2005). *How college affects students: A third decade of research.* San Francisco, CA: Jossey-Bass.

Pascarella, E. T., Edison, M., Nora, A., Hagedorn, L. S., & Terenzini, P. T. (1996). Influences on students' openness to diversity and challenge in the first year of college. *Journal of Higher Education, 67,* 174–195.

Perry, W. G. (1968). *Forms of intellectual and ethical development in the college years: A scheme.* San Francisco, CA: Jossey-Bass.

Raudenbush, S. W., & Bryk, A. S. (2002). *Hierarchical linear models: Applications and data analysis methods* (2nd edn). Thousand Oaks, CA: Sage.

Rest, J. R. (1986). *Moral development: Advances in research and theory.* New York: Praeger.

Sanford, N. (1968). *Where colleges fail: A study of student as person.* San Francisco, CA: Jossey-Bass.

Stage, F. K. (2007). Answering critical questions using quantitative data. In F. Stage (Ed.), *Using quantitative data to answer critical questions* (pp. 5–23). San Francisco: Jossey-Bass.

Whitt, E. J., Edison, M. I., Pascarella, E. T., Terenzini, P. T., & Nora, A. (2001). Influences on students' openness to diversity and challenge. *Journal of Higher Education, 72,* 172–204.

RELIGIOUS PLURALISM AND HIGHER EDUCATION INSTITUTIONAL CONTEXTS

Implications for Research

Peter C. Hill, Keith J. Edwards, and Jonathan P. Hill

It is clear that with increased technology and mobility, people from various faith traditions and worldviews now interact, either by choice or by situation, more frequently. As history attests, diverse groups are either unwilling or unable to constructively regulate worldview differences. In an increasingly multicultural world, understanding and appreciation of religious and worldview differences are potentially beneficial to social functioning. Two factors put the academy in a unique position to foster multicultural understanding and appreciation. First, many campuses are microcosms of the cultural and religious pluralism that reflects the United States society as a whole. Second, the traditional college-age years are critical years in the development of social attitudes and perspectives. For these reasons, we should expect students' experiences in the academy would influence their development of pluralistic attitudes. The findings set forth by Rine and by Bryant Rockenbach and Mayhew show this to be the case. Our purpose here is to discuss how the findings set forth in their chapters both extend the knowledge base on the impact of college and how their findings may stimulate future research efforts on religious diversity.

The Many Meanings of Institutional Pluralism

It is clear from the UCLA Spirituality in Higher Education project (Astin, Astin, & Lindholm, 2011) that institutional contexts greatly differ in terms of facilitating spirituality in students. Bryant Rockenbach and Mayhew also document how institutional contexts have a differential impact specifically on religious and spiritual pluralism. We will discuss the implications of their findings, particularly those that involve conservative religious institutions (i.e., evangelical Protestant), because that is the context of particular focus in Rine's analysis.

Cultural and religious diversity are not evenly distributed throughout our society. Developing a pluralistic orientation among students at a small liberal arts institution in the rural Midwest will likely be a greater challenge than at, for example, Chicago's Loyola University, where 27 percent of the student body speak a language other than English at home. Furthermore, diversity should not be conceptualized only on an individual level; institutions of higher education themselves are diverse with greatly varied mission statements, constituencies, and resources. When applied to the development of an ecumenical worldview, institutional diversity is in some ways magnified even more because, by design, some will be highly pluralistic (e.g., the secular institution, whether public or private) while others will be relatively monolithic (e.g., the evangelical institution). It is not surprising that the institutional context that is most resistant to religious and spiritual pluralism in Bryant Rockenbach and Mayhew's analysis is the conservative religious institution, with Catholic and "other" religious institutions more open to developing an ecumenical worldview.

Indeed, these findings corroborate those of Hill (2009) who found general support for Stark's (1996) notion that religion is promoted in the context of "moral communities" that legitimate religious language, motives, and behaviors when applied to the higher education context. Using nationally representative data, he discovered that, as expected, conservative Protestant institutions were most successful in fostering individual religious practices that align with their legitimated particularities, even if the students did not self-identify as evangelicals (e.g., Catholics). Somewhat surprisingly, however, students attending mainline Protestant-affiliated and Catholic institutions showed larger religious attenuation than students attending nonreligious public institutions. In the religiously diverse public institutions, voluntary collectives that thrive on minority identity (e.g., clubs or local chapters of national organizations such as Campus Crusade or InterVarsity) provide religious meaning and support, thus functionally serving as a moral community.

Essentially, the ecumenical worldview thesis proposed and tested by Bryant Rockenbach and Mayhew and the moral communities thesis tested by Hill (2009) are the opposite sides of the same coin. Our purpose here is to not argue the philosophical merits of either thesis as much as it is to consider their implications for understanding and measuring the importance of the institutional context in developing a worldview. Given, however, that the missional existence of some institutions is to promote a particular religious worldview (the moral communities thesis), religious pluralism in such institutions will have to be framed and measured by a metric different than the one available through the CSBV to Bryant Rockenbach and Mayhew. They recognize this by claiming that, "It may also be that modifications to the ecumenical worldview construct would better reflect the openness toward and appreciation of other faiths that is expressed in nuanced ways within exclusivist traditions" (pp. 98–99). Put another way, how one defines and conceptualizes ecumenicism may be different from one institutional context to another. That is, developing an appreciation of Catholicism or even another Protestant tradition may be as much of a pluralistic jump within an evangelical context as a consideration of other religions in a more pluralistically rich public university. This is *not* to say that the worldview of conservative religionists should exclude an understanding and appreciation of other religious cultures, including those far outside one's own religious boundaries; it is to say, however, that pluralism has different operational meanings that must be accounted for in research. Regardless, it may be the case that the intra- and interpersonal developmental processes in the advancement of a more pluralistic worldview are similar regardless of the institutional context.

Pluralism Within an Exclusivist Framework

Religious Exclusivism

The development of an ecumenical worldview, even if conceptualized and measured more narrowly, is especially challenging within a religiously exclusive framework, as indicated in the chapter by Rine. How the evangelical Christian college navigates its commitment to core religious values while creatively engaging the ever-shifting landscape of the wider culture to a postmodern paradigm is Rine's primary concern. He proposes a fallibilist orientation that allows commitment to core beliefs, including the belief in the existence of an ultimate reality, while also acknowledging the culture-based epistemological limits of ever fully knowing that reality. He introduces two key concepts: 1) *provisionality of belief,* which measures the student's attitude toward his or her own set of beliefs and approach to seeking answers to ultimate questions; and 2) *openness to pluralism,* which stresses interpersonal attitudes of equanimity. Rine's operationalization of fallibilism in terms of provisionality of belief and openness to pluralism is, in our estimation, the type of theoretic and metric adjustment necessary to the study of ecumenicism in the context of a conservative religious institution. We propose that provisionality of belief and openness to pluralism may be less problematic for students with faith commitments because both tenets stress attitudes toward those commitments rather than beliefs about the truth status of other religious worldviews.

We suggest that these three concepts (ecumenical worldview, provisionality of belief, and openness to pluralism) all be included and clearly distinguished in future research. It is our concern that the ecumenical worldview construct confounds openness to pluralism with universalist religious attitudes. Rine's approach to measuring openness to pluralism and provisionality of beliefs separately, as he says, "brings these two seemingly contradictory practices ... into harmony" (p. 74). Indeed, his analysis drawn from the 2007 CSBV survey instrument suggests that certain institutional factors, most notably room for the individual experience of dissonance and what he calls a cultural pedagogy within a campus community that maintains a respect for diverse religious or spiritual beliefs, predict a fallibilist orientation.

Research investigating a quest for religious motivation suggests that a version of the fallibilist orientation is a position held by many conservative Christian college students (Edwards, Hall, Slater, & Hill, 2011). The quest orientation describes those 1) for whom religion is an on-going, open-minded exploration of existential questions; 2) who are willing to accept the fact that many important religious questions do not have clear-cut answers; and 3) who hold a tentativeness of belief that remains open to change as one grows and develops. Though the purpose of the Edwards *et al.* research was to test the construct validity of measures of quest among evangelical students, for our purposes two of their findings are especially significant. First, in their longitudinal analysis across the four college years at eight evangelical colleges, students demonstrated an increase in quest scores on all five dimensions investigated over the course of their college years, with the largest change coming between the sophomore and junior years. Second, certain "soft" dimensions of quest (openness to change and the value of doubts) were more acceptable, regardless of time spent in college, than the more polarized "hard" components of reason over faith and religion conceptualized as only a quest process.

Such research strongly suggests that measures of ecumenical development must be context dependent. Ecumenical worldview development within an exclusivistic context is fundamentally different than it is within the culture at large, and researchers who wish to investigate ecumenical pluralism across institutional contexts are advised to take such differences into account. Rine's constructs of provisionality of belief and openness to pluralism are two additional constructs worthy of consideration.

Nonreligious Exclusivism

Bryant Rockenbach and Mayhew present some surprising results in their analysis of nonreligious students. For these students, challenging co-curricular experiences and the salience of religion/spirituality in academics undermines religious and spiritual struggle. In contrast to their religious counterparts, religious reinforcers actually promote struggling and an ecumenical worldview among the nonreligious. Though rarely thought of in this manner, nonreligious students may demonstrate many of the same cognitive processes as students who maintain a perspective of religious exclusivity (see Hood, Hill, & Williamson, 2005, chapter 8 for a discussion on how some nonreligious individuals display characteristics similar to religious fundamentalists). Research on so-called religious "nones" has found that while most are not openly hostile toward atheists or agnostics, they are not privately religious or spiritual either (Baker & Smith, 2009; Lim, MacGregor, &

Putnam, 2010). Moreover, by adopting no religious tradition, many are symbolically differentiating themselves from organized religion and the conservative politics they associate with it (Hout & Fischer, 2002). These results lead us to believe that most nonreligious students will have a "tin ear" when it comes to religious and spiritual language and ways of seeing the world. Understanding these characteristics of the nonreligious, we believe, helps make sense of the interpretive puzzle presented by Bryant Rockenbach and Mayhew. As the authors note, the elements of the ecumenical worldview might be challenging for a nonreligious student to evaluate. At the most extreme, the nonreligious student may believe that religions of the world are equally invalid and have a generally negative view toward religious belief. This would result in lower scores on ecumenical worldview.

The finding that curricular and co-curricular challenges had a negative impact on religious/spiritual struggle for nonreligious students may reflect the fact that such activities actively reinforce their own nonreligious identity when exposed to religious/spiritual language. The salience of religion in these "secular" experiences may actually increase a negative view of religion and spirituality altogether. On the other hand, the fact that religious reinforcers promoted struggle for the nonreligious might be interpreted as follows: nonreligious students who endorse the religious reinforcer dimensions are students who are choosing to engage in religious activity and social encounters with religious people. It is reasonable to expect they would experience a clash with their nonreligious identity. If they are doing so voluntarily, it may be that such students are open to engagement with religious activities and people. The struggle that would result from such engagement may account for their shift toward an ecumenical worldview perspective. It would be interesting for future research to study the experiences of nonreligious students in these two settings using more in-depth, qualitative methods.

Ecumenical Worldview Hurdles

We wish to conclude our response to these two chapters with a word of caution. When applied to religion and spirituality certain mitigating factors are at work that may present hurdles to the development of a pluralistic perspective that appreciates diversity. Therefore, researchers should not expect that the factors involved in the development of pluralistic responses to other bio-social-cultural forms of diversity (e.g., ethnicity, gender, age) are necessarily at play in the same ways when it comes to religious or spiritual pluralism. Nor should researchers (or practitioners) assume that the effects of institutional contexts will be the same on religious pluralism as they are on other forms of pluralism. Among the many unique aspects of religious and spiritual pluralism, we will consider three: the "ultimate" nature of a religious or spiritual worldview, a perceived secular challenge to religious or spiritual worldviews, and the distinctiveness of moral concerns. Though interrelated, each will be discussed separately.

Religion and Spirituality as Ultimate Concerns

Religious and spiritual worldviews may be held tenaciously simply because religious and spiritual issues are something that many people, including many college students, care deeply about. When questions such as "what makes life worth living?" or "what makes for the 'good' life?" are asked, one is forced to reflect on deeply held values and goals. Research conducted by personality psychologist Robert Emmons (1999) revealed that matters of *ultimate concern*, as articulated by the existential theologian Paul Tillich (1957) and as often understood and articulated through one's religious or spiritual perspective, are not to be taken lightly. If the religious or spiritual answers to such concerns are at all orthodox or conservative in nature, then the very thought of an ecumenical worldview can be highly threatening and discomforting. Considerable research in social psychology (e.g., Liberman & Chaiken, 1992) suggests that a common way of handling a highly threatening message is to adopt a posture of denial; thus, the religious conservative may conclude that perhaps the dangers of a monotheistic culture, or the advantages of religious and spiritual pluralism, are overstated. As a result, the negative effects of personal religious struggle acknowledged by Bryant Rockenbach and Mayhew may actually be a hurdle in the development of an ecumenical worldview.

The Secular Challenge

The view that college tends to have a liberalizing effect on the religious views of students, even to the point of being a "breeding ground of apostasy" (Caplovitz & Sherrow, 1977) remains strong. This view is both supported (e.g., Bryant, Choi, & Yasuno, 2003; Reimer, 2010) and challenged (e.g., Hill, 2011; Uecker, Regnerus, & Vaaler, 2007) by research. When examined longitudinally, Astin *et al.* (2011) found little change in religious commitment and only a slight increase in religious struggle from the freshman to junior years of college, with modest increases in many measures of spirituality. Their findings suggest that religious beliefs are less likely to dramatically change or to substantially decrease during college, as much as they are likely to be re-examined and perhaps modified. The extent to which such modifications are interpreted to represent substantial change may depend upon one's degree of religious conservatism; those who are more conservative may be more likely to see such change as a secular challenge to a prevailing belief system.

The Distinctiveness of Moral Issues

Moral issues, which are often related to one's religious or spiritual perspective, are often handled differently than other issues. For example, the criteria used for determining the legitimacy of differing perspectives appear to differ when making moral versus nonmoral judgments. Nesselroade, Williams, Nam, and McBride (2006) found that students at both a secular and an evangelical religious institution were more likely to rate their own opinion and the opinion of a disagreeing other as equally objective on a nonmoral issue (e.g., foreign vs. domestic cars, buying hard cover vs. paperback books). However, when the opinion dealt with a moral issue (e.g., capital punishment, abortion), both religious and secular college students tended to rate their own opinion as more carefully thought through and more objective than the dissenting other. Though students at the evangelical institution showed this tendency more strongly than did secular university students, the tendency was shared by both groups. These researchers suggested that the tendency to self-enhance on opinion objectivity is greater when "an issue is interpreted to possess significant moral weight and touch on a person's first principles or value structure" (p. 32). People appear to be particularly defensive of their moral judgments and are thus perhaps less open to other perspectives.

Conclusion

We applaud the work of both Rine as well as Bryant Rockenbach and Mayhew for breaking new ground about the opportunities and challenges facing higher education in fostering an appreciation and understanding of diverse religious worldviews. We encourage researchers to follow their lead and, in so doing, to practice what here has been preached. Specifically, researchers too must recognize and appreciate religious diversity not only between people but also between institutional contexts, and such diversity must be allowed for in both our conceptualization and measurement of religious pluralism. No one size will fit all.

References

Astin, A. W., Astin, H. S., & Lindholm, J. A. (2011). *Cultivating the spirit: How college can enhance students' inner life*. San Francisco, CA: Jossey-Bass.

Baker, J., & Smith, B. G. (2009). The nones: Social characteristics of the religiously unaffiliated. *Social Forces, 87*, 1251–1264.

Bryant, A. N., Choi, J. Y., & Yasuno, M. (2003). Understanding the religious and spiritual dimensions of students' lives in the first year of college. *Journal of College Student Development, 44*, 723–745.

Caplovitz, D., & Sherrow, F. (1977). *The religious drop-outs: Apostasy among college graduates*. Beverly Hills, CA: Sage Publications.

Edwards, K. J., Hall, T. W., Slater, W., & Hill, J. P. (2011). The multidimensional structure of the quest construct. *Journal of Psychology and Theology, 39*, 87–110.

Emmons, R. A. (1999). *The psychology of ultimate concerns: Motivation and spirituality in personality*. New York: Guilford Press.

Hill, J. P. (2009). Higher education as moral community: Institutional influences on religious participation during college. *Journal for the Scientific Study of Religion, 48*, 515–534.

Hill, J. P. (2011). Faith and understanding: Specifying the impact of higher education on religious belief. *Journal for the Scientific Study of Religion, 50*, 533–551.

Hood, R. W., Jr., Hill, P. C., & Williamson, W. P. (2005). *The psychology of religious fundamentalism*. New York: Guilford Press.

Hout, M., & Fischer, C. S. (2002). Why more Americans have no religious preference: Politics and generations. *American Sociological Review, 67*, 165–190.

Liberman, A., & Chaiken, S. (1992). Defensive processing of personally relevant health messages. *Personality and Social Psychology Bulletin, 18*, 669–679.

Lim, L. C., MacGregor, C. A., & Putnam, R. D. (2010). Secular and liminal: Discovering heterogeneity among religious nones. *Journal for the Scientific Study of Religion, 49*, 596–618.

Nesselroade, K. P., Jr., Williams, J. K., Nam, R. K., & McBride, D. M. (2006). Self-enhancement of opinion objectivity: Effects of perceived moral weight. *Journal of Psychology and Christianity, 25*, 27–33.

Reimer, S. (2010). Higher education and theological liberalism: Revisiting the old issue. *Sociology of Religion, 71*, 393–408.

Stark, R. (1996). Religion as context: Hellfire and delinquency one more time. *Sociology of Religion, 57*, 163–73.

Tillich, P. (1957). *Dynamics of faith*. New York: Harper & Row.

Uecker, J. E., Regnerus, M. D., & Vaaler, M. L. (2007). Losing my religion: The social sources of religious decline in early adulthood. *Social Forces, 85*, 1667–1692.

PRACTITIONER REFLECTION ON PART III

BECOMING A RELIGIOUSLY ENGAGED GLOBAL CITIZEN

Scotty McLennan

How can religious commitment be preserved in the midst of postmodern higher education? How can college and university administrators help nurture global citizens for the twenty-first century who will be part of the solution of interreligious bigotry and violence rather than part of the problem? These two critical issues are addressed creatively in the chapters of this section, with important implications for crafting college and university contexts that will support both religious commitment and global citizenship. There is a fascinating connection between the pedagogical paradigm of fallibilism and the development of an ecumenical worldview too, which invites further exploration.

P. Jesse Rine's chapter on Christian colleges has lessons for all of us in higher education, not just those in explicitly evangelical institutions. The postmodern challenge to the enlightenment view that there is objective, universal truth affects both Christian certainty and secular confidence that reality can be adequately understood through reason and science. It seems that religious and secular people alike might be able to hold modernist and post-modernist perspectives in creative tension through a fallibilist approach to a free search for truth; namely, asserting that there is an objective reality we all are studying but that our knowledge of it will always be partial and in need of varying perspectives to help elucidate it. This is the point of the Hindu metaphor of the blind men and the elephant. Each is describing the part he is feeling—hard tusk, soft and wet mouth, scratchy and dry hide, broom-like tail—with confidence that he is adequately articulating the whole; yet, if they would all listen to each other, and relax their complete confidence that each knows best, together they could construct a better picture of the reality of the elephant. Many scientists do in fact work this way, and many religionists do too, without falling into either of the twin traps of absolutism or relativism.

Rine's research results teach us that students can be simultaneously committed to evangelical Christian faith and open to pluralism. He was surprised to find that there was a positive relationship between his three subcomponents of fallibilist Christian spirituality: commitment to Christian faith, provisionality of belief, and openness to pluralism. The resulting suggestion that personal faith in Christ and a pluralistic disposition are mutually reinforcing, rather than antithetical, is something that many of us in university chaplaincies observe anecdotally when doing in-depth interfaith programming, like the Rathbun Fellowship for Religious Encounter at Stanford, which I will describe later. Many students come to interreligious engagement with a fear that they might lose their personal faith and their commitment to their own religious tradition; they are astonished to find that they simultaneously deepen their faith and religious commitment as they become more interreligiously literate and relationally adept in understanding other religions and faith stances. Ultimately, many come to feel that this is not surprising after all. Learning about aspects of other traditions that seem useful to their peers—like meditation, fasting, or ritual use of beads—helps students find analogous dimensions of their own tradition. Being challenged about the nature of their own tradition in relation to others leads them to find out more and gain greater appreciation of their own religion. Interacting with other students of faith, especially in a university viewed as highly secular in orientation, provides a new level of comfort and confidence in their own life of faith.

Rine's reflections about the value of fallibilist propositional uncertainty are also worthy of note in relation to the stages of faith development that William Perry, Sharon Parks, and James Fowler have studied and described. Most colleges and universities now operate on the basis of developmental models of their students, even if few staff and faculty are as well aware of stage theory as applied to spiritual development as they are of stages of psychosocial, cognitive, and moral development. I have written elsewhere[1] about the "dependence" and "independence" stages of spiritual development as the two (of six) potential life stages that are most operative in the college and university context.

At the dependence stage, the individual acquires a meaningful outlook on life through following religious doctrine and moral rules with strong peer group support and guidance by a compelling leader or mentor. At this time in the life cycle, God is usually imaged as an idealized parental figure, unconditionally loving, although sometimes deeply judgmental. At the independence stage, one begins to find spiritual authority within, instead of relying on peers, social conventions, and respected elders. It is common to say, "I'm spiritual, but not religious," during this stage, not wanting to be part of any institution or under anyone's control. God usually becomes more impersonal, described as Spirit or Natural Law or Life Force or Energy in the universe, and experienced less as a person who answers prayers or intervenes directly in human affairs.

All major world religions support all stages of faith development, as religious educators for younger children are well aware. However, the college-era stages can become disconcerting to students and their friends, parents, teachers, and university administrators alike if individuals seem to be too dependent or independent, and therefore too vulnerable to "cult" involvement on the one hand or to "losing their faith" or their doctrinal clarity on the other. The fallibilist framework can help students and those around them to retain confidence that they remain within the sphere of their religious tradition and can deepen their faith, even as they are open to substantial change in their personal understanding and feelings about a number of elements of their tradition.

Rine also draws a connection between the pedagogical paradigm of fallibilism and an institutional context that is pluralistic and sees itself as creating a community of inclusion. This relates to what Alyssa Bryant Rockenbach and Matthew Mayhew explore under the rubric of "ecumenical worldview." Rine encourages Christian colleges to admit diverse students, create a welcoming environment, listen to the insights of other cultures and religious traditions, and refine truth claims in dialogue with those representing diversity on their campuses. The resulting counterbalance to the temptation toward absolutist parochialism will allow for a richer and more accurate understanding of Christianity as well as of other areas of study and experience. The same could and should be said for largely secular institutions which can have an absolutist worldview regarding the primacy of science and scientific method, for example, as the best way to arrive at truth and reality. Such institutions need to be pluralistic and inclusive of deeply religious students, faculty, and staff as a way to better refine and express their academic community's truth claims and understanding of reality.

Pluralism is also a critical element in helping students in higher education become true global citizens and leaders, bulwarks against interreligious bigotry and violence. Bryant Rockenbach and Mayhew point to daily news reports from the United States and around the world—each illustrating the discord that different religious worldviews can spawn. College and university context becomes critical in promoting interfaith understanding and cooperation.[2] Much can be learned here by a review of the Principles for Religious Life in Higher Education that were promulgated by the Association of College and University Religious Affairs (ACURA) in 2005 and later affirmed by the National Association of College and University Chaplains (NACUC). The preamble stresses that "Nurturing the religious and spiritual life of students is a critical part of the mission of higher education in the twenty-first century." That is because our colleges and universities are committed to creating global citizens and promoting lifelong civic engagement as well as to developing the whole person. Specifically, "At this challenging time in history, it is clear that interfaith understanding is central to the life of the planet."

There are four parts of the ACURA principles, all relating to college and university context: religious life structures on campus, access and oversight for religious groups, the integration of intellectual inquiry and religious practice, and religious pluralism itself. It is recommended that all institutions of higher learning, public and private, have an office dedicated to religious, spiritual, and ethical life, which is established, funded, and supported by the university or college itself and strategically placed to promote its effectiveness and influence. Among its tasks are fulfilling a coordinating function for religious professionals assigned to the campus and creating and sustaining one or more student interfaith bodies. The office is charged with accommodating diversity of religious expression on campus, both in terms of promoting free exercise of religion and also maintaining a welcoming environment that is free of religious coercion. The office must affirm the compatibility of free intellectual inquiry and religious commitment; this includes promoting academic values of inquiry, multiple perspectives, and critical thinking. Finally, the office should encourage, university-wide, an understanding and respect for the multifaith reality of higher education, while at the same time embracing and engaging the particularity of each religious tradition. This means extending hospitality and meeting the needs of each religious group and individual, especially in relation to under-represented traditions. It also means educating the entire campus community about religious, spiritual, and ethical life.

Bryant Rockenbach and Mayhew describe multiple meanings for pluralism, but operationally they study it in terms of the twelve-item measure for "ecumenical worldview" that was developed from the survey data of the Spirituality in Higher Education study at UCLA. Questions developed for this measure ranged from having an interest in different religious traditions, to believing in the goodness of all people, to affirming that most people can grow spiritually without being religious, to acknowledging that nonreligious people can lead lives that are just as moral as those of religious believers.[3] Bryant Rockenbach and Mayhew understand that ecumenical worldview may track somewhat differently from pluralism; the latter is not necessarily a relativistic stance but often involves making commitments in the presence of diversity.

Their religiously-related findings are that evangelical Christian institutions do a worse job than other colleges and universities in promoting the development of an ecumenical worldview, that religious reinforcers (like attending religious services and having friends who share one's religious views) reduce ecumenism, that entering a student body with religious/spiritual struggles is predictive of greater development of ecumenism, and that having professors who encourage discussion of religion and spirituality in the classroom fosters ecumenical development.

What do these research results mean for creating the best college and university context for an ecumenical worldview, which presumably will help our students to become true global citizens and promote antidotes to interreligious bigotry and violence? First, fallibilism may be the route to a greater ecumenical worldview in evangelical Christian institutions, as discussed above. Religious reinforcers, which have the positive value of deepening students' spirituality and giving them a sense of community, need to be paired, though, with substantial interreligious experiences. As discussed above, those interfaith experiences may paradoxically increase a student's religious faith within their own tradition, while they also help in developing an ecumenical worldview. A key example of this is the interfaith bodies on campus called for in the ACURA principles. The one I am most familiar with, in my chaplaincy work at Stanford University, is the Rathbun Fellowship for Religious Encounter (FRE).

Sixteen students (including undergraduate, graduate, and professional students from any academic discipline) are chosen annually for FRE in a competitive process by Stanford's Office for Religious Life. They receive a $500 annual fellowship and are required to meet over dinner weekly throughout the year on Wednesdays from 5:30 to 7 p.m. with each other and the Dean, Senior Associate Dean, and Associate Dean for Religious Life. Coming from a wide range of religious, spiritual, and secular traditions, they participate in a variety of exercises and engage in sustained interfaith encounter with one another. They must demonstrate a genuine desire to explore religion in their lives and express a willingness to listen to and learn from those of different backgrounds. They are "commissioned" in a ceremony and dinner with the outgoing fellows at the end of the spring quarter. The fall quarter begins with a half-day retreat. There are one-on-one "buddy" meetings every week, so that by the end of the year every individual has had a chance to meet for at least an hour personally with every other student and each of the deans. There are also two public offerings during the year, where the students engage the larger public from on the campus and beyond, through activities like panel discussions and descriptions of "sacred spaces" on campus.

A student group called FAITH (Faiths Acting in Togetherness and Hope) has also been created by FRE "alumni" still at Stanford and others to nurture interfaith student leaders, counter religious bigotry and violence, advocate for human rights from within religious and secular traditions and understanding, and address social issues like preventing deaths due to malaria. The group meets weekly and supports a number of programs on campus from films, lectures, discussions, and interfaith services to days of interfaith service in the larger community, responses to specific instances of anti-religious graffiti and extremist actions on campus, and participation in national conferences.

Many colleges and universities have also created interfaith centers on campus. Stanford's is called the CIRCLE (Center for Inter-Religious Community, Learning and Experiences). It takes up the entire third floor of the student union and includes an interfaith sanctuary for 150 people, a seminar room, a common room, a student lounge, a library, and dedicated prayer spaces and offices for the 35 Stanford Associated Religions (SAR) groups, which include AHA! (Atheists, Humanists and Agnostics); Baha'is; Buddhists; Protestant, Catholic, and Eastern Orthodox Christians; Confucians; Hindus; Jews; Muslims; and Sikhs. It is a place where students of different traditions literally rub elbows with each other, roll up their sleeves to participate with each other's service projects, learn about each other's traditions through joining in others' worship, ritual, meditation, and prayer, and engage in discussions late into the night (the facility is open until 2 a.m.). SAR also has an executive committee that plans programs, staffed by two paid student "Interfaith Fellows," and there are mandatory meetings for the student leaders, professionals, and advisors of all SAR groups three times a year.

The Office for Religious Life at Stanford also co-sponsors Spirituality, Service and Social Change (SSSC) Fellowships in the summer with the Haas Center for Public Service. Six students are chosen competitively and receive $4,000 stipends to work in faith-based community placements in the San Francisco Bay area for ten weeks during the summer. The Dean, Senior Associate Dean, and Associate Dean co-teach a weekly SSSC seminar in the summer for students to reflect on their service experiences and interfaith understanding. The deans teach courses in the regular academic curriculum too, like one entitled "Spirituality and Nonviolent Social Transformation." Offered through Urban Studies and cross-listed in Religious Studies, it examines the American civil rights, anti-war, and farm workers' labor movements of the 1950s–70s, using case studies of religious leaders committed to nonviolence as a way of life who led successful social change movements. Also, the Office for Religious Life consults with professors who would like to help students engage in spiritual and religious inquiry in the classroom, teaching in as far-flung disciplines as psychology, history, computer science, and German literature. I have published do's and don'ts for professors elsewhere,[4] which include modeling personal engagement with issues of meaning and purpose and recognizing that learning to "know thyself" is an important part of liberal education, while at the same time being careful not to proselytize one's own worldview or to use students as tokens of identity categories.

The chapters by Rine and by Bryant Rockenbach and Mayhew substantially expand our knowledge base on how to enact spirituality in higher education. The kind of context created by a college or university makes a significant difference in how students deepen their own spiritual and religious lives. Perhaps even more importantly, for the survival of the planet, contexts that further fallibilism and ecumenical worldview give us the best chance of nurturing the global citizens and leaders we desperately need for the twenty-first century.

Notes

1   Scotty McLennan, *Finding Your Religion: When the Faith You Grew Up With Has Lost Its Meaning* (San Francisco: HarperSanFrancisco, 2001).
2   See, for example, Scotty McLennan, "Interfaith Interaction on Campus," *Journal of College & Character*, Vol. 11, No. 2 (May, 2010).
3   Alexander W. Astin, Helen S. Astin, and Jennifer A. Lindholm, *Cultivating the Spirit: How College Can Enhance Students' Inner Lives* (San Francisco: Jossey-Bass, 2011), pp. 191–192.
4   Scotty McLennan, "Moral and Spiritual Inquiry in the Academic Classroom," *Journal of College & Character*, Vol. VII, No. 4 (May 2006).

PART IV

Outcomes

7

FROM FAITH TO COMPASSION?

Reciprocal Influences of Spirituality, Religious Commitment, and Prosocial Development During College

Jay W. Brandenberger and Nicholas A. Bowman

The development of caring, altruistic, and responsible citizens is a salient social concern, and one that continues to animate various lines of research in the social sciences. Given that most religions promote compassion or caring, religious and spiritual influences are never far from the discussion. Yet as Kohn (1990) points out, the relation between religious orientation and prosocial engagements is complex. Religious faith may prompt care and work for justice, yet differences across religions—heightened in part by the events of September 11th in the United States—continue to yield public conflicts from the local to the international. Fostering skills and abilities to negotiate such tensions is an important challenge for institutions of higher education, both secular and faith-based.

The traditional college years are an especially relevant time for exploring the meaning of faith commitments (Parks, 1986) and for the development of moral reasoning (King & Mayhew, 2004) and civic and social responsibility (Brandenberger, 2005). Although youth may become—by some indicators—less religious during their undergraduate years (Regnerus & Uecker, 2007), students express significant spiritual interest (Lindholm, 2007), and recent research indicates that college may best be described as a period of re-examination (Pascarella & Terenzini, 2005) or a means to prevent religious decline (Uecker, Regnerus, & Vaaler, 2007). Concurrently, most colleges and universities over the last few decades have called for renewed emphasis on service and civic responsibility among college students (see Sullivan, 2000). A groundswell of initiatives—incorporating service-learning, community engagement, and civic action—have recognized, at least implicitly, that students actively seek meaning and purpose during the college years. Yet theoretical grounding for such initiatives is limited (Brandenberger, 1998), and we know little about *how* students' sense of meaning and spiritual purpose develops over the college years.

The Spirituality in Higher Education study facilitated by the Higher Education Research Institute (Astin, Astin, & Lindholm, 2011a) provides an unparalleled opportunity to examine the influence of religion and spirituality on prosocial development in higher education. Do religious commitment and spiritual identification during college predict increased prosocial orientation or behavior? Reciprocally, does prosocial involvement prompt religious or spiritual growth? We address such questions in the current study, utilizing data from 136 colleges and universities.

Literature Review

Prosocial Development

Theorists and researchers define *prosocial* to include cognitive and/or behavioral elements in which individuals focus on or voluntarily commit to actions that benefit others (Eisenberg, Cumberland, Guthrie, Murphy, & Shepard, 2005). Research on prosocial development has focused on both personality factors and contextual influences. In a thorough review, Penner, Dovidio, Piliavin, and Schroeder (2005) emphasized that prosocial development may best be studied through multilevel analyses ranging from the micro (e.g., brain functioning) to the macro level (examination of group behavior such as cooperation or volunteering). Berman (1997) presented a developmental view of a related construct, social responsibility, built on an array of cognitive and social elements, including a sense of care, justice, efficacy, and integrity (for a further discussion of responsibility, see Damon & Bronk, 2007).

Nancy Eisenberg and associates demonstrated age-related changes in prosocial reasoning: as individuals mature, they are able to move beyond hedonistic motivations to considerations of reciprocity (Eisenberg, Carlo, Murphy, & Van Court, 1995) and develop perspective-taking abilities that undergird prosocial responding (Eisenberg *et al.*, 2005). Eisenberg *et al.* (2005) also summarized research that indicates while some age-related changes exist, individuals demonstrate relative continuity across the lifespan in their propensity toward prosocial reasoning.

Research on prosocial development during college is limited, but there are indications that higher education has the potential to foster meaningful attention to prosocial concerns. For example, research at the Higher Education Research Institute (HERI) by Astin (1993) showed a significant rise in students' scores on a measure of social activism over four years, which was the largest gain among six personality types identified at the start of college. In addition, research on moral development (King & Mayhew, 2002; Pascarella & Terenzini, 2005) demonstrated a significant relationship between participation in higher education on moral reasoning (as indicated by the Defining Issues Test or similar measures). In fact, prosocial purpose orientations during the college years predict both prosocial purpose and psychological well-being in young adulthood (Bowman, Brandenberger, Lapsley, Hill, & Quaranto, 2010; Hill, Burrow, Brandenberger, Lapsley, & Quaranto, 2010).

Religious Commitment and Prosocial Behavior

The relation between religion and prosocial orientation is a longstanding question, and one that has prompted various studies in the social sciences and beyond (for example, see Batson, 1983, for a review from the perspective of sociobiology). In an extensive study of altruism conducted by Oliner and Oliner (1988), 15 percent of those who rescued Jews during the Holocaust cited religion, God, or Christianity as one of the reasons they decided to risk involvement. Interestingly, a larger portion (26 percent) of those who were rescued projected that religion was among the reasons prompting the actions of the rescuers. Indeed, most assume that religion is a central force in prompting moral action, so much so that Hunter (2000) argued that declining religious participation across Western cultures portends the "death of character," because character is fundamentally built on the "creeds, the convictions, the 'god-terms'… sacred to us and inviolable within us" (p. xiii).

In a review of the literature, Saroglou, Pichon, Trompette, Verschueren, and Dernelle (2005) suggested that "the theoretical evidence in favor of a possible—probably limited—effect of religion on prosociality is … strong and systematic" (p. 324). The authors noted that the effect of religion is more robust in relation to close "targets" (persons known to the individual) than for outgroup members or universal prosocial themes (e.g., concern for all humanity). In a related study (Pichon & Saroglou, 2009), activation of religious associations among participants prompted more frequent helping responses (for close targets) than secular priming, and participants' just-world beliefs played a mediating role in their prosocial responding. Further, a meta-analysis by Saroglou, Delpierre, and Dernelle (2004) found that the degree of individuals' religious orientation and commitment (among Christians, Muslims, and Jews) predicted the salience of key values, such as a higher valuing of security and benevolence and a lower valuing of universalism. Such studies call for further research to examine the impact of various types of religiosity (e.g., intrinsic vs. extrinsic) and the direction of influence between religious commitment and prosocial orientation.

Religious interest among college students varies significantly by institution, but the majority demonstrates some religious interest and behavior (Astin *et al.*, 2011a). Higher education is a primary context for thousands of youth to encounter the creeds and insights of the world and to face the challenge of examining personal convictions in light of those they encounter. For those of traditional college age, such encounters are especially salient because students' cognitive abilities are sufficiently (though not fully) matured, prompting for many an active (and often critical) exploration (Parks, 2000). Detailed overviews of the religious attitudes of American adolescents and emerging adults are provided in Smith (2009) and Smith, Faris, Lundquist Denton, and Regnerus (2003).

Spirituality

Spirituality is often defined more broadly than religiosity, with a focus on seeking the sacred or ultimate truth without the institutional boundaries of organized religion (Newberg & Newberg, 2008). While some may conceptualize spirituality first as private and individual, it often entails a quality of connectedness (Love & Talbot, 1999). *Faith* is a similar concept that can develop in a religious context or beyond. Parks (1986) argued "that the seeking and defending of meaning pervades all of human life" (p. 14); that is, all individuals must develop a sense of coherent understanding of the world and their place in it. It is this active sense of meaning making—which can be associated with spirituality—that Parks labeled *faith* (which she described as a verb). For some individuals, faith flows from religious foundations; for others, it is built on more secular, personal worldviews.

In a similar vein, Fowler (1995) outlined stages of general faith development, proceeding from egocentric assumptions through more universal considerations. Newberg and Newberg (2008) presented neurobiological evidence for a "developmental spirituality," noting correspondences between spiritual experiences and brain developments common at various ages within Fowler's framework.

Spirituality may also prompt prosocial responding. Indeed, the Dalai Lama claims that compassion and service are necessary components of any definition of spirituality (Dalai Lama XIV, 1999). While there is limited research in this arena—most studies focus on the link between religion and prosocial responding—a study by Saroglou *et al.* (2005) found links between spirituality and helping, empathy, and altruism. The authors also noted that those identifying as spiritual were more likely to extend their prosocial attention to outgroup or universal targets than those categorized as religious. Such differences may be mediated by individuals' belief structures and conceptions of justice (Pichon & Saroglou, 2009), and warrant further exploration.

The Role of Higher Education

Religion has a long-standing role in higher education (Kuh & Gonyea, 2006; Stamm, 2006). Harvard and similar colleges were established for religious training and formation. Over decades, many such institutions became modern secular universities that find encounters with religious issues more problematic than essential. Still, there are hundreds of faith-based colleges in the United States, and increases in enrollment on such campuses have outpaced enrollment in secular institutions since 1990 (Galarza, 2006). Moreover, students arrive on campus with significant religious and spiritual interest. In surveys by the Higher Education Research Institute (2004), 79 percent indicate they believe in God, 69 percent note that "religious beliefs provide strength, support and guidance," and 47 percent say that it is "very important" or "essential" to "seek out opportunities to help me grow spiritually."

While attention to the spiritual and religious life of students has received limited or conflicted attention over the last few decades, colleges and universities have increasingly focused on promoting service-learning and civic engagement (Speck & Hoppe, 2004). Some have suggested that service-learning and related pedagogies may be important means to prompt moral and religious reflection, even or especially at public universities, for such pedagogies may avoid the challenges associated with entangling the religious and the secular (Dalton, 2006). Recently, higher education has shown renewed interest in holistic education (Kronman, 2007; Lewis, 2006) and spirituality on campus (Chickering, Dalton, & Stamm, 2006; Lindholm, 2007; Speck & Hoppe, 2007). Research on the impacts of higher education on prosocial development, as mediated by religion and spirituality, is an important next step.

Reflection on Research in Context

Our work as researchers does not take root in neutral contexts. The authors are part of a larger enterprise of major universities—one faith-based and one public—that care about prosocial development among their students, yet need to negotiate the boundaries of public good and private freedom that come into play in educational contexts. We sense that concern for others gets stirred up by authentic spiritual and religious encounter, yet cannot be implemented homogeneously or through involuntary programs. Reciprocally, we have witnessed that engagement in prosocial efforts can sometimes prompt spiritual and religious interest where little previously existed.

Thus, we have developed research questions that revolve around the potential reciprocal relationships between spirituality, religious commitment, and prosocial behavior. When we turned to the research literature to address such questions, we found little that examines the role of higher education directly. We are excited to address this gap, but we realize that we need to do so with breadth and depth, going beyond the reach of our own institutions. We are also aware that our research framing and conclusions will be influenced by our own personal journeys and institutional contexts. We hope to draw on the best of social science research methods while seeing ourselves and respective conclusions in the context of higher education as a diverse and complex enterprise.

Research Questions

This study examines prosocial development in relation to spiritual identification and religious commitment during the college years. Our primary focus is on prosocial development as an outcome or dependent variable, but we are also interested in the potential impact of prosocial orientation on religious and spiritual outcomes.

While such topics have received recent attention in higher education practice, very little research has systematically examined such constructs or the relationship

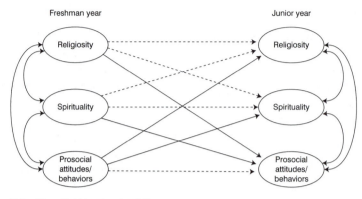

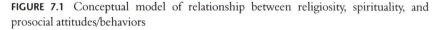

FIGURE 7.1 Conceptual model of relationship between religiosity, spirituality, and prosocial attitudes/behaviors

between them in the context of college. Prosocial orientation, spirituality, and religion are broad constructs that warrant careful definition of terms and measurement, but they are not "ineffable" (Chickering & Mentkowski, 2006). The present research improves on existing studies by using well-documented, multi-item scales and nationwide data through the UCLA Spirituality in Higher Education project.

Figure 7.1 presents a conceptual model that undergirds our study. The direct paths signify potential causal influences, whereas the curved lines with bidirectional arrows represent constructs that are likely correlated. Importantly, multiple indicators of prosocial development were used to convey relevant behaviors, values, and self-perceptions. Three primary research questions were addressed: 1) To what extent are spirituality and religiosity associated with changes in prosocial development? 2) To what extent are prosocial behaviors, values, and self-perceptions associated with changes in spiritual and religious development? 3) To what extent is religiosity associated with changes in spiritual development, and vice versa?

Method

Data Source and Measures

This study analyzed longitudinal data collected by HERI from over 14,000 students during students' first and junior years of college. For dependent variables, we used the existing HERI constructs of *spiritual identification, religious commitment, religious struggle, ethic of caring, charitable involvement,* and *compassionate self-concept*. Of the three prosocial indicators, ethic of caring is attitudinal, charitable involvement is behavioral, and compassionate self-concept is based on self-perceptions. Detailed information about the items and scales used here is provided in Chapter 2 of this book and in Astin, Astin, and Lindholm (2011b).

Students' levels of spiritual identification, religious commitment, religious struggle, ethic of caring, charitable involvement, and compassionate self-concept upon entering college were included as independent variables. Other precollege variables included gender (0 = male, 1 = female), age (1 = 16 or younger, to 10 = 55 or older), and parental education (mean of mother's and father's education; 1 = grammar school or less, to 8 = graduate degree). Several dichotomous variables indicated race/ethnicity: African American/Black; American Indian/Alaska Native; Asian American/Asian and Native Hawaiian/Pacific Islander (a combination of two categories from the CIRP survey); Mexican American/Chicano, Puerto Rican, and Other Latino (a combination of three CIRP categories); and Other. White/Caucasian served as the referent group. Because high school grade point average (HSGPA) was strongly skewed, dummy-coded variables were created for students who reported a "B" average (B– to B+) and a "C" average or less (C+ or lower); students with an "A" average (A– to A+) served as the referent group. The dependent variables and continuous independent variables were then standardized with a mean of zero and a standard deviation of one for inclusion in the analyses. As a result, unstandardized coefficients for continuous independent variables can be interpreted as standardized coefficients (Cohen, Cohen, West, & Aiken, 2003).

Analyses

Pearson correlations were used to examine the relationships between initial levels of spiritual identification, religious commitment, and the three types of prosocial orientation. Fisher r-to-z transformations were conducted to examine whether the correlations between spiritual identification and prosocial orientation differed significantly from the correlations between religious commitment and prosocial orientation.

Hierarchical linear modeling (HLM) analyses were used to explore whether spirituality and religiosity are associated with changes in prosocial orientation, and vice versa. The nesting of students within institutions violates a key assumption of ordinary least squares multiple regression; HLM accounts for this issue by partitioning the variance within and between groups and adjusting standard errors accordingly (Raudenbush & Bryk, 2002). HLM analyses predicting each of the six dependent variables were conducted. Continuous variables were grand-mean centered, and dichotomous variables were uncentered. All analyses included gender, age, race/ethnicity, parental education, HSGPA, and the pretest for the outcome variable as independent variables at the individual level (i.e., at level 1). Spiritual identification and religious commitment at time 1 were highly correlated ($r = .79$), so models predicting the prosocial outcomes were performed separately using (1) spiritual identification as an independent variable, (2) the religiosity variables as independent variables (religious commitment and religious struggle), and (3) all three measures as independent variables. (Note that the correlations between religious struggle and the other two variables were low: $r = .20$ with spiritual identification, and $r = .06$ with religious commitment.) HLM models predicting each form of religious and spiritual development were also examined. Because the three prosocial variables were moderately to strongly correlated with one another ($r = .24$ to $.47$), a separate model was analyzed for each prosocial measure predicting each spirituality/religiosity variable.

Previous research has indicated that the effects of some religious variables predicting spirituality, religiosity, and wellbeing outcomes differ between secular and religiously affiliated institutions (Bowman & Small, 2010, in press; Small & Bowman, 2011). Therefore, preliminary HLM analyses explored whether the slopes of the religiosity, spirituality, and prosocial orientation variables in this study might also vary by institutional type. However, these analyses revealed very few differences between religiously affiliated and secular campuses, so only the fixed-slope analyses are reported.

Intraclass correlation coefficients were calculated to indicate the proportion of variance in the dependent variables that occurred across institutions; these were 15 percent for religious commitment, 13 percent for spiritual identification, 11 percent for charitable involvement, 5 percent for ethic of caring, 4 percent for religious struggle, and 1 percent for compassionate self-concept. Although the values for the latter two variables were somewhat low for the use of HLM (Heck & Thomas, 2009), significant institutional-level differences exist for all outcomes ($ps < .0001$), and the structures of the data used violate the assumptions of multiple regression analyses. Moreover, the use of HLM for all models allows the results of various analyses to be compared with one another.

Limitations

Some limitations to this study should be noted. First, all of the measures are based on students' self-reports of their own attributes and behaviors. Although the use of student self-reports is very common in higher education research (Gonyea, 2005), the use of peer ratings or observations of behavioral outcomes would further bolster the validity of these reports. Fortunately, the longitudinal administration of multi-item scales to measure changes in each religiosity, spirituality, and prosocial construct constitutes a substantial improvement over many such studies (for relevant reviews, see Hill & Pargament, 2003; Koenig, McCullough, & Larson, 2001; Mayrl & Oeur, 2009). Second, as noted earlier, the measures of religious commitment and spiritual identification are highly correlated with one another; as a result, it can be difficult to tease apart the unique effects of religiosity and spirituality. In an effort to alleviate this problem, analyses were conducted separately with spiritual identification, religiosity variables, and both spirituality and religiosity variables as predictors of prosocial development. Third, the sample size was quite large, which increases the likelihood of Type I error and/or identifying significant effects that are actually quite minor in practice. To minimize these potential problems, a conservative significance level ($p < .01$) was used for all analyses.

Results and Discussion

Upon entering college, both spiritual identification and religious commitment are positively correlated with all three prosocial orientation measures, $r = .25$ to $.42$ (see Table 7.1). This finding is consistent with previous research that indicates a positive association between religiosity, spirituality, and prosocial orientation (Saroglou *et al.*, 2005). Furthermore, Fisher r-to-z transformations indicate that, for each of the prosocial measures, the correlation with spiritual identification is significantly higher than with religious commitment. That is, spiritual identification is more strongly related to prosocial orientation than is religious commitment. Of course, this correlational analysis cannot determine whether spirituality contributes to prosocial orientation, or vice versa.

To identify possible direction(s) of influence, HLM analyses explored whether entering levels of spirituality and religiosity are associated with changes in prosocial orientation during the first three years of college. As noted earlier, because religious commitment and spiritual identification are highly correlated, three separate HLM models predicting gains in each prosocial orientation measure were conducted. In Model 1, spiritual identification is positively associated with gains on all three prosocial outcomes (see Table 7.2). Model 2 examined only religious struggle and religious commitment as key predictors; this model suggested that religious commitment is associated with gains in charitable involvement and compassionate self-concept, but not ethic of caring. Religious struggle is not associated with changes on any of the prosocial outcomes. Model 3, which included all spiritual and religious variables, showed that spiritual identification is associated with gains in ethic of caring and compassionate self-concept, whereas religious commitment and religious struggle are not significantly related to growth on any prosocial indicator.

Because the effects of religious commitment on prosocial outcomes disappear when controlling for spiritual identification, students' spirituality seems to mediate

TABLE 7.1 Correlations among students' entering (start of college) levels of spiritual identification, religious commitment, and prosocial orientation

Prosocial measure	Spiritual identification	Religious commitment	Z-value of difference
Ethic of caring	.415**	.275**	12.83**
Charitable involvement	.331**	.272**	5.15**
Compassionate self-concept	.287**	.249**	3.29*

* p < .01; ** p < .001

TABLE 7.2. Unstandardized coefficients for hierarchical linear modeling analyses predicting prosocial development

	Dependent variable								
	Ethic of caring			Charitable involvement			Compassionate self-concept		
Independent variable	Model 1	Model 2	Model 3	Model 1	Model 2	Model 3	Model 1	Model 2	Model 3
Ethic of caring	.481** (.016)	.506** (.020)	.485** (.017)						
Charitable involvement				.372** (.017)	.381** (.016)	.371** (.018)			
Compassionate self-concept							.424** (.018)	.438** (.019)	.426** (.017)
Spiritual identification	.078** (.010)		.116* (.038)	.096** (.020)		.087 (.036)	.086** (.036)		.063* (.022)
Religious commitment		.033 (.019)	-.049 (.044)		.080** (.014)	.017 (.033)		.078** (.019)	.034 (.029)
Religious struggle		.001 (.017)	-.012 (.016)		-.022 (.026)	-.03 (.023)		-.004 (.011)	-.015 (.012)

Note. Standard errors are in parentheses. All analyses are controlling for gender, age, race/ethnicity, parental education, and high school grade point average.
* $p < .01$; ** $p < .001$

the relationship between religiosity and increased prosocial orientation. That is, one's religion may promote prosocial attitudes and behaviors to the extent that it bolsters one's spirituality. Such a view is consistent with the conceptualization of spirituality as internalized beliefs, as opposed to an orientation to the institutional practices and obligations of religion (e.g., Hill & Pargament, 2003). For example, a person may believe strongly in God and the importance of attending church, but such beliefs may only lead to prosocial orientation insofar as they become internalized or integral to the understanding of self. Among many people, organized religion and individual spirituality are strongly linked, so religion is indeed related (though perhaps indirectly) to prosocial development.

Moreover, the current findings are consistent with previous research that suggests religion is associated with prosocial behavior primarily among one's ingroup (Saroglou et al., 2005). Of the three prosocial measures used, ethic of caring is the only scale that includes several items focused on a broad target group (e.g., people throughout the world). In contrast, charitable involvement does not specify to whom the behaviors are directed, and compassionate self-concept contains items that are framed as generalized traits. Thus, people who are prosocial mainly toward their ingroup—regardless of how the ingroup is defined—may be likely to report high levels of charitable involvement and compassionate self-concept, but not ethic of caring. These patterns are borne out in the results for religious commitment versus spiritual identification. Specifically, Table 7.1 shows that the association with prosocial orientation is stronger for spiritual identification than for religious commitment among all three prosocial indicators, and this pattern is much more pronounced for ethic of caring (i.e., the only indicator with a specific focus on a broad target group). Furthermore, as evinced in Model 2 of the HLM analyses, religious commitment is not related to gains in ethic of caring, but it is related to gains on the other two prosocial indicators (see Table 7.2). It should be noted that these results are preliminary and warrant further investigation with measures designed specifically to examine in-group versus more universal targets.

Additional HLM analyses were conducted to examine factors that predict changes in religiosity and spirituality. To minimize potential multicollinearity issues, separate models were conducted with only one of the three prosocial measures upon college entry as an independent variable. As shown in the three columns on the left side of Table 7.3, religious commitment is positively associated with gains in spiritual identification. This pattern provides further evidence for the assertion that religion contributes to prosocial outcomes through promoting students' spiritual development. In contrast, students' initial levels of spiritual identification are significantly associated with gains on religious commitment only in Model 2, but not in the other two models. The lack of a consistent effect of spiritual identification on gains in religious commitment should not come as a surprise, because students who are engaged or not engaged in organized religion can both flourish spiritually (e.g., Bowman & Small, 2010).

TABLE 7.3 Unstandardized coefficients for hierarchical linear modeling analyses predicting spiritual and religious development

	Dependent variable								
	Spiritual identification			Religious commitment			Religious struggle		
Independent variable	Model 1	Model 2	Model 3	Model 1	Model 2	Model 3	Model 1	Model 2	Model 3
Ethic of caring	.026 (.026)			-.007 (.018)			-.038* (.014)		
Charitable involvement		-.012 (.013)			-.041 (.018)			-.062** (.014)	
Compassionate self-concept			-.007 (.011)			-.004 (.011)			-.092** (.019)
Spiritual identification	.456** (.052)	.470** (.042)	.468** (.042)	.070 (.036)	.077* (.029)	.068 (.031)	.107* (.039)	.106* (.036)	.112* (.036)
Religious commitment	.255** (.038)	.253** (.035)	.254** (.035)	.690** (.029)	.694** (.027)	.691** (.027)	.031 (.037)	.037 (.036)	.040 (.036)
Religious struggle	.029 (.013)	.033 (.016)	.031 (.015)	-.029 (.013)	-.028 (.015)	-.031 (.015)	.413** (.020)	.412** (.020)	.399** (.021)

Note. Standard errors are in parentheses. All analyses are controlling for gender, age, race/ethnicity, parental education, and high school grade point average.

* p < .01; ** p < .001

Although the results indicate that initial spirituality and religiosity lead to increased prosocial orientation, none of the prosocial indicators is significantly associated with growth in spiritual identification and religious commitment (see Table 7.3). As implied by the fairly modest correlations between prosocial orientation and religion/spirituality, students who engage in prosocial endeavors are not necessarily religious or spiritual. At many colleges and universities, volunteering and service opportunities are available largely through non-religious organizations, so prosocial behavior—not to mention prosocial attitudes, values, and self-perceptions—can be quite distinct from religious activities and groups. It is interesting to note, however, that in a study by Eyler and Giles (1999), 46 percent of those engaged in service learning reported "spiritual growth" as an important outcome, even though the service experiences and research measures were framed in secular terms.

In the final set of analyses, initial spiritual identification is positively related to increases in religious struggle over time in all three models. It is not obvious why this pattern occurs; it may be that the same forms of reflection associated with spiritual identification also cause students to consider (and sometimes question) their core religious beliefs, or the existence of spiritual identification early in college may indicate that students are primed to explore or react to religious externalities (for more about such struggles during college, see Bryant & Astin, 2008). In contrast, all three forms of initial prosocial orientation are associated with decreases in religious struggle during college. A tentative explanation for this finding follows: if students conceptualize prosocial attitudes and behaviors as part of their religious/spiritual belief systems, later performance of prosocial acts may be construed as living out the tenets of their religion. These students may observe their own prosocial (and, in their mind, religious) actions and feel fulfilled. Because people's attitudes and beliefs are often formed by observing their own behaviors (e.g., Eagly & Chaiken, 1993), these engaged students may be less likely to question their existing religious views. Alternatively, direct engagement in prosocial actions during college may prompt religious awareness and interest.

Reflections and Implications

Our findings are consistent with other research indicating that spirituality and religious commitment predict prosocial orientation, yet in a complex manner. That spirituality is especially predictive of several forms of prosocial orientation is not surprising. Spirituality is often associated with unity and transcendence (Newberg & Newberg, 2008). Peak experiences, as described by Maslow, have been linked with spirituality and characterized by the breaking down of boundaries and prompting of universal concern (see Kunin & Miles-Watson, 2006). Such findings suggest that for many, spirituality is more than a self-focused or private matter.

As researchers committed to the prosocial missions of our universities, we find the outcomes described above—based on data from numerous colleges and thousands of students—to be welcome news. Such empirical support provides important grounding for faculty and administrative efforts to attend to students' spiritual and religious views along with related understandings of prosocial responsibility. Promising practices toward this end (see Chickering et al., 2006; Colby, Ehrlich, Beaumont, & Stephens, 2003; Lindholm, Millora, Schwartz, & Spinosa, 2011) should be enhanced through developmentally grounded research (Brandenberger, 1998, 2005). Given that spirituality, not just religion, is associated with prosocial concern, faculty and staff at secular colleges and universities can introduce relevant opportunities for discussion and learning with less fear of indoctrination.

Our findings raise further research questions. How do students understand spirituality? The concept is fluid and can be highly personal and significantly influenced by culture (Katz, 1978; Newberg & Newberg, 2008). Thus, measures of spirituality need to be well-defined and consistent across studies. In the current study, for example, the term "spiritual" was used in the majority of the items that comprised the spiritual identification variable, yet students may not understand the term uniformly. A second potential research question involves how spiritual concerns may integrate with (or mediate) religious orientation to foster internalized views of social responsibility. A related question is developmental: during the college years, how are students predisposed cognitively and behaviorally to questions of faith and religion? Do the freedoms of college life and pressure to define oneself independently affect the relationships among variables such as spirituality, religiosity, and prosocial orientation? Further, the current research suggests the importance of further exploration of spiritual and religious orientation toward within group or universal targets. Given the need for global collaboration highlighted by broad social and technological change, the importance of fostering respect and concern for those beyond one's close relations is salient within and beyond higher education. Finally, given the shift in higher education toward questions of engagement and purpose, it is essential to examine what elements of the college experience—from undergraduate major to community engagement to the intellectual milieu of the college—may shape spirituality, religiosity, and prosocial outcomes.

To examine such questions, studies following cohorts into the adult years would present a more complete and nuanced picture of development (see Dillon, Wink, & Fay, 2003; Wink, Ciciolla, Dillon, & Tracy, 2007). Our recent research suggests that prosocial purpose during college may be an especially salient predictor of engagement and well-being in young adulthood (Bowman et al., 2010; Hill et al., 2010). Such outcomes may further enhance adults' developmental trajectories, providing ongoing opportunities for spiritual and prosocial growth.

References

Astin, A. W. (1993). *What matters in college: Four critical years revisited*. San Francisco: Jossey-Bass.

Astin, A. W., Astin, H. S., & Lindholm, J. A. (2011a). Cultivating the spirit: How college can enhance students' inner lives. San Francisco: Jossey-Bass.

Astin, A. W., Astin, H. S., & Lindholm, J. A. (2011b). Assessing students' spiritual and religious qualities. *Journal of College Student Development, 52,* 39–61.

Batson, C. D. (1983). Sociobiology and the role of religion in promoting prosocial behavior. *Journal of Personality and Social Psychology, 45,* 1380–1385.

Berman, S. (1997). *Children's social consciousness and the development of social responsibility.* Albany: State University of New York Press.

Bowman, N. A., & Small, J. L. (2010). Do college students who identify with a privileged religion experience greater spiritual development? Exploring individual and institutional dynamics. *Research in Higher Education, 51,* 595–614.

Bowman, N. A., & Small, J. L. (in press). Exploring a hidden form of minority status: College students' religious affiliation and well-being. *Journal of College Student Development.*

Bowman, N. A., Brandenberger, J. W., Lapsley, D. K., Hill, P. L., & Quaranto, J. C. (2010). Serving in college, flourishing in adulthood: Does community engagement during the college years predict adult well-being? *Applied Psychology: Health and Well-Being, 2,* 14–34.

Brandenberger, J. W. (1998). Developmental psychology and service learning: A theoretical framework. In R. G. Bringle, & D. K. Duffy (Eds.), *With service in mind: Concepts and models for service-learning* (pp. 68–84). Washington, DC: American Association for Higher Education.

Brandenberger, J. W. (2005). College, character, and social responsibility: Moral learning through experience. In D. Lapsley & F. C. Power (Eds), *Character psychology and character education* (pp. 305–334). Notre Dame, IN: University of Notre Dame Press.

Bryant, A. N., & Astin, H. S. (2008). The correlates of spiritual struggle during the college years. *Journal of Higher Education, 79,* 1–27.

Chickering, A. W., & Mentkowski, M. (2006) Assessing ineffable outcomes. In A. W. Chickering, J. C. Dalton, & L. Stamm (Eds.), *Encouraging authenticity and spirituality in higher education* (pp. 220–243). San Francisco: Jossey-Bass.

Chickering, A. W., Dalton, J. C., & Stamm, L. (Eds.). (2006). *Encouraging authenticity and spirituality in higher education.* San Francisco: Jossey-Bass.

Cohen, J., Cohen, P., West, S. G., & Aiken, L. S. (2003). *Applied multiple regression/correlation analysis for the behavioral sciences* (3rd edn). Mahwah, NJ: Lawrence Erlbaum.

Colby, A., Ehrlich, T., Beaumont, E., & Stephens, J. (2003). *Educating citizens: Preparing America's undergraduates for lives of moral and civic responsibility.* San Francisco: Jossey-Bass.

Dalai Lama XIV. (1999). *Ethics for the new millennium.* New York: Penguin Putnam.

Dalton, J. (2006). Community service and spirituality: Integrating faith, service, and social justice at DePaul University. *Journal of College and Character, 8*(1), 1–9.

Damon, W., & Bronk, K. C. (2007). Taking ultimate responsibility. In H. Gardner (Ed.), *Responsibility at work: How leading professionals act (or don't act) responsibly* (pp. 21–42). San Francisco: Jossey-Bass.

Dillon, M., Wink, P., & Fay, K. (2003). Is spirituality detrimental to generativity? *Journal of the Scientific Study of Religion, 42,* 427–442.

Eagly, A. H., & Chaiken, S. (1993). *The psychology of attitudes.* Fort Worth, TX: Harcourt.

Eisenberg, N., Carlo, G., Murphy, B., & Van Court, P. (1995). Prosocial development in late adolescence: A longitudinal study. *Child Development, 66,* 1179–1197.

Eisenberg, N., Cumberland, A., Guthrie, I. K., Murphy, B. C., & Shepard, S. A. (2005). Age changes in prosocial responding and moral reasoning in adolescence and early adulthood. *Journal of Research on Adolescence, 15,* 235–260.

Eyler, J., & Giles, D. E. (1999). *Where's the learning in service-learning?* San Francisco: Jossey-Bass.

Fowler, J. (1995). *The stages of faith: The psychology of human development and the quest for meaning.* New York: HarperCollins (original edition published in 1981).

Galarza, C. (2006). More students choosing faith-based college life. *Orlando Business Journal,* March 17. Retrieved November 30, 2009, from http://orlando.bizjournals.com/orlando/stories/2006/03/20/story8.html.

Gonyea, R. M. (2005). Self-reported data in institutional research: Review and recommendations. In P. D. Umbach (Ed.), *Survey research: Emerging issues* (New Directions for Institutional Research, no. 127, pp. 73–89). San Francisco: Jossey-Bass.

Heck, R. H., & Thomas, S. L. (2009). *An introduction to multilevel modeling techniques* (2nd edn). New York: Routledge.

Higher Education Research Institute. (2004). *The spiritual life of college students: A national study of college students' search for meaning and purpose (Full report).* Los Angeles: Author. Retrieved November 22, 2009, from http://www.spirituality.ucla.edu/results/index.html.

Hill, P. C., & Pargament, K. I. (2003). Advances in the conceptualization and measurement of religion and spirituality: Implications for physical and mental health research. *American Psychologist, 58,* 64–74.

Hill, P. L., Burrow, A. L., Brandenberger, J. W., Lapsley, D. K., & Quaranto, J. C. (2010). Collegiate purpose orientations and well-being in emerging and middle adulthood. *Journal of Applied Developmental Psychology, 31,* 173–179.

Hunter, J. D. (2000). *The death of character: Moral education in an age without good or evil.* New York: Basic Books.

Katz, S. (1978). Language, epistemology, and mysticism. In S. Katz (Ed.), *Mysticism and philosophical analysis* (pp. 22–74). New York: Oxford University Press.

King, P. M., & Mayhew, M. J. (2002). Moral judgment development in higher education: Insights from the Defining Issues Test. *Journal of Moral Education, 31,* 247–270.

King, P. M., & Mayhew, M. J. (2004). Theory and research on the development of moral reasoning among college students. *Higher education: Handbook of theory and research, 19,* 375–440.

Koenig, H. G., McCullough, M., & Larson, D. B. (2001). *Handbook of religion and health.* New York: Oxford University Press.

Kohn, A. (1990). *The brighter side of human nature: Altruism and empathy in everyday life.* New York: Basic Books.

Kronman, A. T. (2007). *Education's end: Why our colleges and universities have given up on the meaning of life.* New Haven, CT: Yale University Press.

Kuh, G. D., & Gonyea, R. M. (2006). Spirituality, liberal learning, and college student engagement. *Liberal Education,* Winter, 40–47.

Kunin, S. D., & Miles-Watson, J. (Eds.). (2006). *Theories of religion: A reader.* New Brunswick, NJ: Rutgers University Press.

Lewis, H. R. (2006). *Excellence without a soul: How a great university forgot education.* New York: Public Affairs of Perseus Books.

Lindholm, J. A. (2007). Spirituality and the academy: Reintegrating our lives and the lives of our students. *About Campus 12*(4), 10–17.

Lindholm, J. A., Millora, M. L., Schwartz, L. M., & Spinosa, H. S. (2011). *A guidebook of promising practices: Facilitating college students' spiritual development.* Berkeley, CA: University of California.

Love, P. G., & Talbot, D. (1999). Defining spiritual development: A missing consideration for student affairs. *NASPA Journal, 37*(1), 361–375.

Mayrl, D., & Oeur, F. (2009). Religion and higher education: Current knowledge and directions for future research. *Journal for the Scientific Study of Religion, 48,* 260–275.

Newberg, A. B., & Newberg, S. K. (2008). Hardwired for God: A neuropsychological model for developmental spirituality. In K. K. Kline (Ed.), *Authoritative communities: The scientific case for nurturing the whole child* (pp. 165–186). New York: Springer.

Oliner, S. P., & Oliner, P. M. (1988). *The altruistic personality: Rescuers of Jews in Nazi Europe.* New York: Free Press.

Parks, S. (1986). *The critical years: The young adult search for a faith to live by.* San Francisco: Harper & Row.

Parks, S. (2000). *Big questions, worthy dreams: Mentoring young adults in their search for meaning, purpose, and faith.* San Francisco: Jossey-Bass.

Pascarella, E. T., & Terenzini, P. T. (2005). *How college affects students: A third decade of research* (Vol. 2). San Francisco: Jossey-Bass.

Penner, L. A., Dovidio, J. F., Piliavin, J. A., & Schroeder, D. A. (2005). Prosocial behavior: Multilevel perspectives. *Annual Review of Psychology, 56,* 365–392.

Pichon, I., & Saroglou, V. (2009). Religion and helping: Impact of target, thinking styles, and just-world beliefs. *Archive for the Psychology of Religion, 31,* 215–236.

Raudenbush, S. W., & Bryk, A. S. (2002). *Hierarchical linear models: Applications and data analysis methods* (2nd edn). Thousand Oaks, CA: Sage.

Regnerus, M. D., & Uecker, J. E. (2007). *How corrosive is college to religious faith and practice?* New York: Social Science Research Council. Retrieved November 29, 2009, from http://religion.ssrc.org/reforum/Regnerus_Uecker.pdf.

Saroglou, V., Delpierre, V., & Dernelle, R. (2004). Values and religiosity: A meta-analysis of studies using Schwartz's model. *Personality and Individual Differences, 37,* 721–734.

Saroglou, V., Pichon, I., Trompette, L., Verschueren, M., & Dernelle, R. (2005). Prosocial behavior and religion: New evidence based on projective measure and peer ratings. *Journal for the Scientific Study of Religion, 44,* 323–348. doi: 10.1111/j.1468-5906-2005-00289x.

Small, J. L., & Bowman, N. A. (2011). Religious commitment, skepticism, and struggle among college students: The impact of majority/minority religious affiliation and institutional type. *Journal for the Scientific Study of Religion, 50,* 154–174.

Smith, C., with Snell, P. (2009). *Souls in transition: The religious and spiritual lives of emerging adults.* New York: Oxford University Press.

Smith, C., Faris, R., Lundquist Denton, M., & Regnerus, M. (2003). Mapping American adolescent subjective religiosity and attitudes of alienation toward religion: A research report. *Sociology of Religion, 64,* 111–133.

Speck, B. W., & Hoppe, S. L. (Eds.). (2004). *Service learning: History, theory, and issues.* Westport, CT: Praeger.

Speck, B. W., & Hoppe, S. L. (Eds.). (2007). *Searching for spirituality in higher education.* New York: Peter Lang.

Stamm, L. (2006). The influence of religion and spirituality in shaping American higher education. In A. W. Chickering, J. C. Dalton, & L. Stamm (Eds.), *Encouraging authenticity and spirituality in higher education* (pp. 66–91). San Francisco: Jossey-Bass.

Sullivan, W. M. (2000). Institutional identity and social responsibility in higher education. In T. Ehrlich (Ed.), *Civic responsibility and higher education* (pp. 19–36). Phoenix, AZ: Oryx Press.

Uecker, J. E., Regnerus, M., and Vaaler, M. L. (2007). Losing my religion: The social forces of religious decline in early adulthood. *Social Forces, 85,* 1667–1692.

Wink, P., Ciciolla, L., Dillon, M., & Tracy, A. (2007). Religiousness, spiritual seeking, and personality: Findings from a longitudinal study. *Journal of Personality, 75,* 1051–1070.

8

DEVELOPMENT AMONG ADOLESCENTS AND YOUNG ADULTS

Longitudinal linkages between Spirituality, Religion, and Social Justice

David Chenot and Hansung Kim

Few in academia would argue that educating students to value social justice is a worthless or counterproductive pursuit as faculty attempt to develop prosocial citizens, many of whom are likely to become leaders in society. In fact, increasing justice in society may be viewed as one of the universal goals of higher education. Historically, directives to pursue social justice in very specific ways have appeared in sacred scriptures in most of the world's religions. It is surprising, then, that little attention has been paid to the relationship between religion and social justice in the literature on higher education. In addition, a focus on the influence of spirituality on social justice has been rare. Yet large numbers of students identify spirituality as an important aspect of their lives and many identify themselves as religious (Astin, Astin, Lindholm, Bryant, Szelényi, & Calderone, 2005). If indeed there are relationships between spirituality or religion and social justice among young adults, this would be important for academicians to consider as they promote the concern for social justice. Potential relationships between these constructs have implications for the way the topics of spirituality and religion are managed in academic environments, including general considerations such as the way these subjects are discussed or avoided on campuses, and specific deliberations such as curriculum development and application in various disciplines.

In this chapter, we set out to test associations among spirituality, religion, and social justice. The chapter is based on an analytic model that tests research questions regarding whether relationships among spirituality, religion, and social justice exist among adolescents and young adults over time. We became interested in these potential relationships as academicians that offer instruction to students who are being educated to become professional social workers. Through many years of practicing social work as professionals and offering instruction to new social workers, we have found that spiritual and/or religious issues are extremely important to many of the clients who receive services from social workers. Therefore, no matter how individual social workers view spirituality and religion, they have a professional responsibility to address the issues that are important to their clients. Also, spiritual and/or religious issues are significant personally for many of our students who become practitioners in the field upon graduation. In addition, the pursuit of social justice is a core value in the field of social work that many argue forms the basis for our profession more than any other value or focus (National Association of Social Workers, 2000; Council on Social Work Education, 2008). Therefore, developing social workers are asked to adopt a commitment to social justice practices as part of being professional social workers. With these concerns as the context, we became interested in the relationships among spirituality, religion, and social justice orientation among university students.

Definitions

The definitions of religion and spirituality in this study are based on the concepts of "religious engagement" and "spiritual identification" posited by Astin *et al.* (2005). Religion is an "external" perspective on religious engagement that focuses on identification with religious groups that is manifested through religious behaviors (Astin, Astin, & Lindholm, 2011), whereas spirituality is viewed primarily as a subjective, "inner" pursuit that includes the inclination to perceive the self and others as "spiritual" and an existential search for meaning and transcendence (Astin *et al.*, 2011). The definition of social justice orientation used in this study includes concern for others, a willingness to see that the basic needs of others are met and the propensity to assure equity and human rights for all in society.

Development in Adolescence and Young Adulthood

Developmental considerations are applicable to the current study since many adolescents (65 percent were younger than 20 years old) were included at time 1 of data collection, and the study was longitudinal in nature. This signifies that many in the sample were experiencing a developmental transition from adolescence to young adulthood during the three-year duration of the study.

Developmental theorists have posited that formative components of moral reasoning and attitudes toward justice in society may be situated in adolescence (Gilligan, 1982; Kohlberg, 1984). Others have posited that important aspects of spirituality, religion, or faith formation also occur during adolescence (Fowler, 1981; Fowler & Dell, 2006; Wilber, Engler, & Brown, 1986). In addition, theorists have pointed to the existence of reciprocal relationships between moral reasoning, faith, and spirituality during development (Fowler, 1981; Walker & Reimer, 2006). Empirical findings depict a complex mix of interactive developmental trajectories with moral development independent of religious or spiritual development for some and highly dependent on these influences for others (Walker & Reimer, 2006). Finally, moral development has been posited as a key factor in the formation of social justice oriented attitudes and actions (Kohlberg, 1984).

Religion and Social Justice Orientation

A connection between religion and social justice orientation has existed for centuries in the scriptures of various religions. The connection is obvious in many religions when adherents are extolled to care for the poor, underrepresented groups in society, and those without social support. Current theorists and researchers have also posited relationships between various religions and social justice constructs (Canda & Furman, 2010). Particularly in Fowler's (1981) stage theory, which is supported by empirical findings, one result of faith development (most often in religious contexts) in the highest stages of his theory, is a greater interest in social justice related attitudes and actions (Fowler & Dell, 2006). Fowler and Dell (2006) state that one of the primary indicators of reaching the culminating stage of Fowler's theory of faith development, "universalizing faith," is "activism that attempts to change adverse social conditions" (p. 41). Though the attitudes and actions related to these developmental outcomes are not likely to be fully developed during adolescence, there is empirical support for the notion that at least a nascent sense of importance concerning these attitudes and actions is indicated by many during adolescence (Benson, Leffert, Scales, & Blyth, 1998). Interestingly, at least one set of researchers view religion and social justice as so integrally connected that they have made social justice a dimension of religious commitment in measures that have been used in several studies (Benson, Donahue, & Erickson, 1993).

Spirituality and Social Justice Orientation

A link between spirituality and social justice orientation has not been as clearly delineated. However, conceptual connections between the two constructs have been asserted by many writers (Canda & Furman, 2010; Hay, 2001; Joldersma, 2009). For instance, Canda and Furman (2010) relate spirituality and social justice as essential partners throughout their book on social work practice. In fact, they posit that spirituality and social work share a common focus on social justice. Indeed, some theorists view the connection between spirituality and social justice as an imperative aspect of spirituality. For instance, Gearon (2001) argues that spirituality, without a sense of community, is "self indulgent" (p. 154). The conceptualization of spirituality shared by these theorists includes an inextricable link between "true spirituality" and a concern for others in society such that internally experienced spirituality without externalized action to benefit others would not be considered spirituality at all. In addition, Fenzel (2002) goes beyond positing a conceptual connection between the constructs by viewing social justice as an integral dimension of spirituality in measures composed to test the relationships between spirituality and various outcomes.

Though there have been conceptual treatments of associations between spirituality and social justice, empirical studies are rare. The connection between spirituality and aspects of social justice has been most frequently averred in the positive youth development (PYD) literature (Benson *et al.*, 1998; Lerner, Dowling, & Anderson, 2003; Lerner, Roeser, & Phelps, 2008). For instance, empirically supported links between spirituality and civic engagement and civic contribution are commonly cited in the PYD literature (Lerner *et al.*, 2003; Lerner, Alberts, Anderson, & Dowling, 2006). However, these relationships are often extended beyond generic civic engagement to attitudes and activities related to social justice, such as caring/compassion, charity, political and social activism, and defending the rights of minorities (Lerner *et al.*, 2003, 2006; Sherrod & Spiewak, 2008). For instance, according to Templeton and Eccles (2008), a progressing sense of both morality and spirituality is associated with an "expanding circle of empathy" (p. 198) and caring for greater numbers of people. This expansion is accompanied by "concrete actions that contribute to the welfare of others" (p. 198). In addition, Lerner *et al.* (2003, 2006) explicitly connect both spirituality and religiosity to social justice. For instance, Lerner *et al.* (2006) posit relationships between spirituality, religiosity, and "thriving," while delineating one of the characteristics of thriving as "contributing to social justice and equity for all individuals in society" (p. 63).

There have also been two qualitative studies concerning these variables in the social work literature that found links between spirituality and social justice among some participants in samples of professional social workers (Lee & Barrett, 2007; Wagenfeld-Heintz, 2009). However, there do not appear to be many extant quantitative studies that test the relationships among spirituality, religion, and social justice orientation among adolescents and young adults.

Research Questions

The current study addresses the gap in the literature identified above by reporting on an empirical examination of longitudinal relationships between spirituality, religion, and social justice orientation in a large sample of undergraduate university students, most of whom are adolescents or young adults. Consistent with the suggestion that variables such as those included in this study can be viewed as either independent or dependent variables, the analysis will examine the potential for reciprocal relationships between spirituality, religion, and social justice orientation (Sherrod & Spiewak, 2008). This study addresses the following research questions: 1) Does religion explain the development of social justice orientation among university students over time? 2) Does spirituality explain the development of social justice orientation among university students over time?

Conceptual and Analytic Framework

Conceptually and empirically supported connections between religion, spirituality, and variables related to social justice, such as empathy with others, caring/compassion for others, activism, and concern about equity in society, have been traced in the literature review (Fowler & Dell, 2006; Lerner et al., 2006; Sherrod & Spiewak, 2008; Templeton & Eccles, 2008). Based on these conceptual linkages we expect to discover positive relationships between religion, spirituality, and social justice orientation among adolescents and young adults over time in this study. In order to address the research questions, we employed a cross-lagged panel model to examine the potential longitudinal relationships between the variables of primary interest. This model is appropriate for studies that use two-wave longitudinal data. The cross-lagged panel model estimates synchronous correlations (each variable with the other at the same point in time), autocorrelations (each variable with itself at two time points), and cross-lagged correlations (each variable with other variables at a different point in time) (Kessler & Greenberg, 1981; Taris, 2000). The cross-lagged panel modeling methodology is based on the principle that the causal priority of variables included in the model may be identified by comparing cross-lagged correlations. Following discussions by Taris (2000) and Kessler and Greenberg (1981), the analytic model in this study (Figure 8.1) was developed to explore longitudinal relationships among religion, spirituality, and two dimensions of social justice orientation: attitudes and actions.

Methods

The current study was based on secondary data analysis using two-wave longitudinal survey data collected by the UCLA Higher Education Research Institute (HERI) in conjunction with the Spirituality in Higher Education project (Astin et al., 2005; Astin, Astin, and Lindholm, 2011).

The study variables include religion, spirituality, social justice orientation, and students' socio-demographic characteristics. The following section explains how these variables were measured.

Religion was assessed by using the scale entitled "religious engagement," which was created by Astin et al. (2011, see Chapter 2). Spirituality was assessed using the scale entitled "spiritual identification," which was developed by Astin et al. (2011, see Chapter 2).

We developed measures of social justice orientation using relevant items from the 2007 College Students' Beliefs and Values Follow Up Survey (CSBV) (HERI, 2007). All items were measured on a 4-point Likert-type scale ranging from "Not important" (1) to "Essential" (4). Exploratory factor analysis (EFA) was performed to examine the underlying factor structure without assuming a particular structure (Child, 2006). Results of EFAs supported two sub-dimensions (Table 8.1). The first set of three

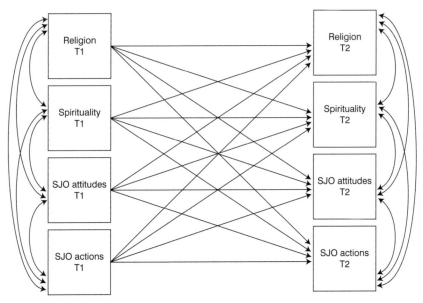

Paths from control variables to endogenous variables were omitted for clear presentation

FIGURE 8.1 The cross-lagged panel model of religion, spirituality, and social justice orientation

TABLE 8.1 Factor loadings from exploratory factor analysis of the 7-item social justice orientation scale

	Time 1 (2004)		Time 2 (2007)	
Items	*Attitudes*	*Projected actions*	*Attitudes*	*Projected actions*
Helping others who are in difficulty	0.51		0.52	
Reducing pain and suffering in the world	0.84		0.89	
Improving the human condition	0.77		0.77	
Influencing social values		0.73		0.71
Participating in a community action program		0.61		0.61
Becoming a community leader		0.68		0.74
Influencing the political structure		0.73		0.71

Note. All items were considered as ordinal-level variables in EFA analyses. Varimax rotation was used to acquire all factor loading values.

items (i.e., helping others who are in difficulty, reducing pain and suffering in the world, improving the human condition) relate to attitudes concerning social justice, while the second set of four items (i.e., influencing social values, participating in a community action program, becoming a community leader, influencing the political structure) represent students' intended behaviors or the actions they are committed to taking to achieve social justice. Overall, the items included in the "projected actions" subscale constitute the types of activities those who develop social justice orientation (SJO) are likely to engage in. In order to perform subsequent analyses, two sub-scale scores were calculated by summing responses to the items in each dimension of SJO. For this sample, Cronbach's alpha values on the SJO attitudes scale were 0.74 at time 1 and 0.75 at time 2. Alphas for the SJO actions scale were 0.76 at time 1 and 0.78 at time 2. These alphas all fall into DeVellis's (2003) "respectable" range, indicating acceptable reliability in the scales at each time point.

Analysis

To explore the longitudinal relationships among religion, spirituality, and social justice orientations, a series of cross-lagged panel models were examined (Figure 8.1). The model was estimated using structural equation modeling (SEM) with the Mplus software program (Muthén & Muthén, 2007). Sample weighting was applied as described in Chapter 2. To evaluate model fit, the χ^2 goodness-of-fit index (GFI), and the root-mean-square error of approximation (RMSEA) were examined. The conventional overall test of fit in structural equation analyses assesses the magnitude of the discrepancy between sample and fitted covariance matrices. A value of χ^2/df less than 3 is considered a reasonable fit (Kline, 1998). GFI evaluates the relative amount of variances and covariances in the observed covariance matrix that are reproduced by the model-implied covariance matrix (Tanaka, 1993). For the GFI, a value of 0.90 is considered acceptable and a value of 0.95 is considered a good fit (Kline, 1998). GFI, however, can be biased by the sample size because GFI does not penalize model complexity (Marsh & Hau, 1996). RMSEA penalizes model complexity and can be used as an alternative assessment of model fit for SEM analyses. RMSEA values below 0.05 are ideal (Kline, 1998).

Limitations

There were some limitations in this study that provide context for the findings. First, the sample was not random but was large and weighted in order to represent the population of university students in the USA. In addition there was substantial attrition in the sample from time 1 to time 2 with approximately 13 percent of the original sample responding at time 2. Due to attrition, the findings of the current study should be interpreted with caution. In addition, the study represented in this chapter employed secondary data analysis. Therefore, the items chosen to compose the social justice orientation scale were limited to the items that were available in the survey that was used in the original study (HERI, 2007). We do not assert that the SJO scales formed for this study capture all dimensions of social justice but we believe they represent both attitudes and actions related to social justice sufficiently to indicate variation of the respondents' orientations toward social justice. Finally, the items that represent SJO actions did not inquire about actions respondents were engaging in at the time of the study. Subjects were asked to project which actions they would take in the future in response to this set of questions. Obviously, this line of inquiry is not as helpful as observations concerning actions respondents were engaging in at the time of the study.

Findings

The results of the analysis revealed that some paths in the full model were not significant. For the purpose of achieving a more parsimonious model, the model was modified by eliminating non-significant paths. Figure 8.2 presents significant path coefficients in the final model (excluding autocorrelations and control variable paths). As a result, the parsimonious final model yielded an overall χ^2 ($df = 17$) value of 30.10, with $\chi^2/df = 1.77$, GFI = 0.99, and RMSEA = 0.008. Once the effects of gender, family income, and race/ethnicity were included, the squared multiple correlation coefficients indicated that the model explained 47 percent of the variance in spiritual identification, 55 percent in religious engagement, 23 percent in SJO attitudes, and 24 percent in SJO actions at time 2.

The results of the path analysis suggest a reciprocal relationship between religious engagement and spiritual identification (Figure 8.2). The path coefficient from religion at time 1 to spirituality at time 2 was $\beta = 0.19$, while the path coefficient from spirituality at time 1 to religion at time 2 was $\beta = 0.10$. It is not surprising that a reciprocal relationship existed in the sample between spirituality and religion. Many researchers have discovered that there is a great deal of overlap between the definitions of these two constructs for most people (Hodge & Chen McGrew, 2005; Zinnbauer & Pargament, 2005). However, it is interesting to note that the effect of religion on spirituality was stronger than the opposite effect between the two constructs. This may indicate that for many in the sample, individual perceptions of their religious engagement play a prominent role in informing conceptions of their spirituality. However, perceptions of personal spirituality also influenced religious engagement. This leads to the conclusion that the inner focus of spirituality is reflected in religious activities among many who consider themselves religious in this sample.

Spirituality at time 1 significantly predicted students' SJO attitudes at time 2 ($\beta = 0.11$). Therefore, higher levels of spirituality at time 1 result in significantly higher levels of SJO attitudes at time 2 after adjusting for the levels of SJO attitudes at time 1. This lasting explanatory relationship was discovered in a formative developmental stage for most of the participants. Though the data in this study do

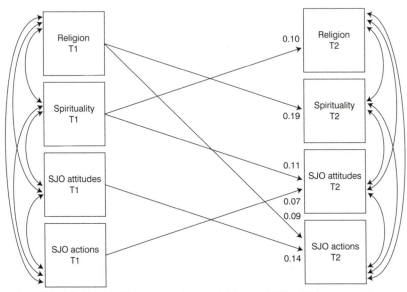

All path coefficients included in this figure were significant at the p < 0.05 level. Paths representing autocorrelations (each variable with itself at two time points) were all significant, but omitted from the figure for clear presentation
β = 0.66 religion time 1 to religion time 2;
β = 0.53 spirituality time 1 to spirituality time 2;
β = 0.34 SJO attitudes time 1 to SJO attitudes time 2;
β = 0.66 SJO actions time 1 to SJO actions time 2).

FIGURE 8.2   Standardized path-coefficients in the final path model

not allow queries about this relationship beyond the end of the participants' junior year in college, there is reason to believe that, for many, the relationship is enduring. This conjecture is based on the stages of development most of the participants were experiencing at the time of data collection which are formative in nature and set the groundwork for mature adulthood. Further research must inquire about the potential ongoing impact of the relationship between spirituality and SJO attitudes.

Religion at time 1 explained students' SJO actions at time 2 ($\beta = 0.09$). The impact religion had on projected SJO actions was not as strong as the explanatory influence of spirituality on SJO attitudes. However, it makes sense conceptually that the practical actions that compose religious engagement would connect directly to SJO actions rather than SJO attitudes. Likewise, spirituality in this study was viewed as the inner pursuit of transcendence and this seems to relate more closely to attitudes than actions.

The paths between SJO attitudes and SJO action resulted in reciprocal relationships. SJO attitudes at time 1 had a significant predictive impact on SJO actions at time 2 ($\beta = 0.14$), while SJO actions at time 1 explained SJO attitudes at time 2 ($\beta = 0.07$). It is important to note that the predictive relationship between SJO attitudes and SJO actions was twice as strong as the relationship between

SJO actions and SJO attitudes. It is not axiomatic that attitudes lead to actions; however, chronologically this order is usually the case (Ajzen & Fishbein, 2005). Developmentally, it seems reasonable to assume that attitudes normally develop prior to self-directed actions (Ajzen & Fishbein, 2005). If a person is not concerned about equity for others or meeting human needs they are unlikely to engage in actions that ensure equity or meet the needs of others. However, the findings were reciprocal and reflect an interactional relationship between attitudes and actions over time. Overall, the findings in this study lead to an assertion of the likelihood that positive attitudes about social justice in adolescence lead to SJO actions later in life.

In addition to the paths between religion, spirituality, SJO attitudes, and SJO action, students' gender (females were coded as 1 and males were coded as 0), family income, and race/ethnicity (Caucasian was coded as 1 and all others were coded as 0) were included as control variables. Gender had a positive relationship with SJO attitudes ($\beta = 0.09$), while race/ethnicity had a negative relationship with religion ($\beta = -0.04$), spirituality ($\beta = -0.06$), SJO attitudes ($\beta = -0.04$), and SJO action ($\beta = -0.05$) (not shown in Figure 8.2). These findings suggest that female students tend to have higher levels of SJO attitudes than male students. In addition, those from racial/ethnic minority groups endorsed higher levels of spirituality, religiosity, and social justice orientation than White students.

Overall, the results depict significant longitudinal relationships between religion, spirituality, and SJO (attitudes and actions) over a three-year period.

Discussion

Because the analyses in this study were longitudinal in nature, the results are revealing concerning the lasting effects of spirituality and religion on social justice orientation for a large group of adolescents and young adults. Though the coefficients signifying these relationships may not be characterized as strong, they are significant and demonstrate the lasting impact spirituality and religion have on SJO during these formative developmental stages. Those who value the formation of concerns about social justice as a goal of development will note that spirituality and religion appear to be significant factors in the formation of attitudes and actions related to social justice in society. Certainly spirituality and religion are not the only factors that lead to social justice orientation but the findings of this study highlight that they are significant factors that should be considered in discussions about improving/increasing social justice orientation among adolescents and young adults.

An additional finding of interest in this study is that there was no significant longitudinal prediction by either SJO attitudes or SJO actions of either spirituality or religion. Reciprocal paths were specified in the models used in this study. We anticipated potential prediction by the SJO variables of spirituality and/or religion since similar variables are viewed as reciprocally influential by some in the developmental literature (Donnelly, Matsuba, Hart, & Atkins, 2006; Sherrod & Spiewak, 2008). The findings in this study lead to the conclusion that spiritual and religious development may be considered antecedents to the formation of prosocial attitudes and actions concerning social justice for many adolescents and young adults. An orientation toward social justice does not appear to influence spirituality or religious engagement in the same predictive manner.

Reflections

Overall, the findings of this study are consistent with the results of research that tested variables that are similar to social justice orientation. For instance, in the positive youth development literature, though the research is much broader in scope than the present study, some of the variables are similar in nature to SJO, particularly in the caring/compassion dimension of "thriving" (Lerner *et al.*, 2003) and the "values" aspects of "internal assets" (Benson *et al.*, 1998, p. 148). Among the primary variables in PYD research, spiritual and/or religious development figure prominently in predicting civic engagement, caring and compassion for others and the adoption of equity and social justice as values. Although this study focused on the effects of spirituality and religion on social justice orientation, similarities to broader PYD studies are clear.

Because the adoption of concern for equity and social justice is commonly valued, encouraging spirituality and positive religious engagement among adolescents and young adults are pursuits that can be promoted as beneficial for society. This leads to the consideration of ways to increase spiritual identification and positive religious engagement among these age groups. Some of this can be accomplished through religious institutions that offer positive experiences that lead adolescents and young adults toward attitudes and actions consistent with a social justice perspective.

However, a growing number of adolescents and young adults do not consider themselves to be religious or do not participate in activities through religious organizations. One of the primary vehicles for societal changes for this group may come through others that directly or indirectly influence a teen or young adult's life. One vehicle for this type of influence has been called "spiritual modeling" by Oman and Thoresen (2003a, b) and is based on Bandura's (1986) social cognitive theory, particularly the concept of observational learning. Oman and Thoresen (2003a) point out that through spiritual observational learning, the "*practical* relevance of religion and spirituality" can be accentuated in ways that improve secular institutions, including "social welfare" (p. 151). Spiritual modeling includes an emphasis Oman and Thoresen (2003a) frame as "the pursuit of social reforms such as social justice" (p. 152). These authors, and Bandura (2003) in his response to Oman and Thoreson, discuss spiritual exemplars that offer "spiritual models" who "contest societal injustices and inhumanities." Bandura (2003) discusses Martin Luther King Jr. and Ghandi in this context. However, spiritual models do not have to be famous "uberspiritual" exemplars. They can be people in individuals' families or social environments that have direct influence on the lives of adolescents and young adults. In fact, Oman and Thoresen (2003b) clarify that Bandura's notion of "diversified modeling" is essential for effective spiritual modeling. Their point is that both "exalted and everyday modeling influences" are needed for helpful spiritual modeling (Oman & Thoresen, 2003b). In fact, they frame the simultaneous need for both types of models as a significant issue that must be integrated into spiritual modeling interventions.

This leads to a consideration of the impact personnel in the educational system have on adolescents and young adults. Oman and Thoresen (2003a) mention the educational system explicitly in the context of spiritual modeling and suggest this is one of the social institutions that could be strengthened through attention to the practical aspects of religion and spirituality. In educational systems with religious affiliations, this can be accomplished with an intentional focus on spiritual modeling and religious practices that lead directly to increased social justice related actions among adolescents and young adults. The finding in this study that religious engagement predicted SJO actions provides empirical support for efforts that target this relationship. Efforts to encourage a focus on these issues in secular educational systems, though, are likely to meet with resistance, particularly when the focus is religion, and perhaps, by association with religion, spirituality. However, most educators in public educational systems that serve adolescents and young adults would agree that increasing social justice in society is one of the missions of their institutions. One of the ways this mission can be accomplished is through the attitudes and behaviors of those who graduate from their institutions and assume various roles in society. In other words, encouraging spirituality among adolescents and young adults in educational institutions can lead to improved social justice in society.

A focus on religious influences may not be acceptable in public education but spirituality does not have to be linked to specific religions. Spiritual modeling in educational systems offers a means for establishing the relationship between spirituality and increasing SJO attitudes and, indirectly, actions in practice (Oman & Thoresen, 2003a, b). However, many faculty have encountered disregard or outright hostility in their efforts to provide spiritual models in university settings (Shahjahan, 2009, 2010). Increased acceptance of spiritual modeling on campuses may be possible to achieve through further research that makes an empirical case for educational reform by convincing administrators and instructors of the importance and effectiveness of this approach in facilitating one of their institution's long-term goals: social justice.

However, some view the relationship between spirituality and social justice as a central access point to improvements in education aimed at increasing the pursuit for social justice. For instance, Erricker (2004) believes the grievous problems of injustice in society have infiltrated educational systems so thoroughly that he calls for "a radical oppositional pedagogy" identified as "spiritual activism." Spiritual activism would focus on the "spiritual and values development of young people, regardless of faith commitments" (Erricker, 2004, p. 169). Gearon (2001) expresses similar sentiments when he encourages a "spirituality of dissent" that mounts "a challenge to the politics of injustice" (p. 154). Proponents of these approaches are convinced spirituality is a primary pathway to social justice through education and advocate a profound overhaul of educational systems that would amplify this path and advance the goal of producing greater social justice in society. However it is accomplished, the encouragement of spiritual growth and religious engagement among adolescents and young adults should be a focus of efforts to increase social justice orientations in educational systems.

The results of the current study included predictive relationships between spirituality, religion, and social justice oriented attitudes and actions among a large group of adolescents and young adults over time. These findings provide empirical support for efforts to improve awareness about social justice and to increase actions that expand social justice in society through a focus on spirituality and religion. The findings are particularly applicable to adolescents and young adults and the specific developmental dynamics they experience. Religiously affiliated institutions can use the results of this study to support curricular changes that directly link religious activities with actions that increase social justice. Within public educational systems, administrators and educators who wish to promote social justice related attitudes and behaviors among their students will be able to use the results of this study as empirical support for efforts to include spiritually specific content in the curriculum or to provide spiritual modeling for their students.

References

Ajzen, I., & Fishbein, M. (2005). The influence of attitudes on behavior. In D. Albarracín, B. T. Johnson, & M. P. Zanna (Eds.), *The handbook of attitudes*, (173–221). Mahwah, NJ, Erlbaum.

Astin, A. W., Astin, H. S., & Lindholm, J. A. (2011). Assessing students' religious and spiritual qualities. *Journal of College Student Development, 52*(1), 39–61.

Astin, A. W., Astin, H. S., Lindholm, J. A., Bryant, A. N., Szelényi, K., & Calderone, S. (2005). *The spiritual life of college students: A national study of college students' search for meaning and purpose*. Los Angeles: Higher Education Research Institute, UCLA.

Bandura, A. (1986). *Social foundations of thought and action: A social cognitive theory*. Englewood Cliffs, NJ: Prentice Hall.

Bandura, A. (2003). On the psychological impact and mechanisms of spiritual modeling. *International Journal for the Psychology of Religion, 13*(3), 167–173.

Benson, P. L., Donahue, M. J., & Erickson, J. A. (1993). The faith maturity scale: Conceptualization, measurement, and empirical validation. *Research in the Social Scientific Study of Religion, 5*, 1–26.

Benson, P. L., Leffert, N., Scales, P. C., & Blyth, D. A. (1998). Beyond the "village" rhetoric: Creating healthy communities for children and adolescents. *Applied Developmental Science, 2*(3), 138–159.

Canda, E. R., & Furman, L. D. (2010). *Spiritual diversity in social work practice: The heart of helping* (2nd edn). New York: Oxford University Press.

Child, D. (2006). *The essentials of factor analysis* (3rd edn). New York: Continuum.

Council on Social Work Education (2008). *Handbook of accreditation standards and procedures.* Alexandria, VA: Council on Social Work Education.

DeVellis, R. F. (2003). *Scale development: Theory and applications* (2nd edn, Vol. 26), Applied Social Research Methods Series. Thousand Oaks, CA: Sage.

Donnelly, T. M., Matsuba, M. K., Hart, D., & Atkins, R. (2006). The relationship between spiritual development and civic development. In E. C. Roehlkepartain, P. E. King, L. Wagener, & P. L. Benson (Eds.), *The handbook of spiritual development in childhood and adolesence* (pp. 239–251). Thousand Oaks, CA: Sage.

Erricker, C. (2004). A manifesto for spiritual activism: Time to subvert the branding of education. In H. A. Alexander, *Spirituality and ethics education: Philosophical, theological and radical perspectives* (pp. 158–171). Brighton, BN: Sussex Academic Press.

Fenzel, M. L. (2002). The development of the Spiritual Involvement Scale: Examining the spiritual lives of late adolescents. Poster presented at the Biennial Conference of the Society for Research on Adolescence. New Orleans, LA.

Fowler, J. W. (1981). *Stages of faith: The psychology of human development and the quest for meaning.* San Francisco: Harper & Row.

Fowler, J. W., & Dell, M. L. (2006). Stages of faith from infancy through adolescence: Reflections on three decades of faith development theory. In E. C. Roehlkepartain, P. E. King, L. Wagener, & P. L. Benson (Eds.), *The handbook of spiritual development in childhood and adolesence* (pp. 34–45). Thousand Oaks, CA: Sage.

Gearon, L. (2001). The corruption of innocence and the spirtuality of dissent: Postcolonial perspectives on spirituality in a world of violence. In J. Erricker, C. Ota, & C. Erricker (Eds.), *Spiritual education cultural, religious and social differences: New perspectives for the 21st century* (pp. 143–155). Brighton, BN: Sussex Academic Press.

Gilligan, C. (1982). *In a different voice: Psychological theory and women's development.* Cambridge, MA: Harvard University Press.

Hay, D. (2001). Spirituality versus individualism: The challenge of relational consciousness. In J. Erricker, C. Ota, & C. Erricker (Eds.), *Spiritual education cultural, religious and social differences: New perspectives for the 21st century* (pp. 104–117). Brighton, BN: Sussex Academic Press.

HERI, Higher Education Research Institute (2007). *2007 College Students' Beliefs and Values Follow-up Survey.* Higher Education Research Institute, Graduate School of Education & Information Studies, UCLA. Los Angeles, CA.

Hodge, D. R., & Chen McGrew, C. (2005). Clarifying the distinctions and connections between spirituality and religion. *Social Work & Christianity, 32*(1), 1–21.

Joldersma, C. W. (2009). A spirituality of the desert for education: The call of justice beyond the individual or community. *Studies in Philosophy & Education, 28,* 193–208.

Kessler, R. C., & Greenberg, D. F. (1981). *Linear panel analysis: Models of quantitative change.* New York: Academic Press.

Kline, R. B. (1998). *Principles and practice of structural equation modeling.* New York: Guilford Press.

Kohlberg, L. (1984). *The psychology of moral development: The nature and validity of moral stages.* San Francisco: Harper & Row.

Lee, E. O., & Barrett, C. (2007). Integrating spirituality, faith, and social justice in social work practice and education: A pilot study. *Journal of Religion & Spirituality in Social Work, 26*(2), 1–21.

Lerner, R. M., Dowling, E. M., & Anderson, P. M. (2003). Positive youth development: Thriving as the basis of personhood and civil society. *Applied Developmental Science, 7*(3), 172–180.

Lerner, R. M., Roeser, R. W., & Phelps, E. (Eds.). (2008). *Positive youth development & spirituality: From theory to research.* West Conshohocken, PA: Templeton Foundation Press.

Lerner, R. M., Alberts, A. E., Anderson, P. M., & Dowling, E. M. (2006). On making humans human: Spirituality and the promotion of positive youth development. In E. C. Roehlkepartain, P. E. King, L. Wagener, & P. L. Benson (Eds.), *The handbook of spiritual development in childhood and adolescence* (pp. 60–72). Thousand Oaks, CA: Sage.

Marsh, H. W., & Hau, K. (1996). Assessing goodness of fit: Is patrimony always desirable. *Journal of Experimental Education, 64*(4), 364–390.

Muthén, L., & Muthén, B. (2007). *Mplus user's guide* (4th edn). Los Angeles, CA: Muthén & Muthén.

National Association of Social Workers (2000). *Code of ethics of the National Association of Social Workers.* Washington, DC: Author.

Oman, D., & Thoresen, C. E. (2003a). Spiritual modeling: A key to spiritual and religious growth? *International Journal for the Psychology of Religion, 13*(3), 149–165.

Oman, D., & Thoresen, C. E. (2003b). The many frontiers of spiritual modeling. *International Journal for the Psychology of Religion, 13*(3), 197–213.

Shahjahan, R. A. (2009). The role of spirituality in the anti-oppressive higher-education classroom. *Teaching in Higher Education, 14*(2), 121–131.

Shahjahan, R. A. (2010). Toward a spiritual praxis: The role of spirituality among faculty of color teaching social justice. *Review of Higher Education, 33*(4), 473–412.

Sherrod, L. R., & Spiewak, G. S. (2008). Possible interrelationships between civic engagement, positive youth development, and spirituality/religiosity. In R. M. Lerner, R. W. Roeser, & E. Phelps (Eds.), *Positive youth development & spirituality: From theory to research* (pp. 322–338). West Conshohocken, PA: Templeton Foundation Press.

Tanaka, J. S. (1993). Multifaceted concepts of fit in structural equation models. In K. Bollen, & J. S. Long (Eds.), *Testing structural equation models*, pp. 10–39. Newbury Park, CA: Sage.

Taris, W. T. (2000). *Primer in longitudinal data analysis.* London, GBR: Sage.

Templeton, J. L., & Eccles, J. S. (2008). Spirituality, "expanding circle morality," and positive youth development. In R. M. Lerner, R. W. Roeser, & E. Phelps (Eds.), *Positive youth development & spirituality: From theory to research* (pp. 197–209). West Conshohocken, PA: Templeton Foundation Press.

Wagenfeld-Heintz, E. (2009). Faith and its application to the practice of social work. *Journal of Religion, Spirituality & Aging, 21*(3), 182–199.

Walker, L. J., & Reimer, K. S. (2006). The relationship between moral and spiritual development. In E. C. Roehlkepartain, P. E. King, L. Wagener, & P. L. Benson (Eds.), *The handbook of spiritual development in childhood and adolescence* (pp. 224–238). Thousand Oaks, CA: Sage.

Wilber, K., Engler, J., & Brown, D. (1986). *Transformations of consciousness: Conventional and contemplative perspectives on development.* Boston: Shambhala.

Zinnbauer, B. J., & Pargament, K. I. (2005). Religiousness and spirituality. In R. F. Paloutzian, & C. L. Park (Eds.), *Handbook of the psychology of religion and spirituality* (pp. 21–42). New York: Guilford.

9

STUDENT–FACULTY INTERACTION AND THE DEVELOPMENT OF AN ETHIC OF CARE

James J. Fleming, Jennie Purnell, and Yang Wang

This chapter can be thought of as the record of a conversation between three educators: a professor, a doctoral candidate, and an administrator—all deeply interested in the transformational power of a college education on the students who experience it and all three working at the same institution of higher learning. We are regularly involved in undergraduate teaching, research on the impact that student–faculty interaction and the choice of pedagogies have on what and how learning takes place, and service to our communities beyond our work in the classroom. The conversation recorded on these pages began a few years before we focused our attention on the HERI data that is the subject of our present discussion. In each aspect of our professional lives (teaching, research, and service) we had the clear sense that, as one of our colleagues said, "there's a lot of human flourishing happening around here." What was not clear to us was whether or not this human flourishing could be quantified in terms of student learning outcomes. Borrowing an archeological metaphor used by others for research methods, we came to understand that our flashlights pointed in the right direction but we needed tools with which to dig. Then came the HERI data and we were handed our shovels and began our excavation.

What we discovered was that student–faculty interactions and pedagogical choices do matter. If we want our students to help create a more caring and just society, then we will want to consider the results of the research in this chapter and throughout the entire book. A just society will prosper when its citizens care for each other. Citizens learn caring. The future citizens of our society are currently on our campuses.

In the often bifurcated world of higher education, affective qualities such as compassion, empathy, and caring for others may be seen as desirable traits to be cultivated in undergraduates through co-curricular activities and programs, but, unlike cognitive and intellectual development, they are unlikely to be defined as crucial learning outcomes. Yet the work of some moral ethicists—those concerned with compassion and caring—suggests that these desirable traits ought to be included in outcome measures, given higher education's renewed emphasis on moral development and civic responsibility. Gilligan (1982), Noddings (1984, 2002), and others argue that caring relationships are the foundation for an alternative understanding of ethics, based not on abstract and general principles of justice but rather on the needs and concerns of individuals in caring relationships. According to Noddings (2002), a "society composed of people capable of caring—people who habitually draw on a well-established ideal—will move toward social policies consonant with an ethic of care" (p. 233). Social justice, for Noddings, "can only be achieved by caring people in caring communities" (Bergman, 2004, p. 151). An ethic of care may also be essential to democracy, especially in diverse societies.[1] Rhoads (2000), for example, argues that "a democratic society thrives only when its citizens have a deep concern for others" (p. 37). Along similar lines, Tronto (1993) maintains that "the practice of care describes the qualities necessary for democratic citizens to live together well in a pluralist society, and that only in a just, pluralist democracy can care flourish" (pp. 161–162).[2]

If there are good reasons for educators to care about caring, how can colleges and universities foster an ethic of care in the students they teach through programs, policies, and practices? This chapter explores how faculty can and do affect their students' development of what Rhoads (2000) calls the caring self: "a sense of self firmly rooted in concern for the well-being of others" (p. 37). We argue that through their mentoring relationships with students and through their pedagogical choices, faculty can encourage students to care more deeply for and about others, and to aspire to become active and caring citizens of local, national, and global communities.

Theoretical Foundations

The idea that our students could learn to care captured our imaginations and held our interests. We further wondered if there were specific types of interactions—both personal and pedagogical—that were more likely than others to influence this learning of care. Since we believed that the social and learning environments on all college and university campuses influence the development of the students who live and learn on them, we began to speculate about how interactions with faculty might explicitly or implicitly foster the development of a caring person. Could the experience of being cared for serve as the foundation for an ethical response to those we meet in our daily lives?

The dominant approach to moral development, both generally and in the literature on higher education, is the cognitive-structural perspective associated with the work of Kohlberg (1984); here the focus is on the development of increasingly complex forms of moral reasoning (King & Kitchener, 1994; Pascarella & Terenzini, 2005; Perry, 1999). Faculty have the potential to contribute to this aspect of their students' moral development through the content of the courses they teach and in their modeling of empirical and normative reasoning. Affective and social learning approaches to moral development, in contrast, emphasize emotions, values, and behavior rather than cognition, and suggest other roles for faculty in fostering moral development. Hoffman (2000) defined moral development in terms of an increasingly complex empathetic response to others. Gibbs (2003) examined the interplay of empathy and cognition in the development of moral values such as caring about others, aspiring to help others, and desiring equality and justice. Bandura (1977) and Sieber (1980) saw moral development as the acquisition of moral behaviors learned through observing others. Building on Gilligan's (1982) concept of an ethic of care, Noddings (1984, 2002) argued, as noted above, that the experience of being cared for is the foundation for an ethical response to others.

In contrast to the literature on cognition and moral reasoning, far less research has been done on values, emotions, aspirations, and behavior as components of moral development during the undergraduate years (Swaner, 2004). At the same time, some studies suggest that higher education does tend to develop values and aspirations linked to an ethic of care. For instance, Pascarella and Terenzini (2005) discuss research that indicates that students experience growth in altruism, humanitarianism, civic responsibility, and social consciousness during college. Likewise, Astin (1993) found that college seniors, after four years of higher education, placed higher value on social activism (defined as helping others who are in difficulty), participating in community-based programs, influencing social values, and influencing the political structure.

Service learning appears to be particularly important in developing such attributes as compassion, empathy, and caring about others. Noddings (1984) argued that caring involved seeing the one cared for as we see ourselves, and thus being moved to act for others as we would act for ourselves: "When we see the other's reality as a possibility for us, we must act to eliminate the intolerable, to reduce the pain, to fill the need, to actualize the dream" (p. 14). When service learning provides personal interactions between students and people in need, a similar dynamic occurs, furthering the development of the caring self (Rhoads, 2000). According to Keen and Hall (2009), service learning can promote dialogue across boundaries of perceived difference and lead students to place higher value on working for social justice. Finally, Saltmarsh (1997) argued that service learning "can provide powerful opportunities for ethical apprenticeships based on relatedness, receptivity, and responsiveness" (p. 84).

Quite a few studies suggest that interaction with faculty can also have an important effect on students' moral values, aspirations, and behavior, as well as their cognitive development. Research cited by Pascarella and Terenzini (2005) showed that faculty–student interaction outside of the classroom promoted student persistence, educational aspirations, and degree completion; when such interactions "reinforce or extend the intellectual ethos of the classroom," they contributed to cognitive development and intellectual growth (p. 189). As in their earlier work (1991), they also found that "principled moral reasoning was enhanced by exposure to and interaction with individuals at more advanced stages of principled reasoning," whether faculty members or peer mentors (Pascarella & Terenzini, 2005, p. 363).[3]

Recent research on spirituality in higher education suggests that faculty spirituality influences the character of student–faculty interaction, as well as faculty views that there are moral ends to higher education. Lindholm, Astin, and Astin (2005) found that faculty who self-identify as spiritual are more likely to consider enhancing students' self-understanding, developing moral character, and helping students to develop personal values as educational goals. Using data from the 2004–05 HERI faculty study, Lindholm and Astin (2008) examined the relationship between faculty spirituality and the adoption of student-centered pedagogies such as cooperative learning, reflective writing, and student evaluation of their own and each other's work. Faculty play a central role in these "student-centered" instructional and evaluative strategies; the interaction between teacher and student is at the heart of the learning process. Lindholm and Astin (2008) reported that faculty who self-reported as being spiritual were much more likely to use student-centered pedagogies, independent of personal characteristics, fields of study, and institutional affiliations.

Both mentoring and teaching through student-centered pedagogies can be seen as modeling a relationship of care; some student-centered pedagogies, such as service learning and student evaluations of the work of others, allow students to practice caring relationships themselves.[4] With reference to student-centered pedagogies, Henson (2003) wrote that "[l]earning occurs best in an environment that contains positive interpersonal relationships and interactions and in which the learner feels appreciated, acknowledged, respected, and validated" (p. 1). More generally, Chickering and Reisser (1993) argued that when "faculty are committed to creating quality learning experiences, when they are consistent in showing respect, caring, and authenticity, and when they are willing to interact with students in a variety of settings, then development of competence, autonomy, purpose, and integrity is fostered" (p. 316).

Mentoring, Pedagogy, and the Development of an Ethic of Care

Existing research demonstrates that students tend to develop values and aspirations linked to an ethic of care during their undergraduate years. We also know that student–faculty interaction is very important to cognitive development and intellectual growth. What drew our attention was the question of whether some particular types of student–faculty interaction have a greater impact on an ethic of caring as a dimension of college student spiritual development. The literature on student–faculty interactions as well as that on the ethic of care suggested two hypotheses to be tested in this chapter using the longitudinal data drawn from the combined HERI CIRP/CSBV survey in 2004 and the follow-up HERI survey in 2007:

1   Students who have had more frequent experiences with student-centered pedagogical practices will place a higher value on the caring self.
2   Students who have had more frequent conversations with faculty about non-curricular matters will place a higher value on the caring self.

Ours is an investigation into the question of whether the content and/or context of student–faculty interactions make any difference with respect to helping students become more caring people. Some faculty do not consider themselves terribly spiritual, are not comfortable talking about spirituality, and find it often inappropriate to talk about spirituality *per se*. Much of what we do as faculty in the classroom isn't spiritual at all … but does it matter? Do faculty need to have spiritual conversations with students in order to help them become more spiritual people? Or do closer student–faculty relationships—a particular type of student–faculty interaction or specific pedagogy—make a difference in and of themselves? The pedagogical questions seemed particularly interesting to us because none of the pedagogical choices offered in the data used for our investigations had anything to do with spirituality and could be adopted in any type of course by any type of faculty.

It could have seemed, at first glance, odd that a political scientist, a statistician, and a higher education policy wonk would find common interest in the possibilities offered to us by the existence of the HERI data. What we have in common, however, is that we share a strong belief about education—especially a liberal arts education at college. We believe that education has the power to transform individuals. As we go about our work as educators, we are sure we will influence and change the individuals who are part of it—our students. An uncritical acceptance of tacit values indeed influences the learner. We feel that it is our obligation to be more explicit about the kind of individuals our students have the potential to be at the end of our shared learning process. "The aim of a university education," wrote Alasdair MacIntyre in his 2010 book *God, Philosophy, Universities*, "is to transform their minds and hearts, so that the student becomes a different kind of individual" (MacIntyre, p. 147). The ontological change required for this real education to take place necessitates that the professor and the learner are explicit about their desires for the outcomes that result from their time together.

Method

Because over 14,000 students from 136 institutions participated in both the 2004 and 2007 surveys, the hierarchical linear modeling (HLM) technique was used to model the dependency among the nested observations (Raudenbush & Bryk, 2002). This resulted in a two-level hierarchical structure—*student* at the first level and *institution* at the second.

Variables

At the student level, a student's development of an ethic of care was the most important variable of the study. Astin, Astin, and Lindholm (2011) identified an "ethic of caring" (see Chapter 2) as one of four measures of qualities related to spirituality (the others being charitable involvement, ecumenical worldview, and compassionate self-concept). The measure consisted of a combination of eight items on the 2007 survey referring to concern and caring for others, and action on behalf of others. After a series of exploratory factor analyses, we added three more items for a modified 11-item "ethic of caring" measure. Table 9.1 represents these items and their factor loadings on the extracted factor using the maximum likelihood method.

These 11 items show reasonable reliability in both survey administrations, with Cronbach's alphas of .86 in 2004 and .88 in 2007. To help visualize the change in

TABLE 9.1   Ethic of care scale: items and factor loadings in 2004 and 2007

		Factor loadings	
Item content		2004	2007
	Original items (Astin, Astin, & Lindholm, 2011)		
1.	Trying to change things that are unfair in the world	.482	.607
2.	Helping others who are in difficulty	.561	.603
3.	Reducing pain and suffering in the world	.668	.725
4.	Helping to promote racial understanding	.656	.682
5.	Becoming involved in programs to clean up the environment	.523	.511
6.	Becoming a community leader	.558	.597
7.	Influencing social values	.594	.633
8.	Influencing the political structure	.514	.526
	Additional items		
9.	Participating in a community action program	.663	.703
10.	Improving understanding of other countries and cultures	.625	.625
11.	Improving the human condition	.710	.716

Note: Item 1 was measured on a 3-point scale: 1 = "Not At All"; 2 = "To Some Extent"; 3 = "To A Great Extent". Items 2–11 were measured on a 4-point scale: 1 = "Not important"; 2 = "Somewhat Important"; 3 = "Very Important"; 4 = "Essential".

the ethic of care, summated raw scores were created and are presented later in the "Descriptive Findings" section of this chapter. For ease of interpretation and in consideration of the factor loading of each item on the scale, factor scores based on regression analysis were computed for both years with means of 0 and standard deviations of 1 (Gorsuch, 1983), thereby providing the factor scores on the measure of the ethic of care in 2007 as the outcome variable, with the earlier 2004 scores used as a covariate for analysis.

Further, using Astin's (1993) *I-E-O Model* to assess the *outcome* (changes in the ethic of care), we considered a number of other *input* and *environmental* variables. In order to test the hypotheses with respect to student–faculty interaction and the development of an ethic of care, we identified ten survey items related to mentoring and nine items related to student-centered pedagogies. Table 9.2 shows details of these items as well as their factor loadings. Most factor loadings are above .40, with the last item "Community service as a part of coursework" as the only exception (factor loading = .33). We hypothesize that this item reflects a professor's student-centered pedagogical practices and therefore included it in the extracted factor even though it has a relatively low factor loading.

Results from exploratory factor analysis indicated that the mentoring items formed two distinct clusters. The first included student–faculty conversations about ethical issues, purpose and meaning, spirituality, and religion; while the second included discussions about graduate study and career decisions and perceived interest on the part of faculty about the students' self-understanding and personal welfare. For brevity's sake, these will be referred to as ethical/spiritual mentoring and academic/career mentoring. The third cluster is referred to as "Student-centered pedagogical practices" and included consideration of such activities as self-evaluation, peer evaluation, and student-selected discussion topics, along with cooperative learning and portfolio assessment. In this chapter, the three factor scores are independent variables at the student level.

In addition to mentoring and pedagogy, the student level variables included student demographic characteristics, degree of religiousness, high school academic achievement, and extra-curricular activities at the exploration stage to explain the available variance. The school level variables included institutional religious type (i.e., public, nonsectarian, Catholic, evangelical, or other church-affiliated). Cross-level interaction effects between institutional religious type and student–faculty interactions were also explored through interaction terms.

Analyses

Hierarchical linear models were carried out in four stages. In the first stage, an unconditional model was built that partitions the total variability in student's ethic of care into within-institution and between-institution variance components. After this, predictors were added at each level to explain the available variance.

TABLE 9.2 Student–faculty interaction items and factor loadings

	Factor loadings		
Scales and items	1	2	3
Mentoring relationships – *Ethical/spiritual mentoring (α = .834)*			
1. Encouraged discussion of religious/spiritual matters	.883		
2. Encouraged personal expression of spirituality	.837		
3. Acted as spiritual models for you	.638		
4. Discussed religion/spirituality with professors	.583		
5. Encouraged exploration of questions of meaning and purpose	.456		
6. Encouraged discussion of ethical issues	.444		
Mentoring relationships – *Academic/career mentoring (α = .778)*			
7. Encouraged you to pursue post-graduate study		.655	
8. Assisted you in your career decisions		.658	
9. Enhanced your self-understanding		.570	
10. Taken an interest in your personal welfare		.602	
Student-centered pedagogical practices (α = .787)			
11. Student evaluations of their own work			.629
12. Student evaluations of each other's work			.611
13. Reflective writing/journaling			.526
14. Portfolios			.508
15. Student-selected topics for course content			.459
16. Cooperative learning (small groups)			.560
17. Group projects			.578
18. Class discussions			.459
19. Community service as part of coursework			.330

Note: Items 1–10 were measured on a 3-point scale: 1 = "Not At All"; 2 = "Occasionally"; 3 = "Frequently". Items 11–19 were measured on a 4-point scale: 1 = "None"; 2 = "Some"; 3 = "Most"; 4 = "All".

More specifically, the second stage included student-level variables such as gender, ethnicity, religiousness, and their ethic of care score upon entry to the institution. In the third stage, school-level variables—institutional religious types—were included and potential interaction effects were explored. The last stage involved adding student–faculty interaction variables and examining their specific contribution to the development of students' ethic of care above and beyond the variables already in the model. The interaction effects between student–faculty interactions and institution types were also examined in this last stage.

In the model building process, each stage was examined as a separate part consisting of several steps. First, all variables within each stage were entered together. Then, those that were not statistically significant were removed one by one and the model was rerun after each removal. After that, the relationships between student-level predictors and the ethic of care were examined across institutions. If no significant variations in student-level slopes appeared across institutions, the student-level slopes were fixed. Otherwise, student-level slopes were set to vary across institutions. Interaction effects were also examined. This model building process was cumulative because only the variables included in the final model at the end of each stage were considered in the following stage.

It should be noted that nine institutions had fewer than 20 students who participated in the surveys. To obtain reliable estimates at the school level, these institutions were removed. Moreover, the school-level variable of interest— institutional religious type—had no missing value, which satisfies the requirement in HLM of having complete data at the second level. At the student level, the listwise deletion method was used for students who had incomplete responses on the items used to create the ethic of care variable and student–faculty interaction variable because those variables were the primary focus of the study. For most other independent variables of interest, the percentages of missing values were minimal (i.e., less than 5 percent). Single stochastic regression imputation was used to impute these missing values. Moreover, the weighting variable was used throughout the analysis to ensure the representativeness of the respondents.

Findings

Descriptive Findings

As mentioned earlier in this chapter, a continuous measure of ethic of care was created for both the 2004 and 2007 surveys by adding the values of the individual items. This resulted in a scale ranging from a low of 11 to a high of 43. Over the course of the three years between surveys, the mean ethic of care score increased from 23.9 (S.D. = 5.87) to 26.2 (S.D. = 6.26). A paired sample t-test showed a statistically significant difference between the two survey administrations ($t(11,291) = 41.05$, $p < .001$).

Table 9.3 shows students' scores on the ethic of care measure upon entry in 2004 and after three years in 2007, and the change in score between 2004 and 2007, by gender and ethnic/racial categories. Among the students who completed all ethic of care and student–faculty interaction items on the two surveys, 55.4 percent were female and 44.6 percent were male. In general, women scored significantly higher than men on ethic of care, both upon entry into college and after three years (2004: $t(10,384) = 18.70$, $p < .001$; 2007: $t(10,211) = 15.13$, $p < .001$). Men, however, experienced a significantly greater increase in ethic of care ($t(10,403) = -2.391$,

TABLE 9.3 Descriptive analysis of the ethic of care by gender and ethnicity

	N	Ethic of care in 2004		Ethic of care in 2007		Ethic of care increase	
		Mean	S.D.	Mean	S.D.	Mean	S.D.
Male	5032	22.77	6.03	25.18	6.57	2.41	6.09
Female	6260	24.83	5.57	26.98	5.89	2.14	5.65
Caucasian	8484	23.40	5.65	25.79	6.16	2.39	5.71
African American	513	25.88	6.62	28.31	6.16	2.43	6.73
Asian American	838	25.54	5.87	27.19	6.20	1.65	5.94
Latino	467	26.27	6.88	28.10	6.86	1.83	6.43
Other race	990	24.80	5.96	26.59	6.45	1.79	6.20

$p = .017$). Men as a group also varied more than women with respect to their level of care.

A large majority (75.1 percent) of the students identified as Caucasian; 7.4 percent as Asian American; 4.5 percent as African American; and 4.1 percent as Latino. All ethnic/racial groups scored higher in 2007 on ethic of care than they did in 2004. On average, Latino students scored highest in 2004 but second highest in 2007. African American students ranked second highest in 2004 and highest three years later, with the greatest increase in ethic of care of all ethnic/racial groups. Caucasian students, the largest of the ethnic/racial groups, scored lowest on average in both 2004 and 2007. Finally, the ethic of care increased least among Asian American students.

One-way ANOVAs showed a consistent statistical difference across ethnic/racial groups on the ethic of care measure in 2004 ($F(4, 11,286) = 73.04, p < .001$); 2007 ($F(4, 11,286) = 41.09, p < .001$), and in the changes between 2004 and 2007 ($F(4, 11,286) = 5.67, p < .001$). Further post-hoc analyses showed several significant pair-wise differences. On ethic of care in 2004, Caucasian students scored significantly lower than all other groups. On ethic of care in 2007, Caucasian students continued to score significantly lower than all the other four groups. In addition, Asian American students scored significantly lower than African American students. For the change in scores between the two years, only two pairs of ethnic/racial groups scored significantly differently—Caucasian students exhibited a significantly larger increase on ethic of care than Asian American students and students in the "other race" category (i.e., American Indians, multiracial students, and those who did not report their ethnic/racial status).

Many students reported that professors had engaged them in conversations about spiritual and religious matters occasionally or frequently during their three years of undergraduate education: 81.9 percent said professors encouraged the discussion of ethical issues; 72.6 percent said professors encouraged them to explore questions of

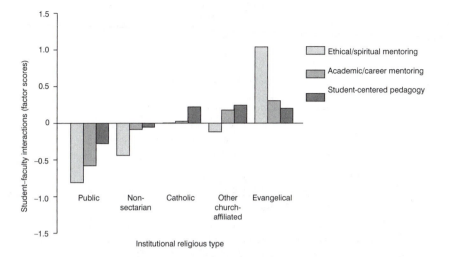

FIGURE 9.1   Student–faculty interactions by institutional religious type

purpose and meaning; 41.2 percent were encouraged to discuss religious/spiritual matters; 36.4 percent reported that professors encouraged their personal expression of spirituality; and 33.5 percent said they had discussed religions/spirituality with professors. Finally, 28.8 percent of students said that professors had acted as spiritual role models for them. Conversations about academics and careers were even more common: 77.0 percent of students reported that professors encouraged them to pursue post-graduate study, and 76.3 percent said that professors assisted them in making career decisions. Large majorities also reported that faculty took an interest in their personal welfare (75.7 percent) and enhanced their self-understanding (71.6 percent).[5]

The number of students who reported experience with student-centered pedagogies was considerable but limited. A full 76.4 percent had regular class discussions; 50.0 percent reported taking courses using small group cooperative learning; and 42.9 percent reported doing group projects. Much smaller percentages of students reported taking courses with professors who employed reflective writing/journaling (12.9 percent), portfolios (8.0 percent), or service learning (4.1 percent).

Moreover, student–faculty interactions varied across different institutions. Figure 9.1 is a visual representation of the relationship between three types of student–faculty interactions (i.e., ethical/spiritual mentoring, academic/career mentoring, experience with student-centered pedagogies) and institutional religious affiliation. The figure highlights the different levels of student self-perceived interactions with faculty members across different school types. Students attending public institutions reported the least amount of student–faculty interactions overall. They also reported an especially low level of ethical/spiritual mentoring compared with students from other types of institutions. Conversely, students from evangelical institutions had the highest level of mentoring interactions with their faculty members.

Hierarchical Linear Model (HLM) Analysis

The unconditional hierarchical linear model constructed at the first stage separated the total variability in the measure of ethic of care into two variance components: the variance among students within institutions and the variance among institutions. Thus, the intra-class correlation coefficient (ICC) was calculated using the following formula:

$$ICC = \frac{\tau}{\tau + \sigma^2} = \frac{0.05491}{0.05491 + 0.84680} = 0.06$$

ICC represents the degree of independence among the students in different institutions. At the end of stage one, 6 percent of the total variance in ethic of care was explained between schools, which supports the use of multilevel models in this study to explore the relationship between ethic of care and student–faculty interactions. Once the total variance in the ethic of care was partitioned, student and school characteristics were added in the subsequent HLM stages to explain the available variance.

In stage two, several student background characteristics were added into the model. Three of them were found to be statistically significant: students' ethic of care in 2004, gender, and the degree of student religiousness. The pre-measure of students' ethic of care in 2004 and their self-reported religiousness were positively associated with the post-measure of ethic of care in 2007. In other words, for every one standard deviation increase in the ethic of care score in 2004, the 2007 score increased by over half of a standard deviation after controlling for students' gender and religiousness $(0.51, t(11,795) = 30.62, p < .001)$. Similarly, the more students self-reported being religious upon entry into college, the higher their ethic of care scores tended to be at the end of their junior year, after controlling for students' gender and the pre-measure of ethic of care $(0.05, t(11,795) = 4.07, p < .001)$. On average, female students scored higher than males after controlling for all other variables in the model $(0.08, t(11,795) = 3.35, p = .001)$. At the end of stage two, these student level variables explained 28.9 percent of the total variance.

Because significant variation remained in the student-level intercept across institutions, institutional religious type was added at the institutional-level in stage three. Results showed that the three student-level predictors remained statistically significant (see Stage 3 in Table 9.4). Moreover, institutional religious type was associated with students' ethic of care. Students from Catholic, Evangelical, and other church-affiliated institutions scored significantly higher than those from public institutions after controlling for all other variables in the model (Catholic: $0.13, t(120) = 2.12, p = .042$; Evangelical: $0.17, t(120) = 2.50, p = .014$; other

TABLE 9.4 HLM analyses: predicting students' development of ethic of care (Stage 3/Stage 4)

Variable	Stage 3 Coefficient (s.e.)	p-value	Stage 4 Coefficient (s.e.)	p-value
Intercept	–0.05(0.06)	.397	0.19(0.04)	**<.001**
Level 1 *Student background*				
Ethic of care (2004)	0.50(0.02)	**<.001**	0.45(0.01)	**<.001**
Female	0.08(0.02)	**<.001**	0.07(0.02)	**.005**
Religiousness (standardized)	0.05(0.02)	**.001**	0.02(0.01)	**.014**
Student–faculty interactions				
Ethical/spiritual mentoring			0.24(0.04)	**<.001**
Academic/career mentoring			0.07(0.03)	**.011**
Student-centered pedagogy			0.06(0.02)	**.001**
Level 2 *Institutional religious type*				
Public (reference group)				
Nonsectarian	0.07(0.06)	.257	–0.06(0.04)	.134
Catholic	0.13(0.06)	**.036**	–0.11(0.05)	**.020**
Other church-affiliated	0.12(0.06)	**.042**	–0.13(0.04)	**.006**
Evangelical	0.17(0.07)	**.014**	–0.32(0.06)	**<.001**
Random components				
Within schools	0.622		0.571	
Between schools	0.011		0.006	
Total residual	0.633		0.577	
Total variance explained	29.8%		36.0%	

Note: p-values smaller than .05 are bolded.

church-affiliated: 0.12, $t(120) = 2.05$, $p = .042$). The addition of institutional religious type variables, however, only helped to explain an additional 1 percent of the total variance, bringing the total variance explained to 29.8 percent. At the end of stage three, significant variation remained in the student-level slope associated with the pre-measure of ethic of care. Therefore, this slope was set to vary across institutions. However, no interaction was found between the pre-measure of ethic of care and institutional religious type.

In the fourth stage, three student–faculty interaction variables were added to the analysis, which allowed us to examine the unique contribution of student–faculty interactions on students' development on the ethic of care. Results showed that all three student–faculty interaction variables were significantly and positively associated with students' development on ethic of care (see Stage 4 in Table 9.4). In other words, the more students reported experiencing ethical/spiritual mentoring, academic/career mentoring, and student-centered pedagogy during college, the greater their growth in ethic of care measured three years after they entered college. It is worth noting that the association between ethical/spiritual mentoring and the development on an ethic of care was especially strong (0.24, $t(11,788) = 6.61$, $p < .001$). For every one standard deviation increase in ethical/spiritual mentoring, students' ethic of care score in 2007 increased by 0.24 standard deviations after controlling for all other variables in the model. For academic/career mentoring and student-centered pedagogy, the increases were 0.07 standard deviations $(0.07, t(11,788) = 2.57, p = .011)$ and 0.06 standard deviations $(0.06, t(11,788) = 3.62, p = .001)$, respectively. In terms of variance components, student–faculty interaction variables explained an additional 6.2 percent of the total variance, with 36 percent of the total variance in ethic of care explained at the end of the four-stage HLM analysis. In the end, some interaction effects were found in the relationship between ethic of care and ethical/spiritual mentoring across institutions with different religious types. A stronger association was found between the ethic of care and ethical/spiritual mentoring among public institutions than other types of institutions. Therefore, the ethic of care would be more likely to develop in students at public institutions as compared with the other types given the same level of ethical/spiritual mentoring from student–faculty interactions. But again, these interaction effects explained less than 1 percent of the total variance in the ethic of care measure.

To explore the impact of student–faculty interaction on the development of an ethic of care in undergraduate students, hierarchical linear models were run in four stages. The results from the regression models largely support the hypotheses. After accounting for the effects of students' backgrounds, their ethic of care score upon entry to the institution, and institutional religious type, student–faculty interactions still accounted for a statistically significant amount of total variance in students' development of an ethic of care. In other words, students who had more mentoring interactions with faculty and more experiences with student-centered pedagogical practices placed a higher value on the caring self, as measured by the ethic of care scale. Moreover, one particular type of student–faculty interaction—mentoring on ethical/spiritual issues—has the strongest association with the development of an ethic of care. Among student background variables, the pre-measure of the ethic of care, gender, and religiousness are also significant predictors of ethic of care three years after college entry.

Reflections

In summary, student–faculty interaction promotes not just cognitive development, persistence, educational aspirations, and degree completion, but also the development of the caring self. Further research would be required to ascertain whether field of study matters; faculty members who teach certain subjects may be more inclined to adopt student-centered pedagogical strategies and mentor students, particularly on ethical/spiritual issues, than faculty who teach in other subjects. Faculty (whether they define themselves as spiritual people or not) who *care* if their students grow in their ability to care deeply for and about others can promote the development of caring selves by *choosing* to engage their students in mentoring conversations (especially about spiritual and religious questions and issues), adopting instructional and evaluative strategies that increase student–faculty interaction, modeling caring for students, and providing opportunities for students to practice caring for others.

College students are deeply concerned with spiritual questions—questions about who we are, why we are, and how we should live together. These questions about the purpose and meaning of human existence also lie at the heart of a liberal arts education. Helping students understand how people have answered these questions in the past and supporting them in their search for their own answers seems like a fundamental task of educators. Serious conversations about how we should live, especially in relation to others and in a variety of campus settings, are a vital part of preparing students for ethical lives of civic engagement.

Given the unique role public universities play in American society and the importance that the ethic of care has in the democratic model, it would seem prudent for public universities to consider the strong correlation between faculty mentoring and the growth of students' ability to care. While direct insistence on certain types of mentoring—such as ethical/spiritual conversations—may not easily fit with the mission of all institutions, finding ways to encourage mentoring, even at large public institutions, could provide a great social benefit.

Notes

1 Both "ethic of care" and "ethic of caring" are used in the literature, the former being somewhat more common. We employ "ethic of care" except when quoting others or referring specifically to the 8-item "ethic of caring" measure developed by Astin, Astin, & Lindholm (2011).

2 On the ethic of care, citizenship, and democratic politics, see also Porter (2006), Sevenhuijsen (1998), and Robinson (1999).

3 See also Terenzini, Pascarella, & Bliming (1996); Kuh (1995); Kuh & Hu (2001); Kuh, Douglas, Lund, & Ramin-Gyurnek (1994); McCabe, Treviño, & Butterfield (2002).

4 Robertson (1999), for example, writes that student-centered pedagogies entail caring relationships between teachers and learners.

5 Percentages refer to students who responded occasionally or frequently to the mentoring items.

References

Astin, A. W. (1993). *What matters in college? Four critical years revisited.* San Francisco: Jossey-Bass.

Astin, A. W., Astin, H. S., & Lindholm, J. A. (2011). Assessing students' spiritual and religious qualities. *Journal of College Student Development, 52*(1), 39–61.

Bandura, A. (1977). *Social Learning Theory* (2nd edn). Englewood Cliffs, NJ: Prentice Hall.

Bergman, R. (2004). Caring for the ethical ideal: Nel Noddings on moral education. *Journal of Moral Education, 33*(2), 149–162.

Chickering, A. W., & Reisser, L. (1993). *Education and identity* (2nd edn). San Francisco: Jossey-Bass.

Gibbs, J. C. (2003). *Moral development and reality: Beyond the theories of Hoffman and Kohlberg.* Thousand Oaks, CA: Sage.

Gilligan, C. (1982). *In a different voice: Psychological theory and women's development.* Cambridge: Harvard University Press.

Gorsuch, R. L. (1983). *Factor Analysis* (2nd edn). Hillsdale, NJ: Erlbaum.

Henson, K. T. (2003). Foundations for learner-centered education: A knowledge base. *Education, 124*(1), 5–15.

Hoffman, M. L. (2000). *Empathy and moral development: Implications for caring and justice.* Cambridge, UK: Cambridge University Press.

Keen, C., & Hall. K. (2009). Engaging with difference matters: Longitudinal student outcomes of co-curricular service-learning programs. *Journal of Higher Education, 80*(1), 59–79.

King, P. M., & Kitchener, K. (1994). *Developing reflective judgment: Understanding and promoting intellectual growth and critical thinking in adolescents and adults.* San Francisco: Jossey-Bass.

Kohlberg, L. (1984). *The psychology of moral development.* San Francisco: Harper & Row.

Kuh, G. D. (1995). The other curriculum: Out-of-class experiences associated with student learning and personal development. *Journal of Higher Education, 66*(2), 123–155.

Kuh, G. D., & Hu, S. (2001). The effects of student–faculty interaction in the 1990s. *Review of Higher Education, 24*(3), 309–332.

Kuh, G. D., Douglas, K. B., Lund, J. P., & Ramin-Gyurnek, J. (1994). *Student learning outside of the classroom: Transcending artificial boundaries.* ASHE-ERIC Higher Education Report No. 8. Washington, DC: George Washington University, School of Education and Human Development.

Lindholm, J. A., & Astin, H. S. (2008). Spirituality and pedagogy: Faculty's spirituality and use of student-centered approaches to undergraduate education. *Review of Higher Education, 31*(2), 185–207.

Lindholm, J. A., Astin, H. S., & Astin, A. W. (2005). *Spirituality and the professoriate.* Los Angeles: Higher Education Research Institute, UCLA.

McCabe, D. L., Treviño, L. K., & Butterfield, K. D. (2002). Honor codes and other contextual influences on academic integrity. *Research in Higher Education, 43*(3), 357–378.

MacIntyre, A. (2009). *God, philosophy, universities: A selective history of the catholic philosophical tradition.* Lanham, MD: Rowman & Littlefield.

Noddings, N. (1984). *Caring: A feminine approach to ethics and moral education.* Berkeley: University of California Press.

Noddings, N. (2002). *Educating moral people: A caring alternative to character education.* New York: Teachers College Press.

Pascarella, E. T., & Terenzini, P. T. (1991). *How college affects students: Findings and insights from twenty years of research.* San Francisco, CA: Jossey-Bass.

Pascarella, E. T., & Terenzini, P. T. (2005). *How college affects students: A third decade of research* (Vol. 2). San Francisco, CA: Jossey-Bass.

Perry, W. G., Jr. (1999). *Forms of ethical and intellectual development in the college years: A scheme* (2nd edn). San Francisco: Jossey-Bass.

Porter, E. (2006). Can politics practice compassion? *Hypatia: A Journal of Feminist Philosophy, 21*(4), 97–123.

Raudenbush, S. W., & Bryk, A. S. (2002). *Hierarchical linear models: Applications and data analysis methods* (2nd edn). Thousand Oaks, CA: Sage.

Rhoads, R. A. (2000). Democratic citizenship and service learning: Advancing the caring self. *New Directions for Teaching and Learning, 82,* 37–44.

Robertson, D. L. (1999). Professors' perspectives on their teaching: A new construct and developmental model. *Innovative Higher Education, 23*(4), 271–294.

Robinson, F. (1999). *Globalizing care: Ethics, feminist theory, and international relations.* Boulder: Westview Press.

Saltmarsh, J. (1997). Ethics, reflection, purpose, and compassion: Community service-learning. *New Directions for Student Services, 77,* 81–93.

Sevenhuijsen, S. (1998). *Citizenship and the ethic of care.* London: Routledge.

Sieber, J. E. (1980). A social learning theory applied to morality. In M. Windmiller, N. M. Lambert, & E. Turiel (Eds), *Moral development and socialization* (pp. 129–159). Boston: Allyn and Bacon.

Swaner, L. E. (2004). *Educating for personal and social responsibility: A planning project of the Association of American Colleges and Universities—Review of the literature.* Retrieved November 30, 2009, from http://www.aacu.org/core_commitments/documents/review_of_lit.pdf

Terenzini, P. T., Pascarella, E. T., & Bliming, G. S. (1996). Students' out-of-class experiences and their influence on learning and cognitive development: A literature review. *Journal of College Student Development, 37*(2), 149–162.

Tronto, J. (1993). *Moral boundaries: A political argument for an ethic of care.* New York: Routledge.

10

INFORMING EFFECTIVE PSYCHOSPIRITUAL INTERVENTIONS FOR COLLEGE STUDENTS

Identifying Mediators in the Relationship between Spiritual Struggles and Substance Use

Carol Ann Faigin

The positive effects of religious and spiritual beliefs and practices have been well documented (Koenig, McCullough, & Larson, 2001). However, when faced with turmoil in life, these beliefs can be threatened or abandoned, effectively destabilizing one's core spirituality, leading to feelings of doubt, confusion, and spiritual disorientation (Exline & Rose, 2005; Pargament, Murray-Swank, Magyar, & Ano, 2005; Pargament, 2007). This process, described as a spiritual struggle, can challenge one's ability to navigate stressors and cope effectively with change; this may be especially difficult for college students who are already undergoing multiple life transformations.

Researchers have identified three types of religious and spiritual struggles: interpersonal, intrapersonal, and divine (Exline, 2002; Pargament, Murray-Swank, Magyar, & Ano, 2005). Interpersonal spiritual struggles refer to spiritual conflicts with friends, family, communities, and/or religious congregations. In contrast, intrapersonal spiritual struggles are marked by personal doubts and questions regarding one's spirituality, faith tradition, or life purpose, or involve conflicts within oneself about morals, beliefs, and practices. Lastly, divine spiritual struggles are expressions of conflict, questions, and tension in relationship to God, such as feeling abandoned by or angry with the divine or questioning if a benevolent higher power exists.

As a psychologist, I am interested in how humans integrate religious and spiritual beliefs in ways that promote health, wellness, increased meaning, and resilience. However, in order to understand the benefits of this critical domain, it is equally essential to explore times when beliefs are in tension or flux. Through working with mentors in life, I began to see the plethora of ways we as humans cope with feeling separated from a higher power, other spiritual supports, or experiences we hold sacred. During such times, many people tend to seek out sources of solace in an attempt to escape the pain or to replace that which they hold sacred. Clinically, I have watched clients wrestle with spiritual struggles, oftentimes to such an extent that a new problem, such as alcohol or other drug abuse, sex addiction, gambling, or self-harm addiction, became the focus of our work together. These behaviors leave in their wake even more sadness and destruction. Therefore, in concert with our clients, we often encourage *sitting with* and *working through* pain to transform it rather than move around it. Although easier said than done, I have witnessed courageous clients employ this transformative approach and have been moved by its power. This has fueled my interest in not only finding ways to better support my clients when grappling with spiritual questioning, but also as a scientist, it has inspired me to investigate whether the data support my personal and professional observations.

Therefore, as researcher I set out to examine the relationship between spiritual struggles and addictive behavior. For my graduate thesis, we found that struggling with one's spiritual and religious beliefs, relationships, and practices was a statistically significant predictor of increased addictive behavior across multiple domains (Faigin & Pargament, 2008). Of course, as with many endeavors, answers usually lead to more questions; subsequently, I became interested in understanding more about *the nature* of the relationship between spiritual struggles and addiction. I wanted to know what dimensions of spirituality contributed to this relationship. The focus of the present study was to investigate possible mediators that could enhance our understanding of the relationship between spiritual struggles and substance abuse, with the hope of gleaning critical information that will guide future clinical interventions to help college students through this pivotal and transformative time.

Spiritual Struggles During College

Although college provides an important and exciting opportunity for personal self-discovery and meaning-making (Chickering & Reisser, 1993; Lindholm, 2006), researchers have found that many students also experience spiritual, religious, and existential tension. In fact, studies have revealed that approximately one-half of students experience spiritual struggles, a normal yet potentially tumultuous component of spiritual development, during college (Astin, Astin, Lindholm, Bryant, Szelényi, & Calderone, 2005; Desai, 2006; Johnson, Sheets, & Kristeller, 2006). It is critical to note that spiritual struggles do not imply religious disengagement, weak faith, low religious maturity, or pathology (Pargament, 2007). Most people experience tension, questioning, or challenges regarding their values and beliefs, which can be a sign of deep engagement and devotion to these beliefs. However, research in adult populations has connected religious and spiritual struggles to psychological distress (feeling depressed, overwhelmed, anxious, stressed), lower self-esteem, less perceived spiritual and religious growth, poorer physical health (Bryant & Astin, 2008), severe levels of psychopathological symptoms (McConnell, Pargament, Ellison, & Flannelly, 2006), panic disorder (Trenholm, Trent, & Compton, 1998), increased suicidality (Exline, Yali, & Sanderson, 2000), and even increased mortality in medically ill elderly patients (Pargament, Koenig, Tarakeshwar, & Hahn, 2004). Ano and Vasconcelles (2005) further corroborated these findings in a meta-analysis of 49 studies on spiritual struggles; they concluded that spiritual struggles are related to poorer psychological adjustment, such as increased self-reported anxiety, depression, and distress.

College-aged youth may be particularly affected by the negative impact of spiritual struggles due to the volatility that often accompanies exploration of beliefs, practices, and values during this time. Research focusing specifically on the college years has identified many deleterious outcomes of spiritual struggles, including lower self-esteem, increased negative mood, anxiety, and depression (Bryant & Astin, 2008; Exline *et al.*, 2000; Pargament, Smith, Koenig, & Perez, 1998). Although there is evidence to suggest that spiritual struggles can lead to spiritual growth (Cole, Hopkins, Tisak, Steel, & Carr, 2008; Hill & Pargament, 2008; Pargament, Desai, & McConnell, 2006), the correlation between spiritual struggles and negative outcomes is consistently strong and underscores the importance of continued empirical exploration, particularly in college settings.

Substance Use in College Students

Students may be particularly prone to utilize substances during college years as a method of coping with the challenges of spiritual development. This appears to be reflected in the literature. According to the U.S. Department of Health and Human Services, college-aged youth have the highest rate of substance use (including tobacco, alcohol, and illicit drugs) across all age ranges (U.S. Department of Health and Human Services, 2007). The long-term health consequences of tobacco use are well-documented and include cardiovascular disease, lung cancer, and psychological distress (U.S. Department of Health and Human Services, 2006). The consequences of college drinking are similarly destructive and include unsafe sex and increased risk of injury and death (Hingson *et al.*, 2002), to name a few. The high level of substance use in college is influenced by many factors (see Marsh & Dale, 2005); however, spiritual tension experienced in the young adult stage of life may be one of the factors.

Although a newly emerging topic, some researchers have begun to explore the intersection of spiritual struggles and substance use in college. Specifically, data have revealed that during college, students who experience spiritual struggles are more likely than non-struggling students to drink alcohol (Johnson *et al.*, 2006;

Lindholm, 2006), use tobacco (Faigin & Pargament, 2008; Lindholm, 2006), and engage in other forms of addictive behavior, including prescription and recreational drug use, food starving, gambling, sex, exercise, work, caffeine use, and shopping (Faigin & Pargament, 2008). Due to the turmoil and crises that often accompany the college years, students may be particularly vulnerable to the dual challenge of spiritual struggle and substance use. However, there is a paucity of research in this area; therefore, the current study examined mediation models that utilize rich measures of spirituality and religiousness to better understand the interaction between spiritual struggles and substance use in a college sample.

Theoretical Framework

Spiritual beliefs and values are often sources of coherence for people (Emmons, 1999). Therefore, individuals who struggle with spiritual questions may experience a void within the most central part of their lives. In response to this void, or spiritual vacuum, individuals may seek out a new form of meaning or significance, including potentially destructive habits, such as substance use. Substance use may serve as an attempt to fill the void created by spiritual struggles by helping a person escape from "mental anguish and suffering" (Gorsuch & Butler, 1976, p. 129). Alternatively, for people with an integrated and strong spiritual/religious framework, belief in a higher power or connection with the sacred can become an organizing force, one that guides and steers them in constructive directions (Emmons, 2005; Pargament, 1997). Other sources of meaning and significance may be seen as unnecessary or inferior to what is understood as sacred; therefore, these individuals may rely less on other methods of coping such as substance use.

Some theorists (e.g., Allport, 1950) have proposed that mature spirituality is a deep, dynamic, and intricate process. Pargament (2007) further expanded these ideas by introducing the notion of well-integrated versus disintegrated spiritual/ religious orienting systems. He stressed that one's ability to effectively draw upon spiritual/religious resources during times of struggle is not determined by ascribing to a particular religious institution, practicing specific spiritual and religious rituals, or espousing a particular set of religious/spiritual beliefs. Rather, Pargament asserts, growth following spiritual struggles is contingent upon how *integrated* one's beliefs and practices are with the context and surrounding community as well as the breadth, depth, continuity, and flexibility of one's spiritual framework. A person with a well-integrated spirituality theoretically will be able to tap into his or her beliefs, regardless of the nature of a crisis, to derive meaning, stabilization, and effective coping. Conversely, an individual with a disintegrated spirituality will likely utilize spiritual pathways that "lack scope and depth, fail to meet the challenges and demands of life events, clash and collide with the surrounding social system, change and shift too easily or not at all, and misdirect the individual in the pursuit of spiritual value" (Pargament, 2007,

p. 136). Therefore, when faced with stress, an individual with a disintegrated spirituality may fail to draw upon his or her beliefs in a way that alleviates an internal crisis, or may experience additional angst from the collision of personal beliefs with the larger societal context, thus leading to further isolation and destabilization.

Drawing upon this theory for the present study, spiritual strugglers who endorse items consistent with a well-integrated spirituality may be able to effectively adjust to challenges and thus be at less risk for substance use as a means of coping. In contrast, those who have a disintegrated spirituality may be at greater risk of substance use due to not having an effective system for coping and stabilization.

Research Questions and Hypotheses

The current study was distinctive in three respects. First, it utilized data from the largest longitudinal study of college student spirituality in the U.S. Second, research in the field of substance use and spirituality has been criticized for using general measures of religiousness, such as religious affiliation or practices (Booth & Martin, 1998; Gorsuch, 1995; Miller, 1998); this study assuaged these concerns by using comprehensive measures of spirituality. Lastly, the current research design investigated spiritual struggles as a *risk factor* for substance use and explored the possible mediators of this relationship. To date, most studies conceptualize spirituality as a protective factor rather than a potential risk factor in relation to substance use.

The hypotheses were as follows. Hypothesis 1: Higher levels of spiritual struggles at Time 1 (first year) would be associated with higher levels of substance use at Time 2 (junior year). Hypothesis 2: Higher levels of spiritual struggle at Time 1 would be associated with higher levels of substance use at Time 2 after controlling for Time 1 substance use, demographic items, and other control indices. Hypothesis 3: The effects of spiritual struggles on substance use would be partially mediated through various spiritual and psychological constructs measured in this study (e.g., Spiritual Quest, Equanimity, etc.) after controlling for demographic items and other control indices. It is important to note that Time 1 measures of spiritual struggles and mediator scales were used rather than Time 2 measures as they more accurately capture experiences at entry to college.

The primary motivation behind this research was to contribute to a better understanding of the underlying nature of the relationship between spiritual struggles and substance use, an understudied yet pivotal phenomenon for college students. The overall aim was to inform the development of targeted interventions to help college students cope with spiritual struggles in an adaptive way, potentially decreasing the propensity towards substance use. Thus, the findings could contribute to a more holistic approach to enhancing the well-being of college students.

Methods

Participants and Procedure

The current project utilized data collected by the Higher Education Research Institute (HERI) as part of the UCLA Spirituality in Higher Education project. The sample included students who completed both the first-year survey (Time 1) in 2004 and the junior survey (Time 2) in 2007 for a total of 14,527 participants. The larger study was described in detail in Chapter 2; however, I will now provide details specific to the current analysis.

Measures

Spiritual struggle, the primary independent variable, was assessed using the Religious Struggle scale developed by Astin, Astin, and Lindholm (2011). This scale measures intrapsychic, interpersonal, and divine spiritual struggles on a three-point Likert scale (1 = "not at all"; 2 = "to some extent" or "occasionally"; 3 = "to a great extent" or "frequently").

Substance use, the dependent variable, was assessed through students' responses to questions regarding the frequency with which they drank beer, wine, or liquor, or smoked cigarettes in the past year. Response options were: 0 = "not at all"; 1 = "occasionally"; and 2 = "frequently" for each of the three items (beer, wine/liquor, cigarettes). Individuals who indicated 1 or 2 on either alcohol use items or the tobacco question were categorized as positive for that item of substance use; students who indicated they did not use these substances were categorized as abstainers on the given item. To better assess these variables and create clearer groupings for analysis purposes, a single "alcohol use" variable was created by collapsing the two alcohol-related items (consumption of beer and wine/liquor), while the tobacco item remained unchanged as a freestanding variable. In addition, all substance use items (tobacco, beer, and wine/liquor) were collapsed to create one composite score for "substance use."

The following scales from the HERI dataset were included as possible mediators of the relationship between spiritual struggles and substance use, all with adequate reliability in both the 2004 and 2007 samples: Spiritual Identification, Spiritual Quest, Equanimity, Religious/Social Conservatism, Religious Skepticism, Charitable Involvement, Ethic of Caring, Ecumenical Worldview, Compassionate Self-Concept, Personal God, All Powerful God, and Mystical God (Astin *et al.*, 2011). Although measures in this study were not designed specifically to overlay upon the concept of spiritual/religious orienting systems, some of the measures share roughly similar theoretical characteristics of a well-integrated versus disintegrated spirituality. Specifically, items that reflect the concept of spiritual integration are consistent with the following scales: Spiritual Identification, Spiritual Quest,

Equanimity, Ecumenical Worldview, Compassionate Self-Concept, Personal God, and Mystical God. Similarly, potential problems with disintegration (e.g., conflict between spiritual beliefs and societal beliefs, firm and absolute opinions regarding the nature of spiritual/religious topics) are reflected on the following scales: Religious/Social Conservatism, Religious Skepticism, and All Powerful God. Some of the measures used in this study (Charitable Involvement and Ethic of Caring) reflect behavioral engagement and do not necessarily fit into one of the dichotomous categories outlined above; however, they were included in this exploratory study.

Previous research utilizing the HERI dataset identified significant correlates with spiritual struggles (Bryant & Astin, 2008). Informed by this research, the control variables in the present study included religious preference, gender, attendance at church-affiliated institutions, college major, discussing politics, religious conversion, and discussing religion/spirituality with friends.

Analysis

First, a descriptive analysis (means, standard deviations) of all items was performed for the full sample. To test Hypothesis 1, a multiple regression was conducted in which substance use at Time 1 was entered into the first block of the analysis as a predictor of Time 2 substance use behavior. Religious Struggles were then entered into the second block and the change in R^2 was examined for significance. To test whether spiritual struggles predict an increase in substance use above and beyond the effects of demographic, religious, and other control variables (Hypothesis 2), a second regression analysis was conducted. Once again, substance use at Time 1 was entered into the first block of the analysis, control variables were entered in the second block, and Religious Struggles were entered into the equation in the final block.

Lastly, to test Hypothesis 3 (identify mediators in the relationship between spiritual struggles and substance use), the mediation method suggested by Baron and Kenny (1986) was employed using the 12 spiritual/religious scales. According to the Baron and Kenny method, each potential mediator (e.g., Ecumenical Worldview) should correlate significantly with both the independent variable (i.e., Religious Struggle) and the dependent variable (i.e., Substance Use). To test for mediation, three separate regression equations were estimated. In Equation 1, the potential mediator (e.g., Ecumenical Worldview) was regressed on Religious Struggle; in Equation 2, Substance Use was regressed on Religious Struggle; and in Equation 3, Substance Use was regressed on both the potential mediator (e.g., Ecumenical Worldview) and Religious Struggle. Mediation was confirmed if the effect of Religious Struggle on Substance Use was less in Equation 3 than in Equation 2. Finally, as Baron and Kenny (1986) suggest, a Sobel test (1982) was used to assess whether the indirect effect of Religious Struggle on the Substance Use via the mediator (e.g., Ecumenical Worldview) was statistically significant.

Findings

As hypothesized, results indicated that Religious Struggle at Time 1 predicted an increase in Tobacco Use (β = .011, p < .000) at Time 2, Alcohol Use (β = .017, p < .000) at Time 2, as well as Overall Substance Use (β = .027, p < .000) at Time 2. According to these findings, students who endorsed spiritual struggles as they entered college subsequently reported increased substance use in their junior year.

However, in order to determine if higher levels of tobacco and alcohol use was a reflection of spiritual struggles at Time 1 (Hypothesis 2), a second regression analysis was conducted thereby accounting for potential confounding variables, including religious preference, gender, attendance at church-affiliated institutions, college major, discussing politics, religious conversion, and discussing religion/spirituality with friends. Findings demonstrated that Religious Struggle at Time 1 predicted an increase in Tobacco Use (β = .063, p < .000), Alcohol Use (β = .042, p < .000), and Overall Substance Use (β = .054, p < .000) at Time 2 even after controlling for potential confounding variables of spiritual struggles (see Tables 10.1–10.3). These results provided further support for the second hypothesis, which suggested that students who endorsed spiritual struggles at freshman year also reported substance use during junior year despite their gender, religious preference, college major, or other religious and spiritual behavior.

TABLE 10.1 Summary of multiple regression analysis for spiritual struggles at Time 1 predicting tobacco use at Time 2

Variable	Model 1			Model 2		
	B	SE B	β	B	SE B	β
Tobacco use Time 1	0.68***	0.01***	.61***	0.67***	0.01***	.61***
Religious preference	−0.02**	0.01***	−.03**	−0.03**	0.01***	−.03**
Gender	−0.04***	0.01***	−.03***	−0.04***	0.01***	−.03***
Attendance at church institution	−0.00	0.01***	−.00	−0.01	0.01***	.00
College major	−0.00***	0.00***	−.03***	−0.00***	0.00***	−.03***
Discussing politics	0.01	0.01***	.01	0.01	0.01***	.01
Religious conversion	0.06*	0.03***	.02*	0.05**	0.03***	.01**
Discussing religion/ spirituality with friends	−0.01	0.01***	−.01	−0.02**	0.01***	−.02**
Spiritual struggles Time 1				0.01***	0.00***	.06***
R^2		0.38***			0.38***	
F for change in R^2		0.38***			0.00***	

*p ≤ 0.05; **p ≤ 0.01; *** p ≤ 0.001

TABLE 10.2 Summary of multiple regression analysis for spiritual struggles at Time 1 predicting alcohol use at Time 2

Variable	Model 1			Model 2		
	B	SE B	β	B	SE B	β
Alcohol use Time 1	0.52★★★	0.01★★★	.52★★★	0.51★★★	0.01★★★	.52★★★
Religious preference	–0.10★★★	0.02★★★	–.05★★★	–0.10★★★	0.02★★★	–.05★★★
Gender	–0.08★★★	0.02★★★	–.03★★★	–0.09★★★	0.02★★★	–.03★★★
Attendance at church institution	–0.12★★★	0.02★★★	–.05★★★	–0.12★★★	0.02★★★	–.05★★★
College major	–0.00	0.00★★★	–.01	–0.00	0.00★★★	–.01
Discussing politics	0.09★★★	0.02★★★	.05★★★	0.09★★★	0.02★★★	.05★★★
Religious conversion	–0.00	0.06★★★	.00	–0.03	0.06★★★	–.00
Discussing religion/ spirituality with friends	–0.05★★	0.02★★★	–.03★★	–0.06★★★	0.02★★★	–.04★★★
Spiritual struggles Time 1				0.02★★★	0.00★★★	.04★★★
R^2		0.29★★★			0.29★★★	
F for change in R^2		0.29★★★			0.00★★★	

$\star p \leq 0.05; \star\star p \leq 0.01; \star\star\star p \leq 0.001$

TABLE 10.3 Summary of multiple regression analysis for spiritual struggles at Time 1 predicting substance use at Time 2

Variable	Model 1			Model 2		
	B	SE B	β	B	SE B	β
Substance use Time 1	0.60★★★	0.01★★★	.59★★★	0.59★★★	0.01★★★	.58★★★
Religious preference	–0.11★★★	0.02★★★	–.04★★★	–0.11★★★	0.02★★★	–.04★★★
Gender	–0.11★★★	0.02★★★	–.03★★★	–0.11★★★	0.02★★★	–.04★★★
Attendance at church institution	–0.13★★★	0.02★★★	–.04★★★	–0.13★★★	0.02★★★	–.04★★★
College major	–0.00★★	0.00★★★	–.02★★	–0.00★★	0.00★★★	–.02★★
Discussing politics	0.10★★★	0.02★★★	.04★★★	0.10★★★	0.02★★★	.04★★★
Religious conversion	0.06	0.08★★★	.01	0.02	0.08★★★	.00
Discussing religion/ spirituality with friends	–0.06★★	0.02★★★	–.03★★	–0.08★★★	0.02★★★	–.03★★★
Spiritual struggles Time 1				0.03★★★	0.00★★★	.05★★★
R^2		0.36★★★			0.36★★★	
F for change in R^2		0.36★★★			0.00★★★	

$\star p \leq 0.05; \star\star p \leq 0.01; \star\star\star p \leq 0.001$

TABLE 10.4 Regression analyses for spiritual struggles and substance use—12 individual spiritual scales as mediator variables

Independent variable	Mediator variable	Dependent variables		
		Alcohol Use	*Tobacco Use*	*Substance Use*
Spiritual Struggles	Spiritual Identification	N/A	N/A	N/A
Spiritual Struggles	Spiritual Quest	N/A	N/A	N/A
Spiritual Struggles	Equanimity	N/A	N/A	N/A
Spiritual Struggles	Religious Commitment	N/A	N/A	N/A
Spiritual Struggles	Religious Engagement	N/A	N/A	N/A
Spiritual Struggles	Religious/Social Conservatism	N/A	N/A	N/A
Spiritual Struggles	Religious Skepticism	1. $\Delta R^2 = 0.003$*** β = 0.053*** 2. $\Delta R^2 = 0.007$*** β = 0.083*** 3. $\Delta R^2 = 0.024$*** β = 0.155*** **Δβ = 0.072** **Z = 3.30*****	1. $\Delta R^2 = 0.003$*** β = 0.053*** 2. $\Delta R^2 = 0.017$*** β = 0.131*** 3. $\Delta R^2 = 0.017$*** β = 0.127*** **Δβ = 0.004** **Z = 31.24*****	1. $\Delta R^2 = 0.003$*** β = 0.053*** 2. $\Delta R^2 = 0.013$*** β = 0.115*** 3. $\Delta R^2 = 0.014$*** β = 0.108*** **Δβ = 0.007** **Z = 3.31*****
Spiritual Struggles	Charitable Involvement	N/A	N/A	N/A
Spiritual Struggles	Ethic of Caring	N/A	N/A	N/A
Spiritual Struggles	Ecumenical Worldview	N/A	N/A	N/A
Spiritual Struggles	Compassionate Self-Concept	1. $\Delta R^2 = 0.001$** β = −0.027** 2. $\Delta R^2 = 0.007$*** β = 0.083*** 3. $\Delta R^2 = 0.007$*** β = 0.082*** **Δβ = 0.010** **Z = 3.19*****	1. $\Delta R^2 = 0.001$** β = −0.027** 2. $\Delta R^2 = 0.017$*** β = 0.131*** 3. $\Delta R^2 = 0.017$*** β = 0.131*** **Δβ = 0.000** **Z = 3.28*****	1. $\Delta R^2 = 0.001$** β = −0.027** 2. $\Delta R^2 = 0.013$*** β = 0.115*** 3. $\Delta R^2 = 0.013$*** β = 0.114*** **Δβ = 0.001** **Z = 2.74*****
Spiritual Struggles	God Image: Personal God	N/A	N/A	N/A
Spiritual Struggles	God Image: All Powerful God	N/A	N/A	N/A
Spiritual Struggles	God Image: Mystical God	N/A	N/A	N/A

*p ≤ 0.05; **p ≤ 0.01; ***p ≤ 0.001

Note: Step 1: Mediator regressed on independent variable (spiritual struggles); Step 2: Dependent variable regressed on independent variable and the mediator; Step 3: Dependent variable regressed on independent variable; β = standardized beta coefficient; Δβ = change in the standardized beta from regression Equation 2 to regression Equation 3; N/A = not applicable because did not meet initial correlational criteria to test for mediation effects (Baron & Kenny, 1986); Z = test of whether indirect effect of independent variable on dependent variable via the mediator is significantly different from zero (Sobel, 1982).

Additionally, the primary premise of this study was to identify underlying spiritual and religious factors that could better illuminate reasons why spiritual struggles appear to pose a risk for substance use during college. Drawing upon theoretical underpinnings of spiritual/religious orienting systems, I was particularly interested in data highlighting the concept of well-integrated versus disintegrated spirituality. One statistical approach to identify contributing factors is to conduct a mediation analysis whereby theoretically founded or exploratory constructs (i.e., 12 spiritual/religious scales) are entered into a regression equation as described above. Findings revealed that Religious Skepticism partially mediated the relationship between Religious Struggle and Alcohol, Tobacco, and Overall Substance Use (see Table 10.4). These results illustrate that a portion of the relationship between spiritual struggles and substance use is partially accounted for by the construct of religious skepticism. Therefore, students who endorsed a skeptical view of religion appeared to be at slightly greater risk of substance use. Potential reasons for this finding will be described in detail below.

Similarly, Compassionate Self-Concept partially mediated the relationship between spiritual struggles and substance use; however, this change is very minimal and should be interpreted with caution. The trend revealed here suggests that students who view themselves as kind and compassionate may be at less risk of substance use even when struggling with spiritual and religious questions. Future research could expand upon this finding to determine if it is truly meaningful or an artefact of the sample at hand. Both mediating variables diminished but did not eliminate the relationship between spiritual struggles and substance use; therefore, Religious Skepticism and Compassionate Self-Concept partially rather than fully mediate this relationship.

Reflections

As hypothesized, spiritual struggles appear to be a significant predictor of increased substance use in this sample of college students. The findings are consistent with the theory that spiritual tensions and conflicts during this developmental stage produce an internal void, which is subsequently filled by reliance on alcohol and tobacco use (Gorsuch & Butler, 1976). As such, results corroborate existing literature that demonstrates a robust link between spiritual struggles and negative health and emotional outcomes (see Ano & Vasconcelles, 2005), specifically alcohol use (Johnson et al., 2006; Lindholm, 2006) and tobacco use (Faigin & Pargament, 2008; Lindholm, 2006). Sample size and homogeneity of some of the previous samples raised concerns regarding the generalizability of results; however, findings from the present study, which queried 14,527 college students from 136 universities nationwide, help to quell those concerns. In addition, this study identified Religious Skepticism and Compassionate Self-Concept as partial mediators in the relationship between spiritual struggles and substance use, which may offer insight regarding the ways spiritual struggles impact college students.

Religious Skepticism

Religious skepticism is marked by affiliation with a secular worldview rather than a traditional religious perspective. In this study, the Religious Skepticism scale included items such as, "What happens in my life is not determined by forces larger than myself," "I have never felt a sense of sacredness," "Whether or not there is a Supreme Being doesn't matter to me." According to the current findings, religious skepticism appears to exacerbate the negative effects of spiritual struggles on substance use. Perhaps this can be understood by drawing upon research regarding religious involvement, the sacred realm, and the nature of religious skepticism and its intersection with traditional U.S. society.

Addiction researchers have consistently identified religion and spirituality as a protective factor in substance use. For instance, in a literature review of general measures of religiousness in adolescents and college students, Booth and Martin (1998) found that religious activities (e.g., church attendance) were inversely related to substance use in seven of eight studies. Koenig and colleagues (2001) also corroborated this finding, concluding from a large review of literature that religious and spiritual beliefs and practices are correlated with lower rates of drug and alcohol use. Although religious preference and church attendance were statistically controlled for in the current study, perhaps individuals who endorsed higher levels of religious skepticism also engaged in fewer religious and spiritual behaviors not measured in the current analyses, thus leading to greater preponderance for substance use. Future research in this area could better illuminate the nature of this relationship and should not be overlooked.

Additionally, perhaps religious skeptics are at risk for substance use during college due to difficulty experiencing a sense of the sacred. The ability to make meaning out of distressing life circumstances has been cited as a critical ingredient in successful adaptation and coping (Davis, Nolen-Hoeksema, & Larson, 1998). Researchers have illustrated the importance of having a sense of sacredness in meaning-making and define sanctification as "the perception of an aspect of life as having divine character and significance" (Pargament & Mahoney, 2005, p. 187). It is critical to note that sanctification applies to those who view the world through a secular rather than religious lens as well. *Any* experience to which one attributes divine qualities, such as transcendence, ultimate value and purpose, and boundlessness can be sanctified, without having to be connected to or anchored in theism. Pargament and Mahoney (2005) assert that sacred aspects of life are approached differently, treated with greater investment, protected and preserved, associated with spiritual emotions, and utilized to build meaning, satisfaction, relationships with others, and strength. Furthermore, loss or desecration of what one holds sacred can result in greater emotional distress, and trauma impact (Pargament, Magyar, Benore, & Mahoney, 2005). Thus, perhaps high scorers on the religious skepticism scale (including items such as "I have never felt a sense of sacredness") experience a potentially disturbing sense of existential isolation and difficulty in meaning-making during distress. Due to these issues, those who endorse religious skepticism in addition to spiritual struggles may be at particular risk to seek substances as a way to cope.

Religious skeptics may also experience social dissonance and isolation due to endorsing beliefs that are contrary to the traditional religious views in a society that encourages such beliefs. Specifically, Pargament (2007) underscores that regardless of the content of a particular set of beliefs and practices (secular or religious), a well-integrated spirituality is "one whose component parts work together in synchrony with each other" (p. 134), which includes the broader context of the society in which one lives. The United States is arguably a religiously oriented society, with upwards of 90 percent of people endorsing a belief in a higher power (Gallop & Lindsay, 1999). This was reflected in the current sample whereby 79 percent of students endorsed believing in God (Astin *et al.*, 2011). Individuals who do not share dominant religious views, especially during such a socially sensitive developmental time as college, may experience greater levels of dissonance, conflict, feelings of isolation, or disorientation from espousing views not shared by peers or the larger society. Religious discrimination and prejudices against minority groups are well documented and have occurred for millennia (Fox, 2007). Perhaps the nature of the distress for this group of students lay in the interpersonal conflict or tension with others regarding their spiritual (secular) beliefs. Therefore, individuals who ascribe to a secular worldview may not experience harmony between their environment and personal beliefs; consequently, these individuals may experience isolation and added distress and therefore may be more prone to seek substances as a way to cope.

Compassionate Self-Concept

Compassionate Self-Concept in this study reflected one's perception of being a kind, compassionate, generous, and forgiving person. Findings revealed that Compassionate Self-Concept buffered the negative effects of spiritual struggles on substance use. However, as mentioned above, this effect is minimal and therefore it is unclear if it is clinically meaningful. Although to be interpreted with caution, it appears that individuals who view themselves through a compassionate lens may be utilizing a well-integrated spiritual orienting system and thus are more apt to counter some of the negative effects of spiritual struggles.

Engaging in spiritual questioning is typically marked by isolation from God, self, and/or others and involves wrestling with concerns that are not perceived as socially acceptable. For instance, social and religious cultures generally dissuade individuals from questioning the divine or disagreeing with fundamental theology related to the divine. Therefore, individuals who are undergoing a spiritual struggle may be feeling isolated from others, the self, and the divine, as well as experiencing guilt or shame about their struggles. Substance use may in turn become a method of coping with isolation and guilt. Perhaps having a benevolent sense of one's being and place in the world enables a person to flexibly utilize spiritual resources in an adaptive way, regardless of the origin of distress (*inter*personally, *intra*personally, or divine), leading to enhanced meaning and less reliance on false substitutes (such as substances) for consolation.

Practical Implications

A primary goal of this study was to identify information to inform targeted and effective psychospiritual interventions to help college students adapt during this critical stage in life. Several implications for practice extend from this study.

Spirituality is clearly identified by college students as an important component of college life and a domain they expect to be addressed on campus (Astin *et al.*, 2011). However, despite this, students appear to be struggling with maintaining stability while experiencing spiritual difficulties, with less than half (42 percent) of students identifying themselves as "secure" in their views on spiritual/religious matters (Astin *et al.*, 2011). Thus, it is critical to bolster the resources offered on campus to help students explore their spiritual struggles in healthy and adaptive ways, and diminish reliance on substances to cope with existential tension. Specifically, interventions that address religious skepticism and compassionate self-concept appear warranted.

In response to the potential isolation that students who define themselves as religious skeptics may experience, college campuses may consider providing a forum in which to share and explore their views and beliefs. As Pargament (2007) notes in his assessment of well-integrated spirituality, it is not necessarily the nature of the belief itself that causes distress, but its integration within the larger community that can also lead to difficulty. Currently, many religious-based campus groups understandably primarily attract believers of a given set of beliefs. However, fewer campus groups allow for interfaith dialogue or opportunities for those who differ from traditional religious perspectives to discuss their beliefs in a respectful and open environment. As such, students who endorse religious skepticism may lack critical social and community outlets for spiritual support and coping within our traditional educational system. Therefore, opportunities for community integration and dialogue may be particularly important for promoting a well-integrated spirituality for these students.

One such non-religious-based group, called *Winding Road*, was piloted at a state university in the Midwest with promising results (Gear *et al.*, 2008). Small groups of students who endorsed experiencing a spiritual struggle were offered the opportunity to participate in a nine-week spiritually integrated psychoeducational group facilitated by psychology graduate students. The purpose of this intervention was not to resolve the struggle or promote a particular set of beliefs, but to reduce self-stigma related to struggle, facilitate greater flexibility and integration of spirituality into daily life, and encourage broadening of one's spirituality in a safe and non-threatening environment; in short, the group aim was to promote a well-integrated spiritual orienting system, based on Pargament's theory (2007). The 12 participants in this study represented diverse religious orientations and included religious skeptics (i.e., Protestants, Catholics, Wiccans, Atheists, Agnostics, and those who were "not sure" about religion).

Findings revealed that *Winding Road* mitigated the negative effects of spiritual struggles including psychological distress, self-stigma related to spiritual struggles, and negative affect related to spiritual struggles. The intervention also promoted congruence between spiritual values and behaviors, improvement in positive affect related to spiritual struggle, enhanced perceived access to effective strategies for emotion regulation during a spiritual struggle, and improved sense of acceptance from a higher power. This study provided compelling support that a structured non-denominational spiritually integrated education group could be an effective environment for promoting integration within one's spiritual framework regardless of one's beliefs. Other campus groups could follow suit and provide an environment for religious skeptics to talk about their views in a supportive and respectful environment, provide mentorship on ways to continue to enhance integration of their beliefs into practice, and find ways to explore new avenues for meaning and support.

Furthermore, campus groups could be developed to educate students and parents that spiritual struggles are normal aspects of human development, regardless of religious heritage or beliefs. This normalization and psychoeducation may help decrease *struggle* in the face of spiritual and religious tension. Additionally, having peer- and mentor-based support during spiritual struggling may enhance one's self-concept and promote a better-integrated spirituality. Letting students know that they are not alone in this process may buffer the feelings of isolation common to those struggling, which in turn may decrease their risk for relying upon substances as a way of coping. Targeted and effective psychospiritual interventions such as these could provide a more holistic approach to supporting and empowering members of the next generation.

Limitations

The present study should be viewed as initial and exploratory. As such, several limitations should be addressed in future research. First, the measurement of substance use in this study was limited. There were only three items assessing alcohol and tobacco use, and the response set for these items was limited to three possible choices. In addition, this study does not include other behavioral and substance-based addictive processes (e.g., gambling, illicit drug use, sex) that are prevalent in college-aged youth. Future studies should consider including broader measures of addiction and include richer response sets to gain a better understanding of the patterns in substance use and abuse.

Second, participation in this study was voluntary; therefore, there may have been a self-selection effect in which students who were either comfortable answering questions related to spirituality or those who wanted a forum for expressing their doubts or dissatisfaction with religion may have opted in, or opted out of participation in this project. Furthermore, although there was no evidence in this study of underreporting, researchers should remain sensitive to anonymity in all sampling procedures, as participants may be hesitant to report illicit substance use or perceived socially unacceptable behaviors in surveys.

Third, the current study queried participants at two time points (freshman and junior years) during their college career. It may also be beneficial to query students at additional time points during and after college to track trends and patterns of use/abuse, as well as resolution or deepening of spiritual struggles over time. Expanding on this already large fund of data can only enhance our perspectives and understanding of the trajectories of spiritual development across different life stages.

Acknowledgment

The author would like to express her gratitude to Dr. Lyuba Bobova for her statistical consultation and Dr. Ken Pargament for his continued support and consultation on this project.

References

Allport, G. (1950). *The individual and his religion: A psychological interpretation.* Oxford, England: Macmillan.

Ano, G. G., & Vasconcelles, E. B. (2005). Religious coping and psychological adjustment to stress: A meta-analysis. *Journal of Clinical Psychology, 61,* 461–480.

Astin, A. W., Astin, H. S., & Lindholm, J. A. (2011). Assessing students' spiritual and religious qualities. *Journal of College Student Development, 52,* 39–61.

Astin, A. W., Astin, H. S., Lindholm, J. A., Bryant, A. N., Szelényi, K., & Calderone, S. (2005). *The spiritual life of college students: A national study of college students' search for meaning and purpose.* Los Angeles: Higher Education Research Institute, UCLA.

Baron, R. M., & Kenny, A. (1986). The moderator–mediator variable distinction in social psychological research: Conceptual, strategic, and statistical considerations. *Journal of Personality and Social Psychology, 51*(6), 1173–1182.

Booth, J., & Martin, J. E. (1998). Spiritual and religious factors in substance use, dependence, and recovery. In Koenig, H. G (Ed.), *Handbook of religion and mental health* (pp. 175–200). San Diego, CA: Academic Press.

Bryant, A. N., & Astin, H. S. (2008) The correlates of spiritual struggle during the college years. *Journal of Higher Education, 79*(1), 1–27.

Chickering, A. W., & Reisser, L. (1993). *Education and identity.* San Francisco: Jossey Bass.

Cole, B. S., Hopkins, C. M., Tisak, J., Steel, J. L., & Carr, B. I. (2008). Assessing spiritual growth and spiritual decline following a diagnosis of cancer: Reliability and validity of the Spiritual Transformation Scale. *Psycho-Oncology, 17*(2), 112–121.

Davis, C. G., Nolen-Hoeksema, S., & Larson, J. (1998). Making sense of loss and benefitting from the experience: Two construals of meaning. *Journal of Personality and Social Psychology, 75*(2), 561–574.

Desai, K. M. (2006). *Predictors of growth and spiritual decline following spiritual struggles.* Unpublished master's thesis, Bowling Green State University, Bowling Green, OH.

Emmons, R. A. (1999). *The psychology of ultimate concerns: Motivation and spirituality in personality.* New York: Guilford Press.

Emmons, R. A. (2005). Striving for the sacred: Personal goals, life meaning, and religion. *Journal of Social Issues, 61,* 731–745.

Exline, J. J. (2002). The picture is getting clearer, but is the scope too limited? Three overlooked questions in the psychology of religion. *Psychological Inquiry, 13*(3), 245–247.

Exline, J. J., & Rose, E. (2005). Religious and spiritual struggles. In R. F. Paloutzin and C. L. Park (Eds.), *Handbook of the psychology of religion* (pp. 315–330). New York: Guilford Press.

Exline, J. J., Yali, A. M., & Sanderson, W. C. (2000). Guilt, discord, and alienation: The role of religious strain in depression and suicidality. *Journal of Clinical Psychology, 56,* 1481–1496.

Faigin, C. A., & Pargament, K. I. (2008). *Filling the spiritual void: Spiritual struggles as a risk factor for addiction.* Poster session presented at the 20th annual convention of the Association for Psychological Science, Chicago, IL.

Fox, J. (2007). Religious discrimination: A world survey. *Journal of International Affairs, 61*(1), 47–67.

Gallop, G. Jr., & Lindsay, D. M (1999). *Surveying the religious landscape: Trends in U.S. beliefs.* Harrisburg, PA: Morehouse.

Gear, M. R., Faigin, C. A., Gibbel, M. R., Krumrei, E. J., Oemig, C. K., McCarthy, S. K., & Pargament, K. I. (2008). The winding road: A promising approach to addressing spiritual struggles of college students. *UCLA Spirituality in Higher Education Newsletter,* 4(4).

Gorsuch, R. L. (1995). Religious aspects of substance abuse and recovery. *Journal of Social Issues, 51,* 65–83.

Gorsuch, R. L., & Butler, M. C. (1976). Initial drug abuse: A review of predisposing social psychological factors. *Psychological Bulletin, 83,* 120–137.

Hill, P. C., & Pargament, I. (2008). Advances in the conceptualization and measurement of religion and spirituality: Implications for physical and mental health research. *Psychology of Religion and Spirituality, 58*(1), 3–17.

Hingson, R. W., Heeren, T., Zakocs, R. C., Kopstein, A., & Wechsler, H. (2002). Magnitude of alcohol-related mortality and morbidity among U.S. college students ages 18–24. *Journal of Studies on Alcohol, 63*(2), 136–144.

Johnson, T. J., Sheets, V., & Kristeller, J. (2006). Identifying mediators of the relationship between religiousness and alcohol use: beliefs, meaning, and perceptions of peer drinking. *Adolescence, 40,* 761–776.

Koenig, H. G., McCullough, M. E., & Larson, D. B. (2001). *Handbook of religion and health.* New York: Oxford University Press.

Lindholm, J. A. (2006). The "Interior" Lives of American College Students: Preliminary Findings from a National Study. In J. L. Heft, (Ed.), *Passing on the Faith: Transforming Traditions for the Next Generation of Jews, Christians, and Muslims* (pp. 75–102). New York: Fordham University Press.

Marsh, A., & Dale, A. (2005). Risk factors for alcohol and other drug disorders: A review. *Australian Psychologist, 40*(2), 73–80.

McConnell, K. M., Pargament, K. I., Flannelly, K., & Ellison, C. (2006). Examining the links between spiritual struggles and symptoms of psychopathology in a national sample. *Journal of Clinical Psychology, 62*(12), 1469–1484.

Miller, W. R. (1998). Researching the spiritual dimensions of alcohol and other drug problems. *Addiction, 93,* 979–990.

Pargament, K. I. (1997). *The psychology of religion and coping: Theory, research, practice.* New York: Guilford Press.

Pargament, K. I. (2007). *Spiritually-integrated psychotherapy: Understanding and addressing the sacred.* New York: Guilford Press.

Pargament, K. I., & Mahoney, A. (2005). Sacred matters: Sanctification as a vital topic for the psychology of religion. *International Journal for the Psychology of Religion, 15*(3), 179–198.

Pargament, K. I., Desai, K. M., & McConnell, K. M. (2006). Spirituality: A pathway to posttraumatic growth or decline? In L. G. Calhoun & R. G. Tedeschi (Eds.), *Handbook of posttraumatic growth: Research and practice* (pp. 121–137). Mahwah, NJ: Lawrence Erlbaum Associates.

Pargament, K. I., Koenig, H. G., Tarakeshwar, N., & Hahn, J. (2004). Religious coping methods as predictors of psychological, physical and spiritual outcomes among medically ill elderly patients: A longitudinal study. *Journal of Health Psychology, 9,* 713–730.

Pargament, K. I., Magyar, G. M., Benore, E., & Mahoney, A. (2005). Sacrilege: A study of sacred loss and desecration and their implications for health and well-being in a community sample. *Journal for the Scientific Study of Religion, 44*(1), 59–78.

Pargament, K. I., Murray-Swank, N. A., Magyar, G. M., & Ano, G. G. (2005). Spiritual struggle: A phenomenon of interest to psychology and religion. In W. R. Miller & H. D. Delaney, (Eds.), *Judeo-Christian perspectives on psychology: Human nature, motivation, and change* (pp. 245–268). Washington, DC: American Psychological Association.

Pargament, K. I., Smith, B. W., Koenig, H. G., & Perez, L. (1998). Patterns of positive and negative religious coping with major life stressors. *Journal for the Scientific Study of Religion, 37,* 710–724.

Sobel, M. E. (1982). Asymptotic confidence intervals for indirect effects in structural equation models. In S. Leinhardt (Ed.), *Sociological Methodology 1982* (pp. 290–312). Washington DC: American Sociological Association.

Trenholm, P., Trent, J., & Compton, W. C. (1998). Negative religious conflict as a predictor of panic disorder. *Journal of Clinical Psychology, 54*(1), 59–65.

U.S. Department of Health and Human Services (2006). *The National Survey of Drug Use and Health Report: Nicotine Dependence.* Retrieved December 14, 2009, from the National Survey of Drug Use and Health (NSDUH) website: http://oas.samhsa.gov/2k8/nicotine/nicotine.cfm

U.S. Department of Health and Human Services (2007). *Results from the 2007 NSDUH: National findings.* Retrieved January 26, 2009, from the National Survey of Drug Use and Health (NSDUH) website: https://nsduhweb.rti.org

ADVANCES IN UNDERSTANDING PRO-SOCIAL DEVELOPMENT IN COLLEGE

Reflections on Spiritual Outcomes Research

Michael D. Waggoner

In his 1971 novel *Love in the Ruins*, Walker Percy's protagonist, Dr. Tom Moore, invented an instrument—an ontological lapsometer—by which he could determine an individual's state of spiritual well-being. Forty years later, while still well short of such a tool, we are further along in measuring spiritual development by more conventional means. Peter Hill and Ralph Hood's important *Measures of Religiosity* (1999) represents a collection of 186 instruments in 17 categories developed since 1935, though only a handful of these measures specifically address spirituality. In the last decade, however, new spirituality measures have been introduced (Astin, Astin, & Lindholm, 2011a; Hall & Edwards, 2002; Hodge, 2003; Raiya, Pargament, Mahoney, & Stein, 2008; Seidlitz, Abernethy, Duberstien, Evinger, Chang, & Lewis, 2002; Underwood & Teresi, 2002). Also, important analytical and conceptual studies have appeared addressing the relationship of religion and spirituality and advances in their measurement (Ashmos & Duchon, 2000; Hill & Pargament, 2003; MacDonald, 2000; Moberg, 2002). The most notable instrument among these recent developments is the College Students' Beliefs and Values Survey (CSBV) (Astin, Astin, & Lindholm, 2011a). The development of the CSBV seems to be a logical next step following the national seven-year UCLA Spirituality in Higher Education study, data from which are the basis for the four studies considered in this outcomes section (Astin, Astin, & Lindholm, 2011b). The use of the CSBV will be central to extending and deepening the knowledge base on the religious-spiritual outcomes of college, including any follow up of the findings of these studies. My reflection will comment on the contribution of these four studies and their place in the higher education religious-spiritual outcomes literature, and will also include observations on possible areas for further research.

Four major themes emerge from the studies in this section, all under the overarching idea of pro-social development in college. They reinforce Pascarella and Terenzini's observation from their review of outcomes research on religious attitudes, values, and identity that development in this area is "more subtle and complex than previously thought" (2005, p. 218). First, those who identify as spiritual or religiously committed are more likely to experience pro-social development in college as defined by ethic of care, charitable involvement, and a compassionate self-concept. Second, spirituality and religious commitment are antecedents to social justice orientation with respect to attitudes and action. Though the influences are reciprocal, individuals identifying as spiritual show significantly more growth over the religiously committed. Third, student/faculty interaction in the areas of ethical/spiritual concerns, academic/career issues, and student-centered pedagogy promote development of the caring self as measured by progression in ethic of care. Fourth, those experiencing spiritual struggles tend toward higher incidence of smoking, drinking, and drug abuse. Religious skepticism mediates these struggles toward increased abuse. Compassionate self-care mediates toward a decrease in these behaviors. In all cases, type of institution (religious-affiliated, secular) makes a difference. All of these themes, while consistent with findings from earlier studies, are much stronger due to their basis in the increased sample size of more than 14,000 students and 136 institutions. At the same time, these four studies note the limitation of the students being in their first three years and suggest research through the conclusion of college and further into the adult years.

Jay Brandenberger and Nicholas Bowman advance our understanding of pro-social development in college. Their findings illustrate the complexity of the interrelationships with results that invite further investigation. One such example (space limitations will keep us from much more) is that "religion may promote pro-social attitudes and behaviors to the extent that it relates to one's spirituality. Such a view is consistent with the conceptualization of spirituality as internalized beliefs as opposed to the institutional practices and obligations of religion." This underscores the importance of separating the analysis of spirituality from religion. The spirituality dimension is largely missing from the outcomes literature summarized by Pascarella and Terenzini (2005) as Astin *et al.* (2011a) observe. Brandenberger and Bowman point also to further complications when examining in-group behavior relative to spirituality and pro-social development. It appears that those who are religiously committed report high levels of charitable involvement and compassionate self-concept, but lower levels of ethic of care. This calls to mind an earlier study of the culture of an evangelical college where a competitiveness around spiritual development and the concomitant unwillingness to admit shortcomings created a tension between the individual's spiritual development and in-group and institutional expectations (Cumings, Haworth, & O'Neill, 2001; Jones, 2002). In such a competitive environment, charitable involvement and an ethic of care could be seen by peers as evidence of spiritual growth. The authors of the study in this volume encourage caution in extrapolating their results and rightfully call for specially developed measures to analyze the nuances of in-group operation. They also raise interesting points regarding spiritual struggle that I will take up in connection with the Faigin study below.

David Chenot and Hansung Kim approach pro-social development using the construct of social justice orientation (SJO). Their findings are consistent with the general thrust of Brandenberger and Bowman, but give a usefully different slant on the issues involved. Chenot and Kim also draw from a different literature, that of Positive Youth Development, adding a dimension to frame the results of their study. They found that religion and spirituality are antecedents to long-term increases in social justice orientation attitudes and actions. The relationship was not, however, reciprocal; that is, the presence of social justice orientation did not predict religious commitment or spirituality. Further, though the relationship between religion and spirituality was reciprocal, the influence of religion on spirituality was stronger. With respect to SJO actions, spirituality was the stronger of the two predictor variables. A nuance in the findings in these two studies points to a locus for further study. Both Brandenberger and Bowman and Chenot and Kim found that religious commitment and spiritual identification contributed to pro-social development. Yet, Brandenberger and Bowman found spiritual identification contributing more than religion, whereas Chenot and Kim found the influence of religion stronger than spirituality in their reciprocal relationship. Granted, Chenot and Kim found that spirituality had a stronger impact on SJO actions than religion, but this nuance bears further study for a deeper understanding of the interactions of religion and spirituality in the multiple dimensions of pro-social development. Also, Chenot and Kim found that females and racial/ethnic minorities ranked higher in religious commitment, spirituality, and social justice orientation than white males. Further survey and ethnographic work should be done to uncover the factors that may contribute to this finding. Of particular interest would be pre-college influences and the impact of college experiences on these factors.

James Fleming, Jennie Purnell, and Yang Wang bring another perspective on the contribution of spirituality to pro-social development in the college years. Their analysis demonstrates that faculty–student interaction contributes to the development of an ethic of care. Increases are found to be greatest among Asians, with the highest scores found among African-Americans and the lowest among Caucasians. Institutional type matters, with public universities showing the lowest level of contact and subsequent development of ethic of care among students. Catholic, evangelical, and religious-affiliated institutions show the highest level of development. Three types of interaction were studied: ethical/spiritual mentoring, academic/career mentoring, and student-centered pedagogy. Ethical/spiritual mentoring was most strongly associated with positive development.

Several intriguing questions arise from the Fleming, Purnell, and Wang study. They note that the field of study of faculty and students may likely make a difference and this warrants investigation. Also, it would be interesting to analyze the relationship of one measure of spirituality that has not been mentioned in the studies in this section—ecumenical worldview—to ethical/spiritual mentoring, academic/career mentoring, and student centered mentoring. For example, this could contribute depth of understanding to questions about in-group effects raised by Brandenberger and Bowman.

Another subset of analyses might involve examining those students identified as low on ethic of care or those students who are indifferent to spirituality or religion but experience a significant increase in ethic of care. Smith and Snell (2009) noted that 25 percent of emerging adults are religiously indifferent and 10 percent irreligious. It would be instructive to learn where there is movement toward the development of the caring self among religiously indifferent and irreligious individuals who represent one-third of the population—and what experiences evoke this change.

One additional avenue for research related to the Fleming, Purnell, and Wang study would be an investigation of student affairs and related staff interactions with students. It has long been maintained that co-curricular involvements figure prominently in student development. Because these are venues in which students closely interact with student affairs staff—residence halls, student activities and organizations, academic and career advising, service learning, counseling services— there are opportunities for mentoring relationships to develop apart from the faculty that can result in development of the caring self.

The last contributor to this section on outcomes, Carol Ann Faigin, offers some provocative findings from her research on the relationship of spiritual struggle to substance abuse. The health and academic problems associated with tobacco, alcohol, and drug abuse on campus are a well-documented bane of higher education life. It would seem that any deeper understanding of root causes and concomitant strategies to mitigate these problems would be a helpful contribution to our understanding of pro-social development in college. Consistent with previous studies conducted on much smaller sample sizes, Faigin found that the experience of spiritual struggle was associated with increases in use of tobacco, alcohol, and drugs through the college years. This was true when controlling for confounding variables (see procedural section of her chapter). Within this overarching finding, she further noted that two variables mediated spiritual struggle. Those experiencing religious skepticism increased their use of these substances, whereas those with higher levels of compassionate self-concept decreased their substance use. These findings raise a number of interesting questions for further inquiry. Faigin raises three in her limitations section. Beyond those, I would like to see a deeper look at religious skepticism, including an analysis by institutional type. What constitutes religious skepticism in a public institution versus a Catholic or evangelical institution may vary, along with the locally acceptable outcomes for resolving that skepticism. For example, a student wrestling with her sexual orientation may have greater degrees of freedom for resolution in an environment that includes a range of liberal to conservative religious and spiritual alternatives than an institution that is more at one extreme than another. Further study of specific spiritual practices and the development of a compassionate self-concept would also be helpful in this connection. There may be practices that could fall under the "wellness" category that could be engaged in by those experiencing religious skepticism. Without violating the integrity of their quest by imposing overtly religious or spiritual language or practice, such practices may gradually foster a self-concept that could aid in the resolution of their existential questioning. Pargament's (2007) idea of a "well-integrated spirituality" should be among those constructs consulted in exploring this further, but as Bryant and Astin (2008) suggest, more sophisticated measures of religion and spirituality will be needed to tease out these nuances.

The research on spiritual outcomes in college reported in this section reinforces, extends, and refines the potential risks and rewards of engaging the arena of spirituality in the college setting. The risks include provoking the disequilibrium of spiritual struggle with the possible outcomes of increased anti-social behaviors including smoking, alcohol, and drug abuse. The rewards include pro-social development resulting in caring individuals who positively contribute to society. These findings underscore the importance of further research on practices that encourage positive spiritual development during college. Further research should be conducted by institutional type given that the orientation of Catholic, Protestant church-related, evangelical, and public institutions have differing ethos, cultures, and norms that define pro-social development and shape the range of allowable resolution of spiritual struggle.

References

Ashmos, D., & Duchon, D. (2000). Spirituality at work: A conceptualization and measure. *Journal of Personality and Social Psychology, 9*, 134–145.

Astin, A. W., Astin, H. S., & Lindholm, J. A. (2011a). Assessing students' spiritual and religious qualities. *Journal of College Student Development, 52*(1), 39–61.

Astin, A. W., Astin, H. S., & Lindholm, J. A. (2011b). *Cultivating the spirit: How colleges can enhance students' inner lives.* San Francisco, CA: Jossey-Bass.

Bryant, A. N., & Astin, H. S. (2008). The correlates of spiritual struggle during the college years. *Journal of Higher Education, 79*(1), 1–28.

Cumings, K. D., Haworth, J. G., & O'Neill, K. (2001). A "perfect standard?" Exploring perceptions of student life and culture at Wheaton College. *Religion & Education, 28*(2), 33–64.

Hall, T. W., & Edwards, K. J. (2002). The spiritual assessment of inventory: A theistic model and measure for assessing spiritual development. *Journal for the Scientific Study of Religion, 41*, 341–357.

Hill, P. C., & Hood, R. W. (1999). *Measures of religiosity.* Birmingham: Religious Education Press.

Hill, P. C., & Pargament, K. I. (2003). Advances in the conceptualization and measurement of religion and spirituality: Implications for physical and mental health research. *American Psychologist, 58*, 64–73.

Hodge, D. R. (2003). The intrinsic spirituality scale: A new six-item instrument for assessing the salience of spirituality as a motivational construct. *Journal of Social Sciences Research, 30*, 41–61.

Jones, S. L. (2002). Response to: "A perfect standard?" *Religion & Education, 29*(1), 90–93.

MacDonald, D. A. (2000). Spirituality: Description, measurement, and relation to the Five Factor Model of Personality. *Journal of Personality, 68*, 153–197.

Moberg, D. O. (2002). Assessing and measuring spirituality: Confronting dilemmas of universal and particular evaluative criteria. *Journal of Adult Development, 9*, 47–60.

Pargament, K. I. (2007) *Spiritually-integrated psychotherapy: Understanding and addressing the sacred.* New York: Guilford Press.

Pascarella, E. T., & Terenzini, P. T. (2005). *How college affects students: A third decade of research.* San Francisco, CA: Jossey-Bass.

Percy, W. (1971). *Love in the ruins: The adventures of a bad Catholic at a time near the end of the world.* New York: Ferrar, Straus, and Giroux.

Raiya, H. A., Pargament, K. I., Mahoney, A., & Stein, C. (2008). A psychological measure of Islamic religiousness: Development and evidence for reliability and validity. *International Journal for the Psychology of Religion, 18*, 291–315.

Seidlitz, L., Abernethy, A. D., Duberstien, P. R., Evinger, J. S., Chang, T. H., & Lewis, B. L. (2002). Development of the spiritual transcendence index. *Journal for the Scientific Study of Religion, 41*, 439–453.

Smith, C., & Snell, P. (2009). *Souls in transition: The religious and spiritual lives of emerging adults.* Oxford, England: Oxford University Press.

Underwood, L. G., & Terese, J. A. (2002). The daily spiritual experience scale: Development, theoretical description, reliability, exploratory factor analysis, and preliminary construct validity using health-related data. *Annals of Behavioral Medicine, 24*(1), 22–33.

QUESTIONS OF SPIRITUALITY ON COLLEGE CAMPUSES

To Engage or Not To Engage?

Donna M. Talbot and Diane K. Anderson

As we read the four chapters in the outcomes section, we realized that context and owning our biases are central to the integrity of our reflections. In our discussions of the chapters, we realized that we, a practitioner and a faculty member, share some commonalities and have some significant differences that informed our perspectives on the research presented. Though we both were raised in Christian households, like our students, how we exhibit our faith and/or spirituality now is different than when we were young. One of us (Diane) attended an evangelical Christian liberal arts college with a mission of integrating faith and learning; since this undergraduate experience, she has attended secular, public institutions and worked at a combination of both private and public institutions. The faculty member (Donna) attended a small, liberal arts college as an undergraduate student; all her graduate degrees have been from large public institutions. Though we have both worked at small, private, and public institutions, our most recent work for more than a decade has been in a mid-sized, public institution in the Midwest.

The institutions represented in these chapters, through the researchers, were largely different than the one in which we exist; therefore, the lenses through which the researchers viewed the topics of religion/spirituality are different than those we are accustomed to using. In public higher education, we continually struggle with the fine line between religion and spirituality experienced by many of our students, as well as wrestle with the role of religion/spirituality in our work. There remains an unspoken rule that "separation of church and state" limits our ability to see religion/spirituality as part of the holistic development of students. This constant tension in public higher education clouds our ability to see that two-thirds of our new freshmen believe that their college experience is very important for them in coming to understand themselves and in developing personal values (Astin, Astin,

& Lindholm, 2011). In other words, their expectation is that college is about much more than gaining knowledge.

Given our experiences in public higher education, we were struck by the ease with which the chapter authors seemed to suggest that integrating spirituality in higher education is an imperative. While we may be willing to consider that assumption, many faculty colleagues at our public institution would bristle at the notion that we should endorse any beliefs that are not closely tied to a traditional academic philosophy. Before we can make recommendations for practice based on the findings of the studies, we felt a need to make recommendations in response to the assumptions of the researchers. The lack of agreement about our role in the university suggests there needs to be more campus-wide discussions about institutional missions and how those missions are interpreted. As professionals in the university community, we need to facilitate a discussion about the university's commitment to developing global citizens and assisting students as they make meaning of their lives. While these conversations take place in small pockets within a public university, they are not community wide. In fact, there are still many faculty who believe that they are responsible only for conveying discipline-specific information to students; they do not see themselves as responsible for facilitating the larger mission of the university, let alone facilitating an ill-defined concept such as "spirituality."

The simplest interpretation of the studies presented in these four chapters is that today's students come to campus with experiences and commitment to a social justice orientation (see Chenot and Kim, Chapter 8); for most of these students, spirituality and religion during their formative years contribute to their commitment to civic engagement, and caring and compassion for others. By the time students come to our campuses, they have already engaged in various civic activities, as well as mission trips and related activities. Brandenberger and Bowman (Chapter 7) found that prosocial behavior (e.g., a commitment to engage in actions that benefit others) is positively associated with spirituality, even more so than religiosity, and includes an ethic of caring for others beyond students' immediate friendship groups. This association continues throughout students' college years.

According to Fleming, Purnell, and Wang (Chapter 9), "student–faculty interaction (across institution type) promotes not just cognitive development, persistence, educational aspirations, and degree completion, but this interaction also promotes the development of the caring self, as measured by growth in the ethic of care." These researchers defined ethic of care with an 11-item scale that included trying to change things that are unfair in the world, helping to promote racial understanding, helping others who are in difficulty, and several other similar attributes. While the authors connect these findings to issues of spirituality, having a student population that reports a desire to affect society positively is a concept that most faculty can embrace regardless of their beliefs about the role of education. Finally, in a study looking at the relationship between spiritual struggles and substance abuse, Faigin (Chapter 10) found that spiritual struggles were a significant predictor of alcohol, tobacco, and other substance use among college students. Given the role of substance abuse in conduct violations on campuses, this finding raises some interesting issues for university conduct officers to consider. Spiritual struggles in adults are also associated with increased depression, lower self-esteem, and poorer physical health. There are also some obvious implications for college counseling staff, especially those working with students referred for alcohol violations.

The implications for practice that stem from these research findings may vary by institution type, require careful interpretation, and demonstrate that ignoring issues related to spirituality and religion could have a negative impact on our students. As a result, we recommend that higher education administrators, student affairs practitioners, and faculty members consider the following questions as they develop best practices on their respective campuses. We will make some recommendations for practice based on our experiences in a public institution.

1   What is our role, in higher education, to nurture and foster spirituality as part of the academic enterprise, both inside and outside of the classroom?
    •   As institutions of higher learning, we need to do a better job defining student success and student wellness in holistic terms, including students' spirituality. We tend to avoid this domain, especially at public institutions, even though it is fertile ground for students as they seek to develop their own identities and make sense of a world riddled with conflict, often laced with underlying religious and spiritual tenets.
    •   Student development theories recognize that we must "meet students where they are" if we are to help them develop while in college. The national data for the past decade suggest that issues of religion and spirituality are central to students' identity. Therefore, we need to be more facile in helping students use their spirituality to support their success in college. For example, if students tell us that exercising or meditating or praying helps them to be more focused for exams, we should encourage them to do whatever helps them succeed.
2   Do institutions have an obligation to engage in deeper conversations about who they are, what they represent, and what they value?
    •   Assuming the answer is "yes," we need to develop "buy-in" and expertise in facilitating meaningful conversations that explore questions of meaning and spirituality. The role of being an educator has changed throughout the history of higher education. In many ways, the role of faculty members in public higher education still reflects the scientific model present in German universities of the 1960s. Given our current student population and their expectations, we need to reconsider this model for the success of institutions of higher education. We may need to return to a more "intimately involved"

faculty—much like that which existed early in the history of U.S. higher education.

3   How do higher education institutions define "good citizens" and "civic engagement" (often found in institutional mission statements)? Do those definitions encompass prosocial behavior, spirituality, and social justice?
   • Many of our institutions have committed themselves, through mission statements, to standards that involve being good citizens and stewards of this world (through sustainability). If we want all members of the campus community to engage in meeting our missions, we must develop workable definitions for terms such as *citizenship, civic engagement, prosocial behavior, spirituality*, and *social justice*. These concepts must be clearly defined and operationalized so that they can be used in creating learning outcomes for courses and co-curricular programs. We must also be transparent in our expectations that all members of the community have a responsibility in reaching our institutional goals and mission.

4   How do we give ourselves (faculty/staff) permission to engage in discussions about spirituality with our students?
   • If we develop more holistic definitions of desired learning outcomes and provide professional development for faculty and staff related to engaging in meaningful dialogues that matter to students and student success, issues of spirituality will naturally rise to the surface. While we are clear, in public higher education, that our goals do not include promoting particular religious views, we cannot let our "fear of religion" keep us from understanding what helps our students succeed in college.

5   How do we better support our students in their exploration and expressions of faith and spirituality both individually and institutionally?
   • The most useful thing we can do for students is to create environments where it is safe for them to talk about their faith-based and spiritual questions. We need not impose our beliefs, but encourage students to explore what is most meaningful for them.
   • As institutions of learning, we need to provide professional development for faculty, staff, and peer mentors focused on spiritual development. As professionals in the institution, we need to be able to understand the challenges and changes that students are engaging.

Perhaps the greatest implication for practice in higher education, particularly in public institutions, is that we need to have "translators" among the faculty and staff who can interpret some of the findings from these chapters in a context that may or may not embrace spirituality/religion as an appropriate concept within higher education. Students come to campus to get a college degree and eventually employment; however, with this education, they are challenged to think critically, to embrace differences, and to make meaning of their educational experiences. In fact, they arrive on our campuses expecting to gain more than just knowledge. The national data collected by the Higher Education Research Institute (2004, 2007) more than suggests that students expect to "find themselves" and refine their values/ beliefs in college. They expect to make meaning of their lives and their life choices after college. Though we may choose to label this differently, many students and practitioners see these deeper explorations as components of spirituality.

Reference

Astin, A. W., Astin, H. S., & Lindholm, J. A. (2011). *Cultivating the spirit: How college can enhance students' inner lives.* San Francisco: Jossey-Bass.

11

THE STUDY OF SPIRITUALITY: AN EPILOGUE

Are We There Yet? If So, Where?

C. Carney Strange

Interest in the spiritual is as ancient as life itself. From the earliest moments, human beings have been drawn to the ultimate mysteries of existence and to the great questions that frame it: Who are we? Why are we here? and Where are we going? Although not inherently spiritual questions, they are often addressed as such, given their potential ultimate nature. While, at first, answers to such wonders presented themselves mostly in a cosmology of natural signs—earthquakes, floods, planets and constellations, parched lands, and bountiful harvests—today they come in the propositional form of insights, creeds, arguments, concepts, frameworks, and factors. From the primitive to the contemporary we have pursued the nature, meaning, and effect of spiritual dimensions in our lives. How close have we come to the point of understanding these aspects? Do we know where we are? What do the data presented here, in the context of other approaches to the topic, have to say about such a complex phenomenon as spirituality, so deep in our human experience but relentlessly elusive? The studies contained in the chapters in this volume contribute important pieces to the puzzle of ultimate questions in students' lives. To appreciate them more fully, though, they must be seen in the context of other approaches to the topic and considered for what they might implicate for future research and practice in this domain.

Exploring Spirituality

The study of spirituality has taken on a number of forms over the centuries. Among traditional approaches were oral and written narratives that depicted the lives of reputed holy men and women who appeared connected in a special way to the sacred and divine. Often referred to as "saints," their lives of prayer, self-denial, and good works in this world were thought to assure a special status or "salvation" in the next (Butler, 1878). Some recluse and others renowned for public service, they were mostly seen as deeply spiritual beings with a special character that clearly set them apart and offered them a special wisdom about the world that others sought. The lessons of their lives were learned through stories of spiritual discipline, temptations overcome, and their widespread influence on others. Emulating them led some to commit their lives to the religious communities established under their charisms (e.g., Franciscans). Understanding the spiritual, then, involved careful study of these people's lives and reflecting on those moments that distinguished them above others in the choices they made. Pursuing the spiritual entailed imitating their actions and engaging in their practices. As important were their examples then, the value of such narratives is certainly not lost on modern culture. In addition to the many historic figures admired, portraits of spiritual heroes today (e.g., Mahatma Ghandi, Mother Theresa, Dalai Lama) continue to inspire many who avail themselves of their stories that remain perhaps among the strongest of influences on what we believe and value.

Contributions of the modern disciplines (e.g., psychology, sociology) have also added much to our understanding of the spiritual. Grounded in the insights of the Enlightenment and tenets of scientific positivism, a wealth of ideas and empirical methods have opened new doors to the inner workings of the human spirit—defining, measuring, and shaping a contemporary context for understanding this dimension. Among the most common schemes for illuminating spirituality and its impact are those that have emerged recently from developmental psychology. Rooted in the work of Piaget (1952), the notions of cognition and meaning making have entered the examination of spirituality with emphasis on a hierarchy of sequential structures that individuals progress through as they approach spiritual questions of the most comprehensive and ultimate kind. Such is the work of James Fowler (1981) whose model of faith development maps out how individuals evolve from an externally defined and dogmatic system of faith (e.g., *mythic-literal faith*) to one that is internalized and contingent (e.g., *conjunctive faith*). With each step or stage evolves a qualitatively different assumption about the nature and source of one's beliefs. Another psychology-based approach is exemplified in the work of Sharon Parks (2000), whose model of "faithing" draws from the various strands of developmental work, including Fowler (1981), Perry (1970), Kegan (1982), and Kohlberg (1969), to construct the spiritual journey of young adults, especially as they encounter the challenge of choice about such matters in a relativistic and often confusing world. In doing so, they shift from an authority-bound dependent meaning-making stage, representing an *adolescent/conventional* faith, to one that is probing but fragile, typical of a *young adult* faith. The continuing experiences of adulthood eventually strengthen levels of conviction and confidence to result in a *mature adult* stage. Each level of development in these models constitutes an intact system of faith or spirituality that approaches the big questions of life in a characteristic manner. The value of such schemes is that they offer a roadmap for understanding how broad meaning-making structures evolve in shaping one's constructions of spiritual concerns. Knowing where individuals are on a scheme indicates from where they have come and more importantly suggests where they are heading, helpful information for understanding them and anticipating what is likely to occur as circumstances change.

In addition to the above models, others are focusing on contemporaneous, rather than developmental, differences that shape various spiritual and faith-based responses. Perhaps indirectly rooted in the work of Jung (1959), Robert Nash (2001), for example, has identified a typology of "religio-spiritual narratives" or stories encountered among college students enrolled over the years in his University of Vermont course on spirituality and education. Among the so-called *mainstream stories* he describes are the narratives of *orthodoxy, wounded believers,* and *mainline* students. *Alternative stories* include *activists, explorers,* and *secular humanists.* Each narrative contains a distinctive resolution to questions of spirituality and faith and orients the student identifying with it toward a characteristic stance that frames how he or she addresses this domain. Similarly, Jenny Small (2011) most recently constructed a multi-faith approach for considering the impact of religious diversity on college campuses, exploring several additional "faith frames" for the most part ignored in previous treatments of the topic, including Judaism, Islam, and atheism/agnosticism. The value of these narrative approaches lies in their capacity to explain and differentiate a diverse range of holistic constructions or "stories" about matters of faith and spirituality that in turn shape how individuals respond to such questions in their lives.

Lastly, another approach (featured in the present volume) draws from the tenets of trait psychology (e.g., Allport & Odbert, 1936; Cattell, 1965; Eysenck, 1991) and identifies a range of personal qualities and broad dispositions thought to be related to students' spiritual development. Accordingly, each quality, trait, or disposition is measured quantitatively, empirically validated and described, and then distinguished from associated phenomena for purposes of defining the component parts of the construct at hand. Thus, Astin, Astin, and Lindholm (2011) have defined and instrumented ten such qualities in their analysis of students' spirituality, associating relative scores on *spiritual quest, equanimity, ethic of caring, charitable involvement, ecumenical worldview, religious commitment, religious engagement, religious/social conservatism, religious skepticism,* and *religious struggle* with a range of independent variables relevant to the post-secondary context (e.g., public vs. private institution, science major vs. art major, freshman vs. senior). Over time, changes on these traits are monitored and effect sizes are observed for any degree of influence attributable to correlated interventions and experiences. Beyond description, the goal of this method is to explain as much variance as possible in the outcome of interest by reference to manipulated input and environmental criterion variables.

Such an approach has led to a more precise and steady mapping of influences that seem to make a difference, suggesting a number of policies and practices, ranging from the encouragement of study abroad and community service to the value of interracial interaction and meditation and self-reflection. Perhaps more than the other approaches discussed here, this one looks and feels more "scientific," due much to its disciplined statistical techniques and systematic methodologies. The expectation is that over time knowledge of the phenomenon accumulates as the "puzzle is solved" piece by piece. The assumption is that some day the edifice of understanding will appear, fully formed and complete. In the meantime, one study leads to yet another and another as the line of inquiry unfolds.

While each of these approaches to spirituality lends itself to only one aspect of the problem, if nothing else, they collectively add to the increasing legitimization of a topic that has long been relegated to the incredible and too often thought of as irrelevant to the interests of the academy. However, a number of critical questions must be raised about the state of the art of spiritual inquiry, especially in reference to the research featured in the present volume. First, to what extent have we succeeded in capturing the breadth and depth of this phenomenon—spirituality in the lives of college students? Second, what is the relevance of this understanding about spirituality to campus practitioners who engage students in these concerns on a daily basis? Third, what lines of inquiry need to guide future efforts to advance these insights and claims? Consideration of such questions suggests that there may be much to do in aligning propositional knowledge of spirituality with the direct experience of it. In brief, spirituality may be a phenomenon that is all too complex and elusive to submit to the empirical process. Consequently, much of what this process yields is only partially recognizable to those who must apply it. In the final analysis, the future of inquiry on this topic might simply warrant a more integrated approach.

The Challenge of Reality is Real

The first concern noted here is the problem of isomorphism: to what extent do claimed representations of a phenomenon reflect the reality of it? In other words, what is the degree of correspondence between what we directly experience in the world and how we explain it? In this case, do our propositions and models with regard to spirituality line up with our experiences of it? To explore this point further consider, for purposes of illustration, the challenge of capturing the totality of a sunrise. How does one come to comprehend and communicate about such a familiar event? One can certainly experience a sunrise directly with focused attention, absorbing its sensual dimensions and basking in its effect. One can also engage it vicariously through stories told by others about one especially phenomenal experience, as warmth, sound, and light came together to create a truly awesome moment. One might also understand the different meanings of such an event from the experience, for example, of a "night owl" who struggles in the early morning hour to appreciate its magic or from the perspective of a hospice resident who gladly welcomes the faithful sign of a new day. The reality for each differs dramatically; a disturbance to one is a source of hope to the other. Still another approach to the problem would be to examine the brightness of a sunrise through a crystal prism, separating its light into a continuum of wavelengths, each with a distinctive hue following its natural order of violet to red. None of these approaches alone can deliver a comprehensive understanding of a sunrise; even the most amazing photograph cannot contain its effect since a single frame misses the point of its rise. Yet all of these approaches together can only nearly approximate a sense of the phenomenon under study.

If the above analogy has merit here, each of these approaches has been employed in the search for understanding the spiritual dimensions of students' lives. None of them alone, including the approach featured in the present volume, can fully comprehend the phenomenon being addressed. More specifically, like the prism separating the light, the data presented here at best reflect only a spectral snapshot of the spiritual questions at hand, bending each wave into measurable components. The "reality" of this dimension in students' lives goes well beyond the qualities and factors identified here. It takes these and more to capture something so complex. In particular, given the assumptions underlying the post-positivist quantitative approach illustrated in these studies, one wonders whether the limits of their analyses in light of the topic addressed are reparable. Is something that renders life whole and connects to ultimate meaning best explored through component parts and fragments? Are precision and stability of measurement the right metrics for something so dynamic and fluid? Is concreteness of definition the right tool for something that is ultimately elusive? Can clarity of explanation replace awe in the experience of the ineffable? Such questions address the challenges that are inevitable in the constraints of this particular line of inquiry, especially concerning the topic of spirituality.

Some Inquire, Others Do

The expressed intent of the research in this volume is to explore systematically the components of spirituality and how they interact with various choices students make and the experiences they encounter during the college years. The suggested goal is to use such information to inform and guide those who engage in the practices that anticipate and respond to the spiritual needs of students. At the risk of oversimplifying the problem, such artisans are probably more pastoral than critical in their orientation to this work. They desire to make a difference in students' lives by encountering them more directly in holistic experiences of a spiritual kind. These individuals are quite comfortable with the language of "soul" and "spirit," for example, seeking neither to operationalize nor confine it to a specific set of attributes and traits. Theirs is a world of the unseen, the miraculous, and the faintly whispered; in short, the ineffable. In contrast, those who pursue research on such topics are more demanding of the language, preferring specificity, clarity, and precision over the obtuse. For many, understandings come in the form of p-values, beta coefficients, and effect sizes. A point worth considering here is whether the manner in which we gather, explore, and communicate our knowledge of student spirituality, especially within the parameters of the scientific paradigm employed here, may not be the way comprehended or appreciated by those whose role it is to enact such understandings on a college campus. While potentially disappointing to the above authors, it should not surprise them to learn that a campus minister, for example, might be less inclined to pick up the present volume of research to understand what may lie ahead in any given week than he or she would be to read a campus news story of a student whose spiritual journey inspired others to commitment and action. More likely, such campus practitioners would rather reflect on the success of a particular experience with students the previous week than consider the effect sizes of observed differences in a large national sample. The formal and fragmented knowledge of the academy couldn't be any further removed from the fluid and holistic experience of spiritual engagement with students. It seems that building a good theory and research base requires just the opposite of what it takes to engage and effect change in the world it hopes to illuminate. While stability and precision inform the one, fluidity and allusion characterize the other. The theory-to-practice conundrum is inherent to any applied field, and although challenging intellectually, it usually proves frustrating for both the theorist and the practitioner who never quite seem to meet on common ground. Nonetheless, the research authors of the present volume have faced this challenge directly and admirably in inviting their counterparts to consider the meaning of their data for the practice of campus spirituality. In the end, if we are to succeed, we must find ways to draw from these various strands of understanding to support the work we consider so important. What else needs to be done to pull it all together? That is probably a question that lies well beyond the next sunrise.

Over the Horizon

The research reported in these pages has clearly advanced the study of student spirituality within the post-positivist frame of understanding, and the authors are to be commended for the discipline and insight they have brought to the problem. Yet, if we are to more fully understand the nature and experience that lies over the horizon, a more holistic and integrated approach is warranted in the scholarship on this topic. A number of critics have noted as much in their reviews of modern behavioral sciences. For instance, Kenneth Gergen (1994) argued the point that "its romance with permanence" is the "primary impetus behind the development of modern science," resulting in a "formidable scientific establishment largely (although not exclusively) devoted to the tasks of locating, documenting, and explaining permanence amid the flux of passing experience" (p. 2). Consequently, in the evolution of the behavioral sciences, associated disciplines have turned their attention to fixed rather than ephemeral phenomena in the quest for a system capable of explaining how the world works. In doing so, they have approached most phenomena with the presumption that what they are studying is more stable rather than fluid. Thus, in the context of the study of student spirituality, exploration of its component parts has become the standard for inquiry on this topic, at least among the studies reported here. Such an approach, while informative, has resulted in a number of imbalances that challenge the validity of the enterprise, according to Guba (1990), who detailed the problem as one of methodological rigor versus relevance, precision in contrast to richness, elegance over applicability, and a penchant for verification instead of discovery. According to his claim, an interest in establishing rigorous methods, precise understandings, elegant research designs, and confirmatory processes, the scientific model has forfeited much of the richness of the phenomena it addresses, attenuating its capacity for discovery, and placing at risk much of its relevance and applicability. His solutions to such tradeoffs entail carrying out inquiry in more natural settings, with an eye toward discovery, and with greater use of qualitative methods to generate theories "grounded" in local circumstances. Assuming the validity of his critique, it makes sense then to consider alternative perspectives and methods as this agenda of student spirituality further evolves.

First, this line of inquiry could benefit from exploring further the potential interconnections of extant threads of understanding on the topic. What is the relationship, for example, between the spiritual and religious qualities featured in the present volume and the developmental stage distinctions described in Fowler (1981) or Parks (2000)? Could it be that gains in *spiritual quest*, *ecumenical worldview*, and *religious skepticism*, for illustration purposes, depend on the deeper structural changes indicated in movement out of a *mythic-literal* or *adolescent/conventional* faith to a *conjunctive* or *mature adult* form? Similarly, from the perspective of contemporaneous differences, are certain religio-spiritual narratives (Nash, 2001) better predictors of these qualities than others? For example, are students who embrace *orthodoxy* more likely to exhibit stronger tendencies toward *religious/social conservatism* and a lesser degree of *ecumenical worldview* than those who identify with *secular humanism*? Furthermore, do some religio-spiritual narratives more than others suggest a quicker ascent through or resistance to the stages of faith described above? How do these aspects of meaning-making change over time and what leads to their development? While cataloguing the correlates of spirituality will add to the body of information available on the topic, how to act on such information is ultimately an ethical challenge that demands the very best of both the sage and the sanctifier.

The power of personal narratives offers a second point for further exploration in the research on student spirituality. What do students say about their own frameworks of spirituality and religion? How did they acquire them? To whom and to what do they attribute their most significant influences in that regard? What are the critical moments that led to their spiritual morphogenesis toward or away from a particular framework, should that be part of their history? How do their spiritual beliefs shape their commitments and day-to-day actions or their choices about life? Parks Daloz, Keen, Keen, and Daloz Parks (1996) studied 100 people whose "long-term commitments to work on behalf of the common good, even in the face of global complexity, diversity, and ambiguity" (p. 5) led to lives of sustained service in their respective communities. Imagine the value of students' stories whose spiritual commitments and choices placed them in positions of leadership to advocate for service and social justice on campus. In addition, developing narratives of ordinary students from different backgrounds could also contribute to the rich texture of understanding in this domain, as nuances of tradition and practice are explored for their meaning. From the beginning to end, how do students' spiritual journeys evolve during the college years? What critical incidents or "shipwreck experiences" (Parks, 2000) set them in motion and to what result? The holistic quality of stories is a critical tool for conveying the complex essence of any phenomenon, where the goal of transferability balances the claim of generalizabilty in the discourse between samples and unique individuals.

Finally, in the increasing multi-faith environment on campus it becomes all the more imperative to recognize and understand how differences of spiritual and religious belief both enrich and threaten our world. What qualities might predispose some students to capitalize on opportunities for inter-faith encounter and dialog on campus? What qualities discourage such border crossings (Tierney, 1993)? Are *religious commitment* and *religious engagement* compatible with an *ethic of caring* and an *ecumenical worldview* under these conditions, especially at a time when tolerance runs thin and battle lines between fundamentals are too readily drawn? What stories do students tell about friendships that evolve from such encounters? What results when roommate assignments intersect with such differences or student organizations form with exclusive purposes around these distinctions? Nash (2001) named religious pluralism as the principal diversity challenge of our times. How can our tools of inquiry elevate our sensitivity to and understanding of these concerns? If nothing else, a more expanded and holistic research agenda on student spirituality can offer more options for awareness and insight, and speak to a greater variety of stakeholders who are committed to supporting and advancing this dimension of students' lives.

Conclusion

The studies of student spirituality featured in this volume offer a good sampling of thoughtful research through the prism of post-positivism. The subsequent reflections also stand in testament to the complex relationship between theory, research, and practice on the topic. Have they advanced our capacity to explain spiritual questions in students' lives? To some extent, yes they have. While the modern totems of objectivist methodology apparent in this approach have added a new level of sophistication to this line of inquiry, they have also produced a mechanistic understanding of the topic that might prove more puzzling than informative for those engaged directly in campus spirituality initiatives. To complement this thread of research, more integrated and holistic approaches are warranted that connect the disparate insights on the topic in the quest for engaging this critically important dimension of students' lives. So, have we arrived yet, in terms of unraveling the topic of student spirituality? I'm not really sure. What appears certain though is that interest in this topic will continue to grow and many of the needs beyond the horizon are as yet unnamed. However, the work of the authors presented here has undoubtedly established a solid basis for further exploration.

References

Allport, G. W., & Odbert, H. S. (1936). Trait names. A psycho-lexical study. *Psychological Monographs, 47(211)*, 171.

Astin, A. W., Astin, H. S., & Lindholm, J. A. (2011). *Cultivating the spirit: How college can enhance students' inner lives*. San Francisco, CA: Jossey Bass.

Butler, A. (1878). *Lives of the saints*. New York: Benziger Brothers.

Cattell, R. (1965). *The scientific analysis of personality*. Baltimore, MD: Penguin Books.

Eysenck, H. (1991). Dimensions of personality: 16, 5, or 3? Criteria for a taxonomic paradigm. *Personality and Individual Differences, 12,* 773–790.

Fowler, J. W. (1981). *The stages of faith: The psychology of human development and the quest for meaning*. San Francisco, CA: Harper San Francisco.

Gergen, K. (1994). *Toward transformation in social knowledge* (2nd edition). Thousand Oaks, CA: Sage.

Guba, E. G. (1990). *The paradigm dialog*. Newbury Park, CA: Sage.

Jung, C. G. (1959). *Psychological types*. New York: Pantheon.

Kegan, R. (1982). *The evolving self: Problems and process in human development*. Cambridge, MA: Harvard University Press.

Kohlberg, L. (1969). Stage and sequence: The cognitive developmental approach to socialization. In D. Goslin (Ed.), *Handbook of socialization theory and research* (pp. 347–480). Chicago, IL: Rand McNally.

Nash, R. J. (2001). *Religious pluralism in the academy: Opening the dialogue*. New York: Peter Lang.

Parks, S. D. (2000). *Big questions worthy dreams: Mentoring young adults in their search for meaning, purpose, and faith*. San Francisco, CA: Jossey Bass.

Parks Daloz, L., Keen, C., Keen, J., & Daloz Parks, S. (1996). *Common fire: Leading lives of commitment in a complex world*. Boston, MA: Beacon Press.

Perry, W. (1970). *Forms of intellectual and ethical development in the college years: A scheme*. New York: Holt, Rinehart & Winston.

Piaget, J. (1952). *The language and thought of the child*. London, England: Routledge & Kegan Paul.

Small, J. (2011). *Understanding college students' spiritual identities: Different faiths, varied worldviews*. New York: Hampton Press.

Tierney, W. (1993). *Building communities of difference*. Westport, CT: Bergin and Garvey.

CONTRIBUTORS

Diane K. Anderson is a student affairs professional with a doctoral degree and 30 years of progressively increasing responsibility at both private and public institutions with varied enrollment sizes. She is currently Vice President for Student Affairs at Western Michigan University. She has extensive experience in collaboration with academic affairs, supervision, organizational change, conflict resolution, and outcomes assessment. She is well versed in the operation of all student affairs functional areas. Diane has proven ability in setting the stage for change within an organization; creating open, trusting and collaborative working relationships within and across divisional and university lines; modeling a participative leadership style with students, faculty, and staff; and building a collaborative team focused on student learning and personal development.

Nicholas A. Bowman is an assistant professor of higher education and student affairs at Bowling Green State University. His research interests include college diversity experiences and student outcomes, religious minority students, the assessment of student outcomes, college rankings, and student retention. He has had more than 30 articles accepted for publication in journals such as *Educational Researcher*, *Review of Educational Research*, *American Educational Research Journal*, and *Personality and Social Psychology Bulletin*. He currently serves on the editorial boards of *Research in Higher Education*, *Journal of Higher Education*, and *Journal of College Student Development*.

Jay W. Brandenberger serves as the director of Research and Assessment at the Center for Social Concerns, and as concurrent associate professor in the Department of Psychology at Notre Dame. He directs research initiatives at the

Center, working with colleagues to examine the developmental outcomes and best practices associated with Center courses and programs. He is the editor of the Center's Research Report Series, and facilitates ongoing longitudinal research focusing on the impacts of community engagement.

David Chenot is an assistant professor in the Department of Social Work at California State University Fullerton. He offers instruction in social work practice (mental health and child welfare), research, and Human Behavior in the Social Environment. Prior to entering academia, David was a social worker in direct practice for many years in public child welfare services and public mental health. He earned his Ph.D. at Case Western Reserve University. David's research interests include: spirituality and religion in social work practice, the public child welfare services workforce, and resilience among vulnerable children and families.

Keith J. Edwards is professor of psychology at Rosemead School of Psychology, Biola University. He holds a Ph.D. in quantitative methods from New Mexico State University and a Ph.D. in clinical psychology from the University of Southern California. He held faculty positions at Rutgers University and Johns Hopkins University before joining the Rosemead faculty in 1973. Dr. Edwards is a licensed clinical psychologist and teaches courses in couple therapy, individual therapy, and research methods. He is interested in spiritual formation and has published a number of papers on measuring spiritual functioning.

Carol Ann Faigin is a licensed clinical psychologist in private practice in central Maine. She received her doctorate from Bowling Green State University in Ohio and completed her residency at VA Maine Healthcare System, specializing in the treatment of PTSD and other trauma-related disorders. Dr. Faigin has lectured and co-authored book chapters and articles on the topic of spirituality and psychological wellness. She is an active contributor to the U.S. Army's *Comprehensive Soldier Fitness Program: Spiritual Resilience Initiative*, which is being administered to U.S. Army soldiers. Dr. Faigin plans to continue developing interventions that integrate psychology and spirituality.

James Fleming is University Vice President & Chief of Staff at Wheeling Jesuit University in West Virginia. Before joining the leadership team at WJU, Fleming worked at Boston College as a faculty member in the Lynch School of Education and as Director of Mission Assessment and Planning where he led a national research project related to the spiritual development of college students through the design and administration of the Boston College Questionnaire about the Undergraduate Experience (BCQ). In 1999 he earned a Ph.D. from the University of California Berkeley where his research focused on higher education policy and assessment.

Sean J. Gehrke is a researcher in the Pullias Center for Higher Education and a Dean's Fellow in the Rossier School of Education at the University of Southern California. His research focuses on the impact of the college environment on student outcomes in higher education by examining the influences of student experiences and campus organization, structure, and culture on these outcomes. His current work is focused on college student spirituality and organizational structure and culture in fostering change in higher education. He is currently pursuing a Ph.D. in Urban Education Policy from the University of Southern California.

Kathleen M. Goodman is an assistant professor in Student Affairs in Higher Education at Miami University. Her research and teaching interests include atheist college students, the impact of college experiences on student learning, diversity and equity in higher education, student development, and quantitative research methods. She is one of a group of scholars selected to participate in the Institute for Higher Education Policy (IHEP) Young Academic Fellows Program, dedicated to evaluating policy-relevant research. She is co-editor, with Sherry Watt and Ellen Fairchild, of "Religious Privilege and Student Affairs Practice: Intersections of Difficult Dialogues" (*New Directions for Student Services,* 2009, #125).

Jonathan P. Hill is an Assistant Professor of Sociology at Calvin College in Grand Rapids, Michigan. His current research focuses on the religious lives of American college students and the institutional factors which shape religion on college campuses. Other research interests include the relationship between religious and secular financial giving, the impact of political affiliation on financial generosity, and the social correlates of beliefs about human origins. He is currently co-authoring a book manuscript on Catholic emerging adults using data from the National Study of Youth and Religion.

Peter C. Hill, Professor of Psychology at Rosemead School of Psychology, Biola University, is a social psychologist with an applied interest in the psychology of religion and spirituality. Dr. Hill's research interests focus on four major areas in the psychology of religion and spirituality: 1) religious/spiritual measurement, 2) religious fundamentalism, 3) positive psychological characteristics such as humility and forgiveness, and 4) the role of affect in religious and spiritual experience. He has served on the Technical Advisory Board for the Higher Education Research Institute's Survey of Spiritual Development in College Students.

Hansung Kim is an assistant professor in the department of sociology at Hanyang University in Korea. He teaches courses in social policy and research methods. He received his B.S.W. from the Yonsei University in Korea, M.S.W. from Michigan State University, and Ph.D. in Social Work from the University of Southern California. Formerly, he was an assistant professor in the department of social work at California State University Fullerton. His research interests include child welfare and social inequality. Some of his current research projects focus on various topics such as child poverty, immigrant families, and child protective services.

Jennifer A. Lindholm is Director of Undergraduate Learning Assessment & Special Projects at UCLA. She also serves as UCLA's Accreditation Coordinator. She directed the decade-long *Spirituality in Higher Education* project and co-authored *Cultivating the Spirit* with Alexander Astin and Helen Astin. Her research and writing focuses on the structural and cultural dimensions of academic work; the career development, work experiences, and professional behavior of college and university faculty; issues related to institutional change; educational assessment; and undergraduate student development.

Peter M. Magolda is a Professor in Miami University's Student Affairs in Higher Education Program. He received a B.A. from LaSalle College, an M.A. from The Ohio State University, and a Ph.D. in Higher Education Administration from Indiana University. Professor Magolda's scholarship focuses on ethnographic studies of college students and critical issues in qualitative research. His recent ethnographic research centers on evangelical student subcultures. In 2011, he co-edited *Contested Issues in Student Affairs* with Marcia Baxter Magolda.

Matthew J. Mayhew is an associate professor of higher education at New York University. He examines how collegiate conditions, educational practices, and student experiences influence learning and democratic outcomes ranging from moral reasoning to ecumenical worldview. Mayhew has published over 30 peer-reviewed articles in *Research in Higher Education, Journal of Higher Education, Review of Higher Education,* the *NASPA Journal, Journal of College Student Development, Ethics and Behavior,* and *Journal of Moral Education.* He has co-authored a chapter in *Higher Education: Handbook of Theory and Research.* Mayhew has also received several grants for exploring the impact of college on student outcomes, including, but not limited to, moral reasoning, spirituality, high-risk drinking, and innovative entrepreneurship. He currently serves on the editorial boards of *Research in Higher Education, Journal of Higher Education,* and *Journal of College Student Development.*

Scotty McLennan is the Dean for Religious Life at Stanford. His duties include providing spiritual, moral, and ethical leadership for the university, teaching, encouraging a wide spectrum of religious traditions on campus, serving as the minister of the Stanford Memorial Church, and engaging in public service. He is a Unitarian Universalist minister and attorney, and has taught courses at the intersection of spirituality and ethics in several faculties, including Urban Studies and Business. He is the author of three books, including *Finding Your Religion: When the Faith You Grew Up With Has Lost Its Meaning* (Harper San Francisco, 2001).

Jennie Purnell is an associate professor of Political Science and the Chair of the Intersections Project in University Mission and Ministry. Purnell's research and teaching explore the ways in which poor and marginalized Latin Americans, especially rural and indigenous peoples, have organized collectively in encounters with local and national governments. As the Chair of the Intersections Project, Purnell facilitates programs that bring together faculty and staff from across the university in conversations about the Jesuit mission and its meaning for teachers, researchers, and administrators at Boston College.

P. Jesse Rine is Director of Research & Grants Initiatives at the Council for Christian Colleges & Universities in Washington, D.C., where he oversees a national research agenda for evangelical Christian higher education. Dr. Rine holds a Ph.D. in Higher Education from the University of Virginia, an M.A.T. in Latin from Washington University in St. Louis, and a B.A. in Christian Thought from Grove City College. His doctoral dissertation, titled 'Pluralism, Provisionality, and Faith: Christian College Persistence in the Postmodern Turn,' was honored with the 2012 Outstanding Dissertation Award by the Religion and Education Special Interest Group of the American Educational Research Association (AERA)." His current research interests include spiritual development during the college years, student learning outcomes assessment, and the population ecology of distinctive institutions of higher education.

Alyssa Bryant Rockenbach is an associate professor of higher education at North Carolina State University. Her research focuses on the impact of college on students, with particular attention to spiritual development, religious and worldview diversity in colleges and universities, campus climate, community service engagement, and gendered dimensions of the college student experience. Her research has been featured in a number of prominent higher education and interdisciplinary journals, including *Research in Higher Education, Journal of Higher Education, Journal of College Student Development, Gender and Education*, and *Religion and Education*. Dr. Rockenbach serves as Associate Editor of the *Journal of College and Character* and is on the editorial boards of *Research in Higher Education, Journal of College Student Development*, and *Religion and Education*. She has been honored with national awards, including the American College Personnel Association (ACPA) Emerging Scholar Award and the Annuit Coeptis Emerging Professional Award.

Jenny L. Small holds a Ph.D. from the Center for the Study of Higher and Postsecondary Education at the University of Michigan. Her research has focused on the spiritual lives of religiously diverse college students, and how students use language to define their identities. Her book, entitled *Understanding College Students' Spiritual Identities: Varied Faiths, Different Worldviews*, is available from Hampton Press. Dr. Small's work is also available in *Research in Higher Education, Journal for the*

Scientific Study of Religion, *About Campus*, and *Religion & Education*. She serves as the Chair Elect of the ACPA Commission for Spirituality, Faith, Religion and Meaning.

C. Carney Strange is Professor of Higher Education and Student Affairs at Bowling Green State University, Ohio, where he has served as a graduate faculty member since 1978. He teaches courses on student development, the design and impact of campus environments, spiritual dimensions of student development, and methods of constructivist qualitative research. He is an associate author of *Involving Colleges* (1991), senior co-author of *Educating by Design* (2001), and co-editor/author of *Achieving Student Success: Effective Student Services in Canadian Higher Education* (2010). Strange was the recipient of the 2010 ACPA College Student Educators-International Contribution to Knowledge Award.

Donna M. Talbot is a Professor of Higher Education & Student Affairs in the Educational Leadership Unit at Western Michigan University. Her research, teaching, and doctoral student mentoring focus on many aspects of diversity and multiculturalism, including religious and spiritual diversity. This work has resulted in nearly 30 publications, and over 75 professional presentations and keynote addresses.

Michael D. Waggoner is Professor of Education at the University of Northern Iowa where he chairs the Graduate Program in Postsecondary Education. His scholarly interests are in the areas of religion and spirituality in education. He is in his 12th year serving as Editor of *Religion & Education* and is also Book Series Editor for Routledge Research in Religion and Education. Dr. Waggoner was recently elected to Chair the AERA Religion & Education Special Interest Group (2012–14). His most recent book was published in 2011 by Routledge: *Sacred and Secular Tensions in Higher Education: Connecting Parallel Universities.*

Yang Wang recently completed a Ph.D. in Educational Research, Measurement, and Evaluation Department from Boston College. She holds an M.Ed. in Language Curriculum Structure & Pedagogical Theory with a concentration in Language Testing. Her dissertation research focused on measuring value-added in noncognitive outcomes in higher education institutions with an emphasis on civic engagement. Her research interests include multilevel and longitudinal statistical modeling, value-added measurement, research methods, and IRT applications in large-scale assessments.

INDEX

When the index entry refers to text within a table, the page number is in bold. When the index entry refers to text within a figure, the number is in italics, e.g.academic/career mentoring 159–**60**, *163*,**165**–6, 189–91. When the index entry refers to a note, "n" plus the note number follows the page reference, e.g.student-centered pedagogies 153–7, 159–60, 163, 165–7, 167n4, 189–90